Doing collective biography

Conducting educational research

Series Editor: Harry Torrance, Manchester Metropolitan University

This series is aimed at research students in education and those undertaking related professional, vocational and social research. It takes current methodological debates seriously and offers well-informed advice to students on how to respond to such debates. Books in the series review and engage with current methodological issues, while relating such issues to the sorts of decisions that research students have to make when designing, conducting and writing up research. Thus the series both contributes to methodological debate and has practical orientation by providing students with advice on how to engage with such debate and use particular methods in their work. Series authors are experienced researchers and supervisors. Each book provides students with insights into a different form of educational research while also providing them with the critical tools and knowledge necessary to make informed judgements about the strengths and weaknesses of different approaches.

Current titles:
Tony Brown and Liz Jones: *Action Research and Postmodernism*
Mairead Dunne, John Pryor and Paul Yates: *Becoming a Researcher*
Stephen Gorard with Chris Taylor: *Combining Methods in Educational and Social Research*
Joe Kincheloe and Kathleen Berry: *Rigour and Complexity in Educational Research*
Maggie MacLure: *Discourse in Educational and Social Research*
Anna Robinson-Pant: *Cross-cultural Perspectives on Educational Research*
John Schostak: *Interviewing and Representation in Qualitative Research*
John Schostak: *Understanding, Designing and Conducting Qualitative Research in Education*
Gary Thomas and Richard Pring: *Evidence-Based Practice in Education*
Lyn Yates: *What Does Good Education Research Look Like?*

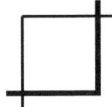

Doing collective biography

Investigating the production of subjectivity

Bronwyn Davies and Susanne Gannon

with
Jenny Browne, Phoenix de Carteret, Suzi Dormer, Anne Britt
Flemmen, Eileen Honan, Lekkie Hopkins, Cath Laws, Hillevi
Lenz-Taguchi, Helen McCann, Babette Müller-Rockstroh,
Eva Bendix Petersen, Margaret Somerville, Sharn Rocco,
Danielle Stewart, Barbara Watson and Monne Wihlborg

Open University Press

Open University Press
McGraw-Hill Education
McGraw-Hill House
Shoppenhangers Road
Maidenhead
Berkshire SL6 2QL

e-mail: enquiries@openup.co.uk
world wide web: www.openup.co.uk

and Two Penn Plaza, New York, NY 10121-2289, USA

First Published 2006

A catalogue record of this book is available from the British Library

ISBN-10   0 335 22044 4 (pb)   0 335 22045 2 (hb)
ISBN-13   978 0 335 22044 1 (pb)   978 0 335 22045 8 (hb)

Library of Congress Cataloging-in-Publication Data
CIP data applied for

Typeset by RefineCatch Ltd, Bungay, Suffolk
Printed in Poland by OZ Graf. S.A
www.polskabook.pl

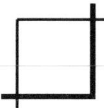

Contents

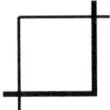

Contributors

Jenny Browne was the Midwifery Program Convenor at the University of Newcastle, NSW, Australia. She is a doctoral candidate at the University of Western Sydney, looking at the work women do to constitute themselves as midwives.

Phoenix de Carteret's PhD research at the University of New England, NSW, Australia, focused on women's experiences of discourses that shape classed and gendered subjectivity. She used collective biography as a research method.

Bronwyn Davies is Professor of Education at University of Western Sydney, Australia. Her work focuses on gender and post-structuralist theorizing and on body/landscape relations.

Suzi Dormer is a psychologist in private practice in Townsville, Queensland, Australia. She is particularly interested in the workings of desire in women's lives.

Anne Britt Flemmen is a lecturer in Sociology at the University of Tromsö in Norway. Her doctoral research focused on how women's fear of sexual violence influenced their activity space, and her current work is on close relationships.

Susanne Gannon lectures in Education at the University of Western Sydney, Australia. Her doctoral research focused on post-structural theory and transgressive writing and research practices.

Eileen Honan is a lecturer in Education at the University of Queensland, Australia. Her PhD thesis was a post-structural rhizoanalysis of the interactions between teachers and syllabus texts.

Lekkie Hopkins teaches Women's Studies at Edith Cowan University, Perth, Western Australia. Her work is feminist, post-structuralist and cross-disciplinary. Her doctoral thesis explores the uses of narrative in re-storying the self in the training of women's services practitioners.

Cath Laws is Principal of Fowler Road School, Sydney, Australia. Her doctoral research focused on children who are marginalized at school, particularly those children who are marginalized as behaviourally/ emotionally disturbed.

Hillevi Lenz-Taguchi is Assistant Professor in Education and Post-doctoral Fellow at the Stockholm Institute of Education, Sweden. Her research concerns feminist pedagogies in higher and in early childhood education.

Helen McCann was a lecturer in Education at the University of Southern Queensland, Hervey Bay, Queensland, Australia.

Babette Müller-Rockstroh is a medical anthropologist and a midwife. She is currently working on a PhD project on ultrasound in Ghana and Tanzania through the University of Maastricht, the Netherlands.

Eva Bendix Petersen is a senior lecturer in the School of Humanities, Communications and Social Sciences at Monash University, Australia. Her research focuses on academic cultures and subjectivities.

Sharn Rocco lectures in Education at James Cook University, Townsville, Queensland, Australia. Her doctoral research investigated women's desire for heterosexual marriage.

Margaret Somerville is Professor of Education (Learning and Development) at Monash University. Her doctoral research focused on body/ landscape relations and her current work also encompasses bodies in workplaces.

Danielle Stewart is a teacher in Queensland, Australia. She was a BEd (Hons) student at James Cook University at the time of the project included in this book.

Barb Watson is an adjunct lecturer in Education and Psychology at James Cook University, Townsville, Queensland, Australia. Her doctoral research was a critical pragmatic analysis of parents living with a child with an intellectual disability.

Monne Wihlborg is a lecturer in Education at Lund University in Sweden.

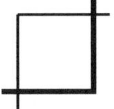

Prologue[1]

This book gathers together the series of projects through which we have developed the research practice of collective biography as a strategy for post-structuralist work in the social sciences. We are a diverse group of women from Australia, Denmark, Germany, Norway and Sweden. Our disciplines, our ages, our academic histories, the material circumstances and trajectories of our lives are vastly different from each other. We are postgraduate students, ex-students, friends, colleagues, and visiting scholars who have come to work with Bronwyn, at her invitation, on furthering the method of collective biography (Davies, 1994; 2000a; Davies and Gannon, 2005). For four years we have gathered, in January and July, usually on Magnetic Island off the coast of Queensland in northern Australia, to work collectively on this task. For a week each time we have grappled with how we might bring post-structuralist thought to bear on our readings of (our own) lived experience. We have taken our memories as data in the research process, inspired initially by and returning frequently to the work of Frigga Haug and her colleagues (1987) in Germany in the 1980s. It was a visit by Haug to Australia that opened Bronwyn's eyes to the possibilities of collective work on memories within feminist/post-structuralist frameworks. Many of us have gone on to use collective biography in our own research. In part because we tap into post-structuralist forms of theorizing and writing, our strategies have developed in surprising ways through all these projects.

This book aims to lay out for a wider readership both our manner of working, and the conceptual/analytical work around the particular topics and themes that we interrogated in our projects. The purpose of this book is, in part, to assist readers to design and conduct their own collective biography workshops. We begin with an overview of our working strategies and of the methodological quandaries that led us to this way of working (Chapter 1). The next four chapters are examinations of particular situated subjectivities: as schoolgirls (Chapter 2), as schoolgirl fiction readers (Chapter 3) and as women at work (Chapters 4 and 5).

In these chapters we engage with the vexed question of agency in contemporary social theory. We analyse the limitations of agency and the ways in which power works to limit the possibilities of agency at the same time as it makes agency possible. One of the features of an agentic position is the capacity for reflexivity and this is what we pursue next, finding that reflexivity is much more demanding and complex than we thought (Chapter 6). We then write about the difficulties and pleasures of our collaborative writing (Chapter 7). This very 'messy text' (Denzin, 1997) is a necessary intervention in the harmonious tale we generally tell of our research practice. The last two of our projects are primarily theoretical in orientation, looking at Foucault's work on power and knowledge (Chapter 8), and at the nature of the subject in post-structuralist theory (Chapter 9). Throughout all these chapters we write and reflect on moments of being, on the ambivalent, slippery subject-in-process – as infant, schoolgirl, writer, teacher, professor, student, lover, wife, daughter/ mother – captured in the remembered *moment of being*, transformed in a process of telling and writing and reading that *moves* us in a variety of ways.

These moments and movements are not towards the transformation of ourselves into new subjects in linear time. Rather, the transformation lies in a particular form of attention to the remembered moment, an attention that makes the subject's vulnerability to discursive power starkly visible while also making visible the constitutive powers of the subject-in-process. The movement is thus not towards a new fixed but transformed subject. It lies in the process of making visible the discursive powers of particular discourses and the modes of subjection they entail. It is that visibility that makes transformation possible, not just of ourselves as individuals, but of our collective discursive practices, of our social contexts, of our capacity to imagine what is possible. We use the term *mo(ve)- ment* to bring together this detailed attention to particular remembered moments with the possibilities of transformation, within the ethical reflexive research practice that we call collective biography.

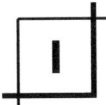

The practices of collective biography[2]

Qualitative research and social science

Much qualitative research in the social sciences depends on the memories of those we interview and on their elegant – or sometimes clumsy – attempts to answer the questions we put to them about *what is (or was) going on here – or there.* An interview can be described as the interviewee's best attempt to describe or explain, in the particular dialogic context of the interview, what he or she remembers, based on a particular history of observation and experience. Similarly, our analysis of the interview transcript is our best attempt, based on what we remember having seen or heard or read, both 'in' the data and outside the data, to make sense of what is said. Sometimes we attempt to make this sense-making more 'scientific' by engaging in elaborate forms of coding and quantifying, or following the carefully laid out steps of a particular, recognized method, or producing elaborate transcription formats that reveal what is 'really going on'. We comfort ourselves with methodic terms like 'triangulation', hoping that if the question has been approached from three sides, surely the answer is reliable. At the same time we draw on (more or less) sophisticated theoretical concepts to enable us to make sense of what we see and hear, theoretical concepts that are in effect refined tools the theorist develops to make sense of his or her observations and experiences. Just as the interviewee is engaged in interpreting and thus constituting his or her world, either in telling us about it or, in ethnographic research, engaging in it in such a way that we can observe it, so too, we as researchers, in collecting and analysing data or in theorizing about it, are engaged in interpreting and analysing (Scheurich, 1997). This is so, no matter how much we might try to convince ourselves, or our audiences, that we have got hold of 'reality' via the methods we have used. At every turn we rely on the powerful and flawed capacities we each have to remember and to make sense of what we remember.

In the social sciences our practices are deeply rooted in realist traditions. It is now generally assumed that discourse plays a powerful part in shaping what we take to be real, and that 'the real' is a more or less powerful set of fictions, albeit fictions with powerful effects. There are nevertheless interesting debates about whether we can afford to let on to the general public that our knowledges are not absolute – that we are not able to provide authoritative truths in the way we once thought we could (see, for example, Parker, 1998). The United States government went so far recently to legislate that what would count as (fundable) research would be research carried out in realist and positivist traditions favouring scientific and quantitative paradigms (see, for example, Lather, 2004). In reply there has been an upsurge of interest in, talk about, and passion for, the values of qualitative research. In qualitative research we are careful to explore the limitations of what we take ourselves to know through our research; to lay out the theoretical and methodic (and sometimes chaotic) pathways we have traced in order to arrive at a particular way of knowing; and to make sense of the potentially powerful effects of those ways of knowing, for our research subjects and for ourselves.

Recent methodological work in the social sciences foregrounds the precarious nature of the claims to knowledge that we might make. Paradigms such as feminism, post-colonialism and postmodernism have questioned what can be known and who can know it (Gannon and Davies, forthcoming). Post-structuralist theorizing has brought attention to the discursive contexts within which knowledge is constituted. Validity, reliability and objectivity have been challenged from diverse locations. New approaches, aimed at inclusive and ethical research practices, proliferate (Denzin, 2003; Denzin and Lincoln, 2000; Lewin and Somekh, 2005; Scheurich, 1997; Stronach and MacLure, 1997). In many of these research practices, the subject and object of research are brought much closer together. The researcher is no longer invisible in the work of research. In work with memories, the 'evidence of experience' is no longer treated as innocent or transparent but is seen to be constituted through language, discourse and history (Davies and Davies, forthcoming; Scott, 1992). What can be known is shaped as much by the researcher and what he or she is able to think as by whatever our 'data' might be. And what can be known emerges not only out of the methodic practices, but also out of what Somerville (2005) calls the spaces-in-between – the contemplative moments where something else, something surprising, can come to the surface and disrupt our thinking-as-usual, calling into question that which we had thought, until then, was self-evident and not open to question.

Alternative approaches to social science

Critiques of traditional approaches to research have led to the proposal of alternative research practices. These practices attempt to bypass the problems for the social sciences that traditional methods, based on the physical sciences, pose. These alternative approaches search for ways to engage with the epistemological and ontological challenges of working with human subjects who, unlike the objects of the physical sciences, have language, and are constituted within the social in a multitude of ways and in a multitude of contexts, including the context of the research. One of these new practices is autoethnography (Ellis, 2004). By taking oneself and one's own ongoing experiences as the data, in autoethnography the gap between memories and the interpretive analytic work of research is closed. According to autoethnography the richness, subtlety and complexity of the researcher's own embodied thinking and being in the world can be told, brought to the surface of memory and language. In this work it is assumed that the detail of how the researcher is discursively constituted will give insights into how the researcher, like others, is made human in particular ways through their engagement in the social world. Autoethnography seeks to make relevant those aspects of being that are suppressed by analytic strategies that draw a veil of silence around emotions and bodies. It becomes possible then to interrogate this lived experience theoretically, enabling the extension of theory and of ways of knowing and representing memory (Gannon, 2006).

Another strategy that shares a similar agenda, and that we set out in this book, is collective biography. Embodiment and sociality are crucial dimensions as lived experience is re-membered in the research. In collective biography a group of researchers works together on a particular topic, drawing on their own memories relevant to that topic, and through the shared work of telling, listening and writing, they move beyond the clichés and usual explanations to the point where the written memories come as close as they can make them to 'an embodied sense of what happened'. In working in this way we do not take memory to be 'reliable' in the sense of providing an unquestionable facticity, nor do we take what initially surfaces as being truer, or more valid, than the texts that are worked and reworked in this approach. We take the talk around our memories, the listening to the detail of each other's memories, as a technology for enabling us to produce, through attention to the embodied sense of being in the remembered moment, a truth in relation to what cannot actually be recovered – the moment as it was lived. This is not a naive, naturalistic truth, but a truth that is worked on through a technology of telling, listening and writing. In a sense it is the very *unreliability* of memory that enables this close discursive work.

The truth that is accomplished in this process interests us, not as a means to generate knowledge about the individual self of each storyteller, but as a means to provide knowledge about the ways in which individuals are made social, are discursively constituted in particular fleshy moments. We do not seek totalizing truths but particular, local and situated truths. Our methodological question is not whether or not truth is found but what kind of truths are produced and through what technologies. In the projects of collective biography included in this book we have been particularly concerned to interrogate the materiality of our lived experience through the conceptual apparatus enabled by post-structuralist theory. Our project has been to bring theory into collision with everyday life and thus to rethink, collectively, both the discursive contexts within which our lives make sense and the uses to which we might put theory.

Collective biography draws on the collaborative strategy of memory work developed by Haug and her colleagues in Germany in the 1980s and published in English as *Female Sexualization* (Haug et al., 1987). Memory work involves the writing and subsequent analysis of remembered stories told and written by the researchers themselves. It is an explicitly feminist approach that was developed to address the gap that Haug and her colleagues found between Marxist theory and their own experiences as women. They set out through their memory-work to discover the constitutive means by which they had formed themselves into particular individuals, focusing on 'the way individuals continuously reproduce society as a whole: the way they enter into pre-given structures, within which they reproduce both themselves, and the categories of society' (Haug et al., 1987: 40). In this way Haug and her colleagues set out to disrupt existing theory by insisting on a starting point in their own experiences as girls and as women, and then going back to theory to see how it might be changed in light of those experiences.

Our approach has not been embedded in this kind of quarrel with Marxism. Our theoretical framework is post-structuralist, and we take this not to be a dogmatic framework that is in need of quarrelling with. Quite the reverse; it assists us in examining those thoughts and practices that are usually taken for granted, and usually assumed not to be in need of inspection. By making the ordinary objects and subjects of everyday life worthy of inspection, we can ask what the social conditions are that hold their apparent certainty in place. Foucault works with the questions that come up for him in his everyday life (in which he includes his work). And he says that: 'in order to establish the right relationship to the present – to things, to others, to oneself – one must stay close to events, experience them, be willing to be effected and affected by them' (Rabinow, 1997: xviii). The challenge of Foucault, Rabinow adds, 'is not to replace one certitude (*évidence*) with another but to cultivate an attention to the conditions under which things become "evident"' and in becoming evident, cease to be 'objects of our attention', becoming instead 'seemingly fixed, necessary and unchangeable' (Rabinow, 1997: xix). By developing imaginative strategies of being close to events, as though we are re-experiencing them, seeing how we are effected and affected by them, and telling and writing them in the ways we have developed here through collective biography, we create our own documentary materials through which we can search out the ways in which things were made evident, fixed and apparently unchangeable. Our stories, in showing the detail of our own collective enmeshment in that fixed world, set out to make it more fluid, more open to other possibilities.

In taking up our own approach to post-structuralist theory and developing it in ways Foucault did not envisage, we take the texts of Foucault and other post-structuralist writers as rhizomatic, as open, in a Deleuzian sense, to the work that we want to do with them. As Grosz says of such an approach to text.

> Instead of a Derridean model of the text as textile, as interweaving – which produces a close, striated space of intense overcodings, a fully semiotized model of textuality . . . texts could, more in keeping with Deleuze, be read, used, as modes of effectivity and action which, at their best, scatter thoughts and images into different linkages or new alignments without necessarily destroying their materiality. . . . Instead of the eternal status of truth, or the more provisional status of knowledge, texts have short term effects, though they may continue to be read for generations. They only remain effective and alive if they have effects, produce realignments, shake things up. In Deleuzian terms, such a text, such thought, could be described as fundamentally moving, 'nomadological' or 'rhizomatic'.
>
> (Grosz, 1995: 126–127)

We should caution here that embodied practices of remembering and writing do not give some direct access to 'buried' moments. In producing memories that have sensual texture as if they are happening in the moment, collective biography evokes some resonance with, or even makes visible, some trace on the body of the unrecoverable 'real'. The practices of collective biography, in Grosz's words, 'have effects, produce realignments, shake things up'. The discursive and material practices of collective biography can make visible, palpable, hearable, the constitutive effects of dominant discourses. And in working post-structurally, those effects, while understood as real, are not taken to be inevitable – we are not *determined* by those dominant discourses. In examining how discourse and practice work on us, we open both ourselves and discourse to the possibility of change.

One branch of social scientists inspired by Haug and her colleagues has sought to contain their strategies in a method with explicit rules to be followed (Crawford et al., 1992; Onyx and Small, 2001; Schratz, Walker and Schratz-Hadwich, 1995). Working initially within the discipline of psychology, such elevation of method over theoretically focused, rhizomatic explorations, has created a parallel path where our interests in Haug and her colleagues' strategies both overlap and diverge. The English translator of *Female Sexualization*, Erica Carter (1987: 13), summarizes the memory-work methodology, as it was originally developed by the Haug collective, and characterizes it as avoiding strict methical guidelines:

> [C]hoosing a theme connected with the body . . . and calling on members of the group to write down their memories of past events that focus on this physical area, . . . the stories are circulated amongst the group, discussed, reassessed and rewritten. The group searches for absences in the text, for its internal contradictions, for clichéd formulations covering knots of emotion or painful detail. Rewritten in the light of collective critique, the final version becomes a finely textured account of the process of production of the sexualized female body.

We quote from the translator's preface because, in the body of their text, Haug and her colleagues do not give explicit instructions as to how aspiring memory-workers can go about it. Indeed, in 1987, they actively resisted such a formulation. Haug suggested 'there might well be no single, "true" method that is alone appropriate to this kind of work . . . the very heterogeneity of everyday life demands similarly heterogeneous methods if it is to be understood' (Haug et al., 1987: 70–71). They did, however, describe in considerable detail the particular work they did and various strategies that they found useful at different moments during their research process and with different topics (Haug et al., 1987: 56–70). This is what we have chosen to do here in this collective work – each chapter presents a different story about the way in which the group working on each chapter has chosen to tell the details of how we went about evoking our memories, writing them and then writing *about* them. In each case, the particular topic we have chosen, and the configuration of the research collective, has shaped each project differently.

Another difference between our own work and that of Haug and her colleagues arises when we look at the way that they focus very strongly on what might be called 'therapeutic outcomes' of their work. Their primary intention was political; they wanted to bring about change by developing in themselves a greater capacity for resistance to oppressive versions of femininity (Haug et al., 1987: 58). While participants in collective biography projects often remark on the therapeutic effects of their engagement in the collective work, we have consistently maintained that we are not 'doing therapy' – we are doing research.

At the same time we understand that the research itself is transgressive and potentially transformative, and that the work we do in our collective biographies makes visible, and therefore revisable, the discourses through which we make meanings and selves; and it powerfully deconstructs the idea of the individual as one who can exist independent of various collectives, of discourse, of history, of time and of place (Davies, 2000a). While some contemporary therapies might share some of these aspirations, we think it would be quite dangerous to claim that we offer therapy in our workshops, since it could shift the focus of our work towards individuals and their problems and away from the collective task of interrupting the taken-for-grantedness of everyday discourses and practices.

Our primary interest lies in developing the process of collective biography as a means of learning to read/write embodied social selves. We use that reading/writing to produce a textual base through which we can explore various aspects of the processes of meaning-making through which we become subjects and go on becoming subjects. This critical reading and writing practice contains within it possibilities for a different kind of agency; not in the enduring sense that most forms of therapy might hope for, and not through memories that might be fixed and interpreted scene by scene, but through memories as mo(ve)ments.

The remembered moments detail discursive habits that we peel away, not to find the 'real' embodied self hidden beneath, but in order to see the movement, the flow, the working of 'organisms, forces, energies, materials, desires, thoughts, etc' (Foucault, 1980a: 97). Through a very intense, focused gaze on the particularity of our own memories, we hope to arrive at an understanding of the social, of the way individual subjectivities are created and maintained through specific kinds of discursive practices, within particular historical moments, in particular contexts that in turn afford particular interactions and patterns of meaning-making. We are interested in our research to understand the processes of selving, rather than to discover particular details about individual selves. It verges on the paradoxical, we suggest, to require a detailed and loving attention to individual selves, and their memories, in order to arrive at new understandings that do not take as their central focus those individual selves. But it is a paradox we must live with in order to do this work.

Haug and her colleagues were strongly influenced by Foucault and the discursive turn that came with post-structuralism. The new modes of thinking made possible by Foucault were influential in the thinking of the collective. Ultimately, however, in that time and place, as feminists and as Marxists in the 1980s, they rejected Foucault's work, concluding that:

> [h]uman beings who make their own history have no place in Foucault; instead, [in Foucault] human beings are the effects of the structure (the 'order') that attains its goals by the most devious means, and remains impervious to willed efforts to change it.
>
> (Haug et al., 1987: 203)

In this rejection of what they read as Foucault's determinism, there is a lingering humanist faith in the individual (and the collective) and in the possibility of liberation as a consequence of re-education. Yet their work was also infused with post-structuralist scepticism both of 'reality' as any sort of veridical truth and of social scientific method as inflexible or as guaranteeing truth.

The methodic (and sometimes chaotic) practices of collective biography

We have taken up our practice of collective biography both with and against the original idea of memory-work. While remaining open to changing the strategies of using our memories, depending on the topic we are exploring and the theorizing we are currently attempting to do, there is a describable pattern that has emerged in what we set out to do in our collective biography workshops. Although it is possible to run a collective biography workshop for half a day or a day, our strong preference is for a small group of us, usually six or seven, to meet for a week, working into our topic through reading, discussion, storytelling and writing and analysis of those stories. It is possible for one of the researchers to write a paper from this work, only working with the other members of the group as consultants on her writing (e.g. Davies, 2000a; Gannon, 2001, 2004). Our practice in the papers gathered together here, though, has been to maintain each group of workshop participants as a collective who writes the paper out of the workshop, only sending it to our own wider group (that is, all of those listed as part of this book's collective), and to other colleagues, for comment when it is almost complete. Although this can be a fraught and chaotic process (as we discuss in Chapter 6), all the papers included in this book have adopted this collaborative writing process.

So, briefly, and by way of introduction, what is it that we do in conducting a collective biography workshop? This process has evolved and goes on evolving as we discover what works and what does not work, and as we think of new strategies. The particularities of a number of different workshops are elaborated later in this book. The brief summary that follows here is a thumbnail sketch of a workable workshop.

Selecting the group to work on the project

This is a very variable but important part of the process. Haug initially drew together participants for her projects through her networks in socialist women's organizations and the journal *Das Argument* and selected participants who were committed to meeting regularly and working on the project over two years (Haug et al., 1987: 21–22). Our own shifting membership of each of the projects you find here began with whichever of Bronwyn's students could get away for the particular week-long bi-annual workshop, and grew to include guests from among local colleagues and guests visiting from other universities and other countries. Participants make a commitment to participate on the understanding that they must do preparatory work, reading about collective biography if they are attending their first workshop, and reading about the chosen topic for study. They must also be willing to commit themselves to the long and complex haul of collective work.

Selecting the topic

Before a workshop begins, a topic, arising out of our ongoing research and writing, is selected for investigation, and we begin looking for and circulating reading around that topic. Usually before, but also during the collective biography workshop, we negotiate the detail of the memory questions to be asked. These are usually in the form of 'what is your first memory of . . .'. Those questions usually arise from an engagement with the readings that inform the topic and are circulated to the group beforehand, usually, in our case, by Bronwyn, as group leader, so that participants can reflect on their memories before coming to the workshop.

Structuring the workshop

Two to three hours are devoted to each memory question, including the telling, writing and reading back of the chosen memories. This means that no more than two sets of memories can be generated each day. On the first day we begin by reconnecting with each other and by introducing ourselves to any new members. We take time to revisit the process we are involved in and to discuss the topic we have gathered to work on, including a discussion of the readings we have done beforehand. Apart from the sessions dealing with the memory questions, several hours are generally allowed on the last day to plan the collaborative process of analysing and writing up the memories we have produced. In many of the workshops we have also created space for participants to talk about, and get feedback on, some aspect of their own ongoing research.

Memory-telling

Each memory that is told in response to the agreed question inevitably leads to the generation of new memories. Sometimes these memories are of moments that had until then been completely forgotten. Often those who arrive with 'no memories' are amazed at how quickly stories begin to come to them once the storying begins. In this sense each memory is threaded on to the last. As we each tell our stories, the others of us listen carefully, probing for details and images that could help us imagine and bring to life in our own bodies each other's remembered stories. At the same time, we remember new stories of our own that take off from points in the discussion or from moments in others' stories. In this way the topic in hand is brainstormed and body-stormed; we actively excavate what was buried, amazing ourselves with what we find in our own and each others' memories. This remembering is difficult, provocative, challenging, funny, sad and pleasurable, evoking laughter and tears and a lot of intense questioning about exactly what happened: how did it feel, how did it look, what were the embodied details of this remembered event?

Memory-writing

After this memory-telling and listening and questioning, we separate out, each into a quiet space, to write one or two of our own memories. In this process of writing we focus on the writing itself as a constitutive act, reminding ourselves not to use clichés and explanations. Instead we focus on writing from the body, not telling the story how it should be told, but as it is lodged in the body. In this sense we write *from* the body. When the stories are long and complex we a find a key moment to focus on, and write only about that moment. The focus on the moment and the body helps us also to resist the effects of narrative structures that are inclined towards linearity, causality and closure. As a rule of thumb the memory should take place in one or two minutes, though this rule is often broken. If the explanations seem crucial to comprehending the moment, we write them as separate to the memory, a little in the way the Japanese poet Basho wrote explanatory notes as background to many of his poems.

Reading stories

The written stories are read to the group, each member of the group again listening carefully to the words with the explicit intention of entering into the experience as it is told in the memory, and also noting where, in the text, explanations or clichés have crept in to block or obscure their capacity to imagine the emotional and embodied detail of the story. Stories are often then rewritten in light of the discussions that follow. That rewriting generally takes place at night and the new day begins with a reading of any rewritten stories being brought back from the previous day's work. Again, attentive, embodied listening is brought by the listeners to the stories that are read.

Through the telling of and listening to the spoken and written stories, and through the questions and answers, we aim to open up spaces in which our stories become not merely autobiographical, but are the means to make visible the discursive processes in which we each have been collectively caught up. The stories no longer primarily signify individuals' identities, but in their similarities and differences we become visible as constituted and constitutive beings. In this process we do not aim to construct a pre- (or post- or apart and outside of) discursive self, but to see some of the invisible threads within which we are entangled and to make visible and open for interrogation the discourses in which we have constituted others and have ourselves been constituted as particular kinds of subjects – as girls, or boys, as students or teachers, as moral or immoral beings, and so on.

In this process we identify strategies of surveillance that operate socially and that we take up as our own. In discussing panopticism and the power of the gaze, Foucault analyses the way we become subject to our own controlling gaze, becoming both controller and controlled:

> He who is subjected to a field of visibility, and who knows it, assumes responsibility for the constraints of power; he makes them play spontaneously upon himself; he inscribes in himself the power relation in which he simultaneously plays both roles; he becomes the principle of his own subjection.
>
> (Foucault, 1979: 202–203)

In this way, the power that weighs on us and subjects us becomes invisible; its touch is so light that we do not know it is there. What collective biography does is to make this turn on oneself visible – the mechanisms of power at work in oneself and on oneself become available for inspection. The identity accomplished in that taking on of power over oneself may no longer be, in that new awareness, the precious, naturalized, essentialized object to be maintained at all costs, but an observable way of being taken up both by oneself and by others, a way of being that enables certain things to be accomplished and forecloses others.

In collective biography we catch ourselves in remembered acts of turning on ourselves, seeing how we take up forms of power and strategies of surveillance. We attend to the ambivalent processes of subjection. We develop and refine our capacity to reflexively turn our gaze on ourselves in remembered moments of turning, of constituting ourselves and being constituted.

The methodological advantages of this process are that we are not dependent on research subjects who may or may not be willing or able to tell us what we want to know, since we are our own subjects; and we do not need to accept versions of events as they are told to us in response to our questioning, since we are free to interrogate each other until sufficient or appropriate detail is provided that enables us to enter the remembered moment in a way that is satisfying in relation to the particular quest we are on in that particular workshop. The questioning and challenging of each other's stories can, indeed, take on a ruthless quality as we pursue the detail that might otherwise be obscured by the clichéd phrases that announce: 'this is what anyone would know and recognize'. This (sometimes) difficult process is aimed at breaking open platitudes with which anyone could agree, and pursuing the detail that makes it possible for something else to take its place. We must hasten to add, here, that this ruthless pursuit can only work where a profound level of trust and mutual commitment has already been established among the workshop participants.

The writing of memory stories does not seek merely to document what we said when we first told our memory (as if that telling captured some kind of authentic truth about our own individuality), but to tell the memory in such a way that it is vividly imaginable by others, such that those others can extend their own imaginable experience of being in the world through knowing the particularity of another. In this sense, working with memory stories does not work with discourse-as-usual, or with the gathering of the sedimented practices of telling that are taken to 'reveal' the world that the teller inhabits. Memory-work attempts to go beyond the clichéd practices of everyday life, by attuning the telling and writing of stories to the embodied detail of the memory. The telling and writing of the memory stories attends to language itself as it is in the present and as it worked in the past to constitute the embodied self, but it also struggles to find a new way of working with language that begins with the cells of the body, the senses of the body, as they were in the remembered moment – to relive the moment as far as possible, and to open it up for reliving by those who are listening to it, and interrogating it. This imaginability comes not out of the repetition of predictable or familiar storylines, nor out of the retrieval of pristine 'authentic' memories, but out of the collective detailed attention to embodied detail in the collective memories that brings a new and unexpected view of what happened to light. This does not involve any kind of deliberate fictionalizing or fabricating of the memory, but, ironically, goes in a different direction – seeking to evoke the remembered moment through attention to touch or sight or smell or taste, or through the particular attention to the muscles and flesh of the body in the particular moment being told. Often, additional details of the memory arise during the telling of others' stories, and during the discussions. These new details are not only remembered because they are the same as the detail in those other stories, but also because the details in another's story draw attention to gaps and silences in one's own story. Sometimes the additional details do not become available until the writing, or later rewriting, is taking place, as we each struggle, alone, to put ourselves again in the body of the child or woman experiencing that moment. While we insist that we write out of what we can recall, rather than 'what might have been', it is also true that we are, in remembering and in writing, engaged in a constitutive act in which the remembered subject is re-created on the page and in the imagination of the others and ourselves. Although we attempt to avoid words that the remembered child would not have known, memory is not a veridical act that reproduces the original, it is necessarily always constituted from a particular time, place, discursive frame and present self of the writer. The ethical and aesthetic practices of collective biography begin to dissolve a binary that sets 'true' representation against good fiction.

We aim in rewriting our memories within the collective for what we call 'embodied writing'. In *Female Sexualization* the body is recognized as the central site of female subjectification to the social. The female body is the site of Haug and her collective's investigation as it is in our own and other work with memories. (This is not to say that male bodies cannot be similarly used in collective biography – see, for example, Davies, 1994.) Although the body is recognized as the site of production for memories, the idea of 'embodied writing' is rarely directly addressed in the memory-work literature. Feminist writers have written about embodied writing and memory in other contexts. Virginia Woolf, for example, saw memory as a physically embodied practice rather than an intellectual practice. Writing memories, she wrote, '[I was] hardly aware of myself, but only of the sensation. I am only the container of the feeling of ecstasy, of the feeling of rapture.' She gained access to embodied memories not from the 'direct gaze' of the intellect but 'by side glances and hints, in the effects of sound, light, smell, touch' (cited in Benstock, 1991: 1053). Basic to the collective memory project is the attempt to reclaim embodied memory, to mine the hints and glances and to uncover the things that one does not remember in the first full direct gaze. It could be claimed that any good writing, that is, writing that is evocative, detailed and multidimensional, is embodied in this way. But we engage in embodied writing not just to produce good writing, but to access the body's knowledge. Focusing on the corporeality of subjectivity, Grosz (1994: vii) suggests that:

> [A]ll the effects of subjectivity . . . can be adequately explained using the subject's corporeality as a framework as it would be using consciousness or the unconscious. All the effects of depth and interiority can be explained in terms of the inscriptions and transformations of the subject's corporeal surface. Bodies have all the explanatory power of minds.

The memories that are excavated and analysed in collective biography provide the data for tracing such inscriptions and transformations as they manifest on and in bodies. Learning to write from the body is to learn to align the words as closely as possible to the remembered embodied moment, so that in reading the words on the page, the reader also knows in her (or his) body, relives, that particular moment.

The final stage of our practice of collective biography comes with the writing of an analytical text using the written memories. The collective carefully unravels the discursive nets in which their individual memories are caught, rewrite them and present their understandings of the cultural and social processes of subjectivity and subjectification along with the memories. This practice was initiated by the text of *Female Sexualization* (Haug et al., 1987). The writers of that text constructed a 'we' who speaks – more or less – for them all through the pages of the book, although Haug maintains authorial responsibility with her name alone being on the title page, and as the author of the chapter on method. Although configurations change in different chapters of the text, the voice of the author herself (her-selves) remains a plural voice. The individualistic labour of writing is reconfigured in the plural: the authorial voice becomes 'we'. Cixous claims that 'the moment there is an author in the place there is a kind of air of authority that blows . . . a kind of poisoned air' (1990: 28). In *Female Sexualization* the 'air of authority' is dispersed among the collective.

Collective writing of the final text, where each person works 'both on and with' the memory texts (Haug et al., 1987: 42), has also been a practice followed by several other research collectives. In this work, the 'we-ness' (Crawford et al., 1992: 10) of the published text is presented relatively seamlessly. We seek to unravel this seamlessness by bringing to the surface, in Chapter 6 of this book, the struggle to write collaboratively. While two of us have written much of that chapter and this one, and have gathered together and edited the papers in this book, there are 18 authors who have been part of the 'we' who write this book. Each chapter carries the names of those who participated in its original writing, and all have been consulted over the collective task of putting those chapters together as this book.

Finally, our work differs from the work of memory-work practitioners who generate theory from memories. Our work begins, proceeds and ends with a focus on theory, as we understand it through the lens of lived experience, with our bodies and our memories as discursive/textual sites. We see bodies and theory as integral to one another. Indeed, in the ways that we take ourselves up in the world through particular storylines and ways of being, and that we foreclose on others, we might claim that bodies are 'always in theory' and 'always already deferred to'; we might even claim that '[t]heory-making is a labor of the body' (Zita, 1998: 204). Collective biography, as a research practice, grants us the space to examine this labour. It enables us to begin to unravel, collectively, the discursive nets within which our bodies, and our ways of understanding lived experience, are constituted, and to imagine how they might be constituted otherwise. In this way we work to trouble the mind–body binary and to work with all that our minds–bodies make possible.

In the next four chapters we work with memories from our lives as girls/women in the specific situations of school, of fiction reading and of work. In the first of these four chapters we focus on the concept of subjectification, drawing on our own embodied experience of becoming appropriate(d) schoolgirls. We draw on Butler's and Walkerdine's theorizing of the processes through which we become subjects. In the chapter we tease out the ambivalence of the process of subjectification – its subjection of us and its construction of us as active, agentic subjects.

2

Becoming schoolgirls: the ambivalent project of subjectification[3]

[Y]oung girls of primary school age are presented with, and inserted into, ideological and discursive positions by practices which locate them in meaning and in regimes of truth.

(Walkerdine, 1991: 87)

Our agreed task in this workshop was to examine more closely the processes of subjectification – and to do so through locating the meanings and the regimes of truth through which we became, and go on becoming, speaking subjects. What we have chosen to write about here is the ambivalence of the project of becoming schoolgirls. What our stories make visible is our passionate desire to be appropriate, recognizable, valued subjects, and at the same time how painful and how tenuous our grasp was on being those subjects.

Walkerdine, in *Daddy's Girl* (1997), writes about 'fictions' that function as truths about what a schoolgirl is, and that are constitutive of what she becomes. Our memory-work project takes us into the moments when we struggled to become as we 'should be', as schoolgirls. It lays bare the complex patterns of desire to become that schoolgirl. The stories we told, on that shady verandah in the tropical heat of Magnetic Island, made visible the (often silent) battles we fought as schoolgirls, and still are fighting as women, weaving ourselves into the fictional fabrics of 'proper' school and university practices. They also show flashes of cautious pleasure, and even exhilaration, when correct positioning was achieved or gaps exploited. They recover the joy and the pain of our always provisional achievement of autonomy in school settings. They show how we worked conscientiously at our inscription as appropriate subjects within the social order of schools. They show, as well, the simultaneous struggle to submit to and to master the 'conditions of possibility' made available in that order. As Butler (1995a: 45–46) says of the paradoxical simultaneity of mastery and submission:

> The more a practice is mastered, the more fully subjection is achieved. Submission and mastery take place simultaneously, and it is this paradoxical simultaneity that constitutes the ambivalence of subjection. Where one might expect submission to consist in a yielding to an externally imposed dominant order, and to be marked by a loss of control and mastery, it is paradoxically marked by mastery itself . . . the lived simultaneity of submission as mastery, and mastery as submission, is the condition of possibility for the subject itself.

It is that paradoxical simultaneity of submission and mastery, and the related ambivalence, that we explore here. The dual nature of subjection is so readily (mis)understood in the binary structure of western languages as necessarily *either* submission *or* mastery, but not both. Like Butler, we understand that they cannot so easily be separated, and that the conditions of possibility for the subject itself require both. And so it is to the necessity of that simultaneity that we give flesh in the analysis of our embodied stories.

What we have enacted in this project is a strategy for interweaving theory with embodied knowledge. We have used post-structuralist theory in a productive relationship with our own subjective embodied experiences, and at the same time have made our embodied experiences productive in relation to theory. Our use of 'experience' here, is not in the sense of individuals *having* experiences, but about subjects who *constitute themselves and are constituted as experiencing subjects*:

> Experience in this definition then becomes not the origin of our explanation, not the authoritative (because seen or felt) evidence that grounds what is known, but rather that which we seek to explain, that about which knowledge is produced.
>
> (Scott, 1992: 25–26)

The collective biography project

Our starting point for each day's topic of the collective biography work was a fragment from Judith Butler's extensive theoretical work on subjection (1995a, 1995b, 1995c, 1997a). Bronwyn had selected these fragments and posed, as an organizational strategy for our daily programme, a topic for memory-work connected to each of those theoretical fragments. These topics included first memories of:

- existing, of desiring existence, in a school setting, and of how that existence was conferred

- mastery in a school setting of an externally imposed dominant order
- being an autonomous subject in a school setting and being deprived of autonomy
- working with discursive possibilities in school, and of being worked by them.

As has been our practice as we settled into the storying of our own subjectification, we invented the method of collective biography afresh to suit the topic, ourselves, and the time and space we found ourselves in. Each day we began with informal talk as we 'caught up' with each other, and made cups of tea and coffee. On this occasion we used essential oils as an aid to memory, to awareness of the body and to receptivity (Jefferies, 1999). We then settled to describing and talking through particular memories sparked off for us by the topic for the day and by the associated provocative lines from Butler. Most of us had arrived with at least one story in mind that we wanted to tell. As we listened to each other's stories, and probed the detail with careful questioning aimed at enabling us to imagine the experience being described, old forgotten stories leapt into consciousness and long forgotten details came vividly to mind. After telling each other our stories, we separated to write one or two of the stories we had told. Following this intense period of writing we joined together again to read our stories aloud to the group. As we opened ourselves into the current of memory, and the space of writing, we discovered that in the writing, our memories gathered more details of the context, of the interactions, of our bodies located in time and space and discourse. We found, as others have found who are engaged in similar work, that the telling of stories, written and spoken, produces a web of experiences that are at once individual, interconnected, collective – and political.

The space we create for memory-work is a place of speaking and also of writing where we are at once the script and the page. The work of finding the embodied memory, of letting go of clichés and tired explanations, requires a particular attitude to writing in relation to the embodied self. As Hélène Cixous (in Cixous and Calle-Gruber, 1997: 41) says of the position of writing:

> The initial position is a leaving oneself go, leaving oneself sink to the bottom of the now. This presupposes an unconscious belief in something, a force and materiality that will come, manifest itself, an ocean, a current that is always there, that will rise and carry me. It is very physical.

Also, our storying made visible how talking and writing memories in a collective context, and teasing through them in detail, in critically reflective talk, enables the writers to move towards 'a revelation of the social and discursive processes through which we become individuals' (Davies,

1994: 83). Our stories are woven from/with/through the discourses and storylines which construct our particular historical/geographical/spatial/ social selves-in-process.

The contexts of our subjectification as 'individuals' and as schoolgirls were differently located, culturally, historically, geographically, economically and philosophically. One of us is from Sweden and completed all her schooling in a Swedish public school. Another grew up and attended a privileged Catholic boarding school in England as a 'charity student' before migrating to Australia as a young adult. The rest of us were born in Australia, had variously experienced urban and rural living, poverty and privilege, and extreme and temperate climates. Our schooling experiences included both single-sex and co-educational schools, and both religious (Catholic and Anglican) and public schools. In the religious schools, many of the practices of schooling were related to religious observance and ritual. There was an age range of 20 years between us. While none of us had experienced physical violence on our own bodies in schools, some of the Australian stories told of acts of violence that were surprising and shocking to Swedish ears. The emphasis in our own memories was on achieving *self*-regulation − of our bodies, of our tongues, of particular school practices. As we discuss in later chapters, the emphasis on self-regulation appears to have increased since our childhoods. Self-regulation is generally understood now, as it was then, in terms of the contradictory humanist discourses of individuality, of choice and consequences, of autonomy and responsibility (Henriques et al., [1984] 1998; Laws and Davies, 2000). Our own position differs from the humanist position, since we focus on the paradox that while self-regulation is the condition of possibility for the subject itself, the mastery of self-regulation is at the same time an act of submission.

Embodied knowledge and theory

It was not our intention to find a way of reading and writing that escapes subjectification, but rather to recognize how bodies are subjected within available discourses and thus become the selves we take them to be. This process of subjectification both reduces us to clichéd binaries (such as mind–body) and at the same time gives us the power to deconstruct those same binaries:

> Bodies learn to recognize themselves through clichés. Bodies learn to separate mind from body. Yet bodies can also learn to use the very powers they gain through being subjected, to turn their reflexive gaze on the discursive practices and the habituated ways of being those practices make possible, making them both visible and

revisable, and opening up the possibility of developing new ways of knowing.

(Davies, 2000a: 168)

One of our stories reveals an early dramatic splicing off of self from body – a body distanced as having 'disgusting' and 'unspeakable needs' that should not interfere with the higher work of the mind:

As the afternoon wears on, she becomes aware of the need to go to the toilet, but she cannot find a way that she is happy with to ask for this. She knows she must put up her hand and ask, 'Please, Sister, can I leave the room?' but it seems disgusting to draw attention to herself in this way, as having this unmentionable bodily need. She wants to be a good girl, doing her schoolwork. She hopes if she ignores it, it will go away but eventually she feels the hot liquid release through her pants, soaking through the serge and then dripping from the wooden seat onto the stone floor. A puddle forms underneath her. She eyes it with some curiosity but admits no sense of responsibility. A change in the classroom activity allows her to move to another place but she can't escape so easily. The teacher notices the puddle. The child there now is indignant and dry and the teacher discovers her wet dress. The teacher is sympathetic, kind and smiling, but the girl still tries to ignore the wet heaviness of her pants and dress, feeling as though it didn't really happen to her . . .

She wants to be a good girl. She knows the correct form for gaining permission to go to the toilet, but her desire is to leave her body to one side so she can fully concentrate her mind on the work the teacher wants her to do. But her body betrays her – attention to it cannot be abandoned completely, yet she persists in her desire to splice it off from herself in her effort to be good – and thus to come to learning.

In telling and writing our stories, we deliberately set out to make our storying an embodied process that would produce a site evocative of the unexpected, the forgotten and the foregone. We created a purposeful interactive space where the writer, as well as the listener and reader, might acknowledge her temperature rise or her stomach cramp with anger or embarrassment at a moment past, where she may feel exhilarated by her own daring or the daring of others, or might laugh as joy or pleasure flow from her, where her eyes may leak silently, her body flush or shudder, where she might experience grief, frustration or relief at the telling, or where she may feel her bladder surprisingly full and insistent as it did that day when she wet her pants in kindergarten. In so doing, we wanted to (re)value and (re)view the experiences of bodies and emotions in the processes of subjectification.

We found that paying too much attention to theory in the phase of talking and writing led us easily into explanations that impeded the storying of memories as embodied. In this way we had to temporarily 'leave go' of our rational teacher/educator/researcher selves. In order to resist the discursive inclination of these selves to theorize our stories of school subjectification until after they had been written and read back to the group, we attended with vigilance to the ways stories were told and written and to our discussions of them. The theoretical excerpts from Butler were useful in provoking the memories in the first place, but they were sometimes in danger of hijacking the stories and overwhelming or obscuring their detail. As we found this happening, on occasion, we considered how such theorizing was, for us, in this context of a research workshop, 'usual practice' that was both difficult but important to resist. We practised letting go of that 'usual practice' in order to produce our stories, and then we retrieved and refined it in the writing of this chapter.

After the week together, working both on this and our own individual projects, and storying our previously unspeakable or unspoken biographical moments, we geographically separated and took it in turns to write successive drafts of the chapter. We began with a first draft written by Sue, then sent it by email in succession to each member of the group. We have each written two drafts, with Bronwyn taking responsibility for the final draft. Apart from the first draft it has not been possible to tell who has written which sentences. This strategy for collective writing also called for a 'leaving go' of ourselves as individual writers, as authors of our own texts, as clever girls who will be lauded for our independent thinking and writing. This process has required us to abandon our precious and highly desired status in academia as individuals, whether PhD students and/or academics.

The ambivalence of subjection

We are all women who have been successful in 'getting the goodies' of formal schooling. We did learn to desire, and to be, the right sort of student to complete pre-school, primary, secondary and tertiary studies to the point where we are all engaged in or have completed doctoral studies. We are/were subjected, as successful students, to desiring recognition through achievement, acknowledgement and status. This subject position is/was not achieved without vulnerability and resistance. One of the stories tells of a moment of deep ambivalence at being positioned as good student:

I am in the canteen, which is the basement of the church/school. There are two other girls here. They are going through all the things they might need to know for the scholarship exam. I am supposed to do this too – for the sheer joy of it even though I can't sit for the exam. Means tested out – how can my family be rich? The windows are all frosted glass – I can't even look out. It's summer – hot and sticky but at least the basement is cooler than the classroom. That's a relief. I am hotter than I should be – the anger sending my face red. If I can't sit the exam why do I have to do this? Why can't I do the other stuff the kids are doing like making Christmas decorations? I should be allowed to be a dummy if I want to be! These girls are really smart and they can prepare for the exam themselves. They ask me a question and I know the answer – something about the Nile. I tell them what I know. But I am so angered at the waste of my time and this is all consuming. I imagine saying 'No' to the teacher tomorrow – 'I don't want to study for an exam that I'm not sitting for'. But I know I can't do that and I'll be here again. It's supposed to be a privilege so I'll keep on doing this.

Butler argues that: 'Subjection exploits the desire for existence, where existence is always conferred from elsewhere; it marks a primary vulnerability to the Other in order to be' (1997a: 20–21). In marked contrast to Butler's position, humanist discourses, which are the dominant constitutive discourses in schools, locate existence 'inside' the individual. People are who they are either because they choose to be so, or because of their biological/social/economic inheritance – or some combination of both. What is generally not visible to teachers who understand themselves and their students in terms of the humanist model, is that choice stems not so much from the individual, but from the conditions of possibility – the discourses which prescribe not only what is desirable, but what is recognizable as an acceptable form of subjectivity (Laws and Davies, 2000). Modern forms of schooling are understood, in humanist terms, as not shaping through coercion, but through the subject taking up for herself the desire to be appropriate. What our stories show is the implicit coercion in this benign process of shaping schoolgirls. The girl child desires the teacher's approving gaze, works hard to achieve it, and is always at risk in doing so. The 'individual', and, by extension, individuality, is taken to be highly valued within humanist discourses, yet the girl student who innovates, and in so doing challenges established practice, may always be subject to immediate correction and control:

I copied the sums off the board, ruled two straight lines underneath for the answers. I worked out the answers and wrote them neatly and correctly between the two straight lines. I looked up, pleased with being in school where teachers actually noticed if you did things well. Everyone else was still working. I glanced in the new teacher's direction to see if she had noticed that I had finished. She had not. I looked back at the page, at my neat answers. I saw how I could make them even better. With ruler and pencil I joined up the two straight lines to make a box for the answers. Careful, laborious. I wondered what comment she would make about these interesting boxes. Finally, when we were all finished, she told us we could line up at her desk to have our work marked. Without a word, she put a cross beside each of my sums and told me to do them again. I stared with disbelief at my page. I went back to my desk, and checked the sums. They were still correct. Confused, I asked permission to come out again to her desk. Politely, I told her I couldn't find how they were wrong. She looked for some time at the page. Then pointing to the lines I had added, she said, 'I thought they were ones. Rub them out'. But they could not be mistaken for ones! She was lying! Silently, I went back to my desk, and rubbed out the lines. It looked messy. I hated her. I longed for my real teacher to come back – the one who knew who I was.

This schoolgirl dared to innovate, because she knew she had achieved the signifiers of good student: she was obedient, quick and her answers were both correct and neat. These signifiers of good student gave her room for movement with her regular teacher. The error of judgement that she made here was to assume that a new teacher would be able and willing to read these signifiers, and to accord her the space to engage in pleasurable deviation – a deviation that quietly and unobtrusively filled the space while everyone else finished. The failure of recognition on the part of the new teacher, generated a longing for the teacher who did recognize her as correctly signifying 'good student' and who accorded her spaces for autonomy. Her longing for her regular teacher is accompanied by an emotional rejection of her present teacher's authority *at the same time as* she obeys her commands.

Both of these girls silently submitted to the (unreasonable) authority their teachers wielded, and they experienced strong and antagonistic emotions in the very same moment that they submitted to that authority.

For love of the teacher

At the same time as she is the subordinated Other in the male–female binary, the teacher is the One in whom power is invested in the discursively constituted teacher–student binary (Davies, 2000b). It is the teacher who, within the discourses of schooling-as-usual, is constituted as the one with authority, who determines what will be counted as 'reason', who has knowledge and the 'objective' capacity to recognize the 'nature' of the students. It is she who will confer the rewards of schooling – not only the ability to read, write and count – but also the possibility of being – in particular of being recognizably a 'good' subject, recognizably desirable in the conditions and enabling limits of the school setting. It is the teacher's power to recognize and to constitute as desirable, and it is also sometimes her youth, her beauty and her benevolence that makes the schoolgirl 'love her'. As Erica McWilliam (1996: 374) observes, many of the conditions, contexts and practices of gender difference are held in place by the politics of desire:

an elating and elated teaching body is often the sight/site out of which future scholars are propelled into an on-going love affair with their disciplines . . . the body of the teacher is crucial inasmuch as it performs what it looks like to have a love affair with a body of knowledge and this performance is enacted and observed as erotic, a manifestation of desire which is necessarily ambiguous and duplicitous . . .

The schoolgirl's desire to occupy the ascendant subject position of good, desirable 'student' shapes her body and her perception into a conscious performance of conformity. The girl child with whom we began this chapter, who spliced herself off from her unspeakable body, concentrates her attention on the teacher, and the knowledge she offers, in an attitude of love:

> *Her black serge school uniform is hot and thick against her legs, solid and prickly, a harsh barrier between her soft bottom and the hard wooden seat. She gazes raptly at the teacher, a young nun, fresh face surrounded by a halo of black and white. She loves her and does not want to miss one word of what she says – this is more important than physical comfort. This is what she has been waiting for – to do reading, writing and counting. Her lips are pursed in concentration, her eyes and ears watchful and alert, a frown on her forehead.*

The intensity of concentration achieves a separation of mind and body. She knows already that subordinating the body to the mind promises the possibility that she will not be positioned as the abject other, who does not or cannot control her body, that abject other from whom she must split herself off. She achieves this splitting at the same time as she comes to love the teacher, and to love what it is that she has to teach her.

The tenuous process of achieving and maintaining appropriate(d) subjecthood

On entering school, the child is already familiar with taboos controlling the body and its 'private' functions. The 'abject', according to Butler's (1990: 133) reading of Kristeva, is a 'structuralist notion of a boundary-constituting taboo for the purposes of constructing a discrete subject through exclusion'. To be not-abject is to have control of the body and its functions, but the *recognition* of abjection or non-abjection is regulated and authorized by the hierarchical discourses and practices of schooling. Within this relational state of play, the child's positioning of herself and her positioning of and by others is always tenuous and open to re-inscription, as other and as abject.

The location of the schoolgirl's self as of lesser value in this relational hierarchy may not stem from acts or meanings over which she has any control. In one of our schools, the children were required to bid, on their first day at pre-school, for symbols to place beside their coat hooks and on their belongings. Without any visible prompting by the teacher, the children treated these symbols as visible signs of their relative positions in the hierarchy of the classroom. Powerful children, it seemed, knew instantly which were the valuable symbols and bid for them. Absent children had no choice:

> *It is after circle-time and I am sent out to meet my friend. She is coming in late that day after having been sick for the first three days of preschool. She is my friend from before we started school.*
>
> *The day before, when my friend was absent, the teacher had let us choose from a pile of colourful stickers that she placed before us, the symbol that would mark our place in the classroom, that would signify our hanger in the cloakroom, our books and belongings. My friend was given the symbol that everyone else had avoided, that was left over after we had all tentatively or aggressively made our choice.*
>
> *As I walk out in the hallway my heart starts beating very hard. She comes through the door smiling happily. I greet her but there is no excitement in my voice and my body feels heavy as we walk the few steps to the wall where our hangers are. As I point to her hanger and the symbol she has been given the day before in her absence – a blue armchair, I instantly feel like covering up my own symbol, a white daisy, with the other hand so she will not see it. For an instant I consider the possibility of saying: 'You can have mine', but I don't.*
>
> *She turns pale, and I can see her thinking: 'Am I supposed to be that name – the blue ugly arm-chair?' She begins to sob out loud.*
>
> *The teacher comes out in the hall. I explain to her why my friend is crying. The teacher then signals to the other children to come out in the hall and comfortingly declares that these symbols are just a practical way for us to recognize our things. She says they do not mean anything, and there is no symbol that is better than the other. I look at the other children around me. Some of the faces are fearful and some proud, and it seems that the hierarchy amongst us is set.*

Through her late entry, her absence and the allocation to her of a rejected, arbitrary symbol, the 'innocent' schoolgirl becomes the abject other, the excluded subject. Although the writer dreads being the bearer of the tragic news, it becomes starkly evident to her in this moment of emotional conflict, that her own existence as non-abject, as occupying an acceptable position in the hierarchy of the class, is conferred by *and in part depends upon* the arrival and labelling of the abject other. The teacher, meanwhile, as faithful subject and conveyor of liberal humanist discourses of democracy, equality and freedom of choice, persists with established practice. She is apparently unaware of how the children's positioning within the discourses of schooling-as-usual, already makes visible to them the hierarchical meanings to be ascribed to the plastic stickers that signal 'who they are'. She assumes they are too young to read their names and that the picture is preferable.

No matter how hard any schoolgirl works to achieve the signifiers that can be read as competence, her appropriation is tentative and vulnerable – the subject position of good student is always provisional. She may have no power in relation to her assignment to a low-status category. She may work hard at achieving the right signifiers and yet always she is at risk of running up against definitions of correct practice that she does not know about:

> *Thursday afternoon we all filed in after lunch knowing it was time for 'Composition', wondering what the teacher would expect us to write about, glancing at the board to see if the title was already displayed there. We sat at our desks, backs straight, Composition books open at a new page, margin ruled with red biro on the left hand side of the page, date at the top on the right hand side, facing our teacher expectantly.*
>
> *'Today', she says, 'You can write about anything you like.'*
>
> *Stunned silence. Children glancing at each other in trepidation, excitement, anticipation, disbelief, holding back the inclination to chatter, to express our wonder.*
>
> *I could not believe my luck! To be granted this freedom the very day after having a friend over to play. I had something to write about. I took up my pen as I gathered my thoughts, checking my pen grip and the angle of the book across the desk. I wrote about the bus ride home, about what we'd had for afternoon tea, about having a hit of tennis, about feeling disappointed when it was time for Meg to leave. My story flowed onto the page disguising my anxieties about neat handwriting, correct spelling, the teacher's judgement.*
>
> *Soon we were being asked to put down our pens and pass our open books to the person on our right until all the books were in tidy piles at the end of each row of desks and someone was chosen to collect the piles and carry them to the teacher's desk for marking. I felt confident, sure the teacher would enjoy hearing about my afternoon with a friend and maybe even a little impressed with the description of my family home and our having a tennis court in the back yard. I looked forward to the next day when our books would be returned. Maybe this time my story would be noteworthy, maybe even 'the best' . . .*

The schoolgirl reveals herself in her story as competent in, and observant of, all the ritualized practices of the classroom. She has mastery over her body and is quite confident that the content of her composition is worthy. She is not in confrontation with the imposed order of the school, but relishes its practices and the display of her own mastery within them. But:

> *The teacher sat at her desk and called our names, handing our books back one*

by one. I took the book from her hand, outstretched beyond her expressionless face. I sat back at my desk and gazed at the page, at the blood red gash with which she had marked my story. Shame and disbelief rushed through my still, silent, obedient body. There was apparently something wrong with 'a hit of tennis'. She had crossed out 'hit' and written 'game' neatly above it. Everything had changed. My pride in my family, in my story, my hopes for success and acknowledgment were shattered and focussed with the slash of her red appropriating pen.

Her downfall is a tiny slip-up, the word 'hit' used as a noun instead of a verb. Her use of a colloquial spoken form of Australian English is deemed inappropriate for a school composition. The teacher in this state school polices 'proper' usage of English, in conformity with the English teaching practices of the 1960s and with the cultural cringe of Australian intelligentsia of the time. For this student, despite her submission to and mastery of school practices, her insufficient mastery of the language of the 'masters' is enough to remove the 'possibility for the subject' herself to exist as a competent subject in that class(room). The language she has used is the language of her family, which now is marked as wrong, as inappropriate speech, as having lesser status in the social hierarchy. The child feels she has been positioned as of a lesser class, as someone with insufficient grasp of 'correct English'.

Insufficient mastery of language provided us with multiple possibilities for embarrassment, and for exposure as incompetent subjects. Our memories of slippages in mastery of language were deeply etched. What these stories reveal is that the struggles for mastery can never be complete – appropriate subjection is an ongoing project, and moments in which we are recognized as appropriately subjected give rise to deep ambivalence. There is a deep anger against the one who reveals that our mastery is incomplete, and an extreme vulnerability associated with the gaps in our knowledge of 'correct practice'. The power of the other (usually the teacher, but also often the other students) to rob us of our position of masterful subject, makes our hold on subjecthood tenuous, and something we learn to struggle continually for.

Mastery of the body

Walkerdine (1991: 88) argues that the willing acceptance of the conditions of possibility come not from the girl but from the power of the practices themselves:

> That the girl appears willingly to accept the position to which she is classically fitted does not, I would argue, tell us something basic about the nature of the female body, nor the female mind, but rather tells

us of the power of those practices through which a particular resolution to the struggle is produced.

Bodily control is read by schoolgirls as one means of becoming a recognizably appropriate(d) and valued subject. Such control is not only of
bodily functions and of emotions, but also of the fine motor control
required for such skills as writing:

> *I lean forward in my seat, bracing my forearms on the desk, feet barely
> touching the floor. The lines on the page in front of me demand my attention.
> I must get my hand-writing to fit the order prescribed by the heavy lines at
> top and bottom, the lighter ones inside them and the dotted line in the
> middle . . .*

The schoolgirl is ever conscious of the lines, literal and metaphoric, that
she must not transgress within the conditions and practices of schooling as
usual. One blot of ink is enough to indicate that mastery is incomplete.
Mastery is incomplete because submission is insufficient – submission to
the rules of the lines on the page, to the necessity of bodily control:

> *I dip the pen into the inkbottle, careful to wipe off excess ink. I can imagine
> the ugly blot if I let a drop spill on the page to spoil it – please don't let it
> happen – sometimes these things seem beyond my control. My hand aches
> from the effort of control, my whole body is tightly sprung. The capital 'A'
> starts at the top line, a smooth curve down, done with a heavy stroke, then it
> must start up again, a lighter stroke this time, and meet back where it started.
> I am good at this but there is no room for relaxation – the lines insist on being
> obeyed. Start down again, break away just exactly on the dotted line – ink
> stains my forefinger, my tongue sticks to the roof of my mouth in concentra-
> tion. 'A is for Actil sheets.' It's a long slow journey, laboriously making the
> correct marks on the paper, until I reach 'Z is for . . .', but determination
> steels my muscles. I will win the award again.*

Ultimately, when 'Z is for . . .' is complete, the correct form of writing
achieved and no blots mark the page, her 'lived simultaneity of submission as mastery' will be publicly rewarded. Existence as a subject is conferred again by the Other, by the teacher who is the One who controls/
administers the external reward system. It is through being subject to the
repetition and relations of power within schooling-as-usual that she
comes to know she 'will win the award again'. With such concentrated
effort and repetitious practice, and with the repeated receipt of awards,
she will be established in relations of power in which failure to recognize
her as appropriate(d) will become less and less likely.

In the following story the schoolgirl again achieves her bodily self as
competent in relations of power in which abject others interrupt the
smooth flow of the day's beginning in boarding school. She struggles to

behave appropriately, to submit herself beautifully to the institutional practices involved in the commencement of the day:

> *A room of my own albeit small and cramped with a window and radiator. The bed was tucked into a corner with the door at the foot of the bed. In the mornings I would snuggle under my old gold eiderdown – warm and cosy with even my head encased – hearing vague noises as the nun worked her way down the corridor – knock, announce, response and step. Sometimes the student would be tardy and then it would be knock, announce, announce again, sleepy response and step. My turn soon – I would prepare by swallowing and salivating in order to be able to voice the response, struggling up through the layers of sleep, savouring those seconds. My knock, gentle today, blur of black and white, I like to be able to identify the face, voice insisting 'Bene dicamus domino' – pushing my head up and out and my clear response 'Deo Gratis' – an awareness that I could respond clearly, loudly, while drifting in half-sleep. I knew how to sound alert like a good girl should yet knowing I would also grasp the possibilities of a few more minutes of warmth, sleepiness and encasement.*

Although she is compliant in her submission to the ritualized performance, her memory presents this very submission as control, as mastery. She has learned the tricks of the trade – how to *sound* alert when she is not. She presents herself as a competent self-regulating subject who knows how to recognize appropriate behaviour and how to choose, unlike others, to perform that behaviour. Although she presents the ritual as a 'performance' over which she has control, there is no other way to be recognized as appropriate(d) in that place.

The conditions of existence for the subject in the dormitory of the boarding school, and in the writing lesson, reveal that the perfect subjection of the schoolgirl's body leads to a pleasurable sense of well-being, of secure knowledge that her appropriateness will not be called in question, and that she will be accorded the recognition of herself as having some value. At the same time, the abject other, who does not gain such a pleasurable sense of well-being, is always present, not only as other, but always, potentially, as herself.

The illusion of autonomy: reading against the grain of correct practice

Until now we have focused on the work the child does to constitute herself inside the conditions of possibility made available to her. At the same time, running *within and against* the grain of available/correct practice is the desire to be recognized as someone who is worthy of notice. In this section we examine the ways in which running against the grain is fundamental to autonomy, which is also, paradoxically, fundamental to being recognizably an appropriate(d) humanist subject. In the first story here, the child is angry with her teacher for withholding important knowledge – the knowledge that guarantees access to correct answers. She discovers 'for herself' the secret knowledge, and understands herself in doing so to have passed a crucial test. At the same time, she judges herself negatively for taking so long to gather the secret knowledge:

> *Why hadn't Miss Carver told her this secret? Because she is so mean. Maybe it is a test to see if it can be discovered. Will discovering it count or will just getting it right matter? Should she tell that she has discovered the secret? She decides that she shouldn't tell the secret. It's her turn. She gets it right and the fear is gone but she does not relax. Her body is still tense. It took too long for her to understand it – just getting it right doesn't really count inside her.*

The child theorizes about the way the world works. She reads herself as having worked to make sense of it, and to locate herself in desirable spaces within it. At the same time she does not thus find satisfaction in her positioning. She stands aside from herself and finds herself not yet adequate. She takes this judgement up as her own, quite independent of what the mean Miss Carver knows about her. In this way she judges the gaze of the Other as insufficient. In doing so she opens herself to self to doubt as to her own appropriate(d)ness, and also, ironically, finds the source of a sense of autonomy – of the capacity to know herself differently, and for herself.

Autonomy was often read by us, in the stories we told, as moments of power. In these moments of power we present ourselves as individual subjects who choose to act independently, who differentiate ourselves from those others who are still rule-bound, or bound by the gaze of the Other. Our remembered selves somehow subvert the 'natural order' of the institutional practices of the school and get away with it. As Butler points out, the processes of exclusion and differentiation are covered over and concealed in the experience of autonomy. The schoolgirl subject comes to believe she is autonomous, as long as she can no longer see her dependence on the Other for her recognition and her recognizability:

> In a sense, the subject is constituted through an exclusion and a differentiation, perhaps a repression, that is subsequently concealed, covered over, by the effect of autonomy. In this sense autonomy is the logical consequence of a disavowed dependency, which is to say that the autonomous subject can maintain the illusion of its autonomy insofar as it covers the break out of which it was constituted. This dependency and this break are already social relations, ones which precede and condition the formation of the subject.
>
> (Butler, 1995a: 45–46)

The achievement of autonomy, then, is based on an illusion of separateness from a system from which she can never float free. She is dependent on the recognition of others, which may or may not be bestowed. The schoolgirl cannot willingly enter into a situation in which she knows she will be recognized as incompetent – as inappropriate(d). Yet her dependence, combined with a moment of exclusion and differentiation, may well lead to a recognition of herself as autonomous, which blots out, for the moment, the relations of power in which and on which she is dependent:

It was the secondary school Scripture exam. Each student sat, separated from the others, at a small wooden desk. The wooden dividers between the classrooms had been pulled back to make one large hall. The headmistress sat on the stage, waiting for the clock to turn to 9.30 when she would begin to read out the questions. I was feeling confident and happy. Last year, in 6th grade, I had sat the secondary school spelling exam and while I had not come first, I had got a prize for doing so well in a test for secondary students. And now Scripture – I had listened to the Headmistress each morning in prayers, and I had reflected deeply on what she said. I had listened and debated with Archdeacon in Divinity lessons. I had imagined in minute detail what it felt like to be Job with his boils, and Abraham holding the knife over his son's heart – (Isaac, my son, Isaac) – I had pondered the implications of all those stories since I was six years old.

She read out the first question: What are the first ten books in the Old Testament? Genesis, Exodus, Leviticus, Numbers, Deuteronomy . . . but what came next? I couldn't think of it. The questions kept coming: what was the name of . . . where did such and such a thing happen? These were not the details I attended to in listening to the lessons. It was the questions of moral existence that interested me. I knew none of the answers. I was on the verge of being publicly humiliated – of becoming a noticeable failure, right in the Headmistress's gaze and in front of the entire secondary school, to which I was a newcomer. I took out the tissue from my pocket, and deliberately blew my nose as hard as I possibly could. My nightly nosebleeds would now have to come to my rescue – please God. My tissue filled with blood, pouring out of my nose, like a tap, into my cupped hand. I raised my other hand and asked to leave the room. I went to the toilets and kept my nose pouring with blood for the two long hours of the exam. Finally – sound of doors opening, girls' voices, hubbub of talk at the end of an exam. Relief. I was saved and I could now try to stop the flow of blood.

Next day the Headmistress called me to her office. She must have noticed that I had written nothing even though I had been in the exam room for at least ten minutes before my nose bleed. I knocked on her door.

'Ah yes dear, you must be very disappointed to have missed the exam. Come

to my office tomorrow morning at 10.30 and I will give you the exam ques-
tions here.'

'Thank you, but it's OK really, I don't mind. I don't want to put you to
such trouble' (stay calm, stay calm).

She accepted my words!

I managed to stay home on the day of the Scripture exam every year
after that.

The schoolgirl retained her position as the good/clever schoolgirl, avoided
'being publicly humiliated . . . becoming a noticeable failure' by forcing
her nose to haemorrhage. She exploited a weakness in her own body to
save her from the humiliation of losing her positioning as good student.
She was then able to use her positioning as 'good student' to save herself
from the second possible act of humiliation. Not only did she twice escape
an undesirable positioning – she also found a way to avoid the apparently
inevitable, to stand apart from it without anyone noticing that she had
done so.

In both these examples, the schoolgirl recognizes herself as separate, as
autonomous, as able to know differently from the teacher. One girl judges
the teacher as mean and as withholding knowledge, and herself as clever
enough to gain access to the withheld knowledge – yet still not safe, not
yet secure in the knowledge of her own competence. The other schoolgirl
sees the teacher as having asked unimportant questions (with elusive
answers), and she too discovers knowledges with which to sustain herself
as both competent and yet different. Both find their teachers lacking,
and while their own positions are still insecure and need to be struggled
over, they each take an interesting first step in constituting themselves as
autonomous, conforming subjects.

And so . . .

In this chapter we problemize the humanist subject using collective biography as a strategy for remembering moments of our own subjectification,
and interpreting these in light of post-structuralist theorizing such as that
of Butler and of Walkerdine, we have been able to put flesh on the bones
of the concept of subjectification. We have been able to show the hard
work of becoming appropriate(d) – both its necessity and its risky fragility.
There is no guarantee that even the most conscientious schoolgirl will be
able, repeatedly, to produce herself as that which she has come to desire
for herself. Her knowledge of herself as acceptable depends on both a tight
disciplining of the body, and a capacity to dis-attend the body and its
needs. It depends on a capacity to read what the teacher wants and to
produce it, but more than that, to want it for herself. At the same time, it

depends on a capacity to distance herself from the Others, on whose approving gaze she is dependent, and to know herself *in contrast* to them. She must, paradoxically, find these points of contrast at the same time as she takes herself up as recognizable through the very same discourses through which she and they are constituted.

We have shown through our own stories that subjectification is necessarily an ambivalent project. One must submit in extraordinary ways in order to gain mastery. Yet mastery need not bind us to the very terms and conditions of our subjection. The idea and the ideal of autonomy, which our theorizing recognizes as fictional, is nevertheless the conceptual and practical linchpin of the appropriate(d) subject. The subject submits to the fictions of the self and gains mastery through them; and that mastery – of language, of the body – provides the conditions of possibility for inventing something new, of seeing afresh, of creatively moving beyond the already known. Our elaboration, we hope, gives new life to Butler's (1997a: 14) words when she writes:

> Power acts on the subject in at least two ways: first, as what makes the subject possible, the condition of its possibility and its formative occasion, and second, as what is taken up and reiterated in the subject's 'own' acting. . . . The notion of power at work in subjection thus appears in two incommensurable temporal modalities: first, as what is for the subject always prior, outside of itself, and operative from the start; second, as the willed effect of the subject. This second modality carries at least two sets of meanings: as the willed effect of the subject, subjection is a subordination that the subject brings on itself; yet if subjection produces a subject and a subject is the precondition of agency, the subjection is the account by which a subject becomes the guarantor of its resistance and opposition.

Subordination is thus the precondition for resistance and opposition. We submit in order to become masters of autonomy, to become schoolgirls who depend on teachers for recognition and at the same time, and through the very acts of submission, come to the possibility of seeing otherwise. Now, in the writing of this chapter, we use collective biography to come to know our own pasts differently – against the grain of humanist discourses, so prevalent in explanations of what it is that happens in schools, that shapes desire, that makes life possible:

> coming to know differently, through your own remembered past and the past of others . . . is also about transgression, about finding other ways to speak and write with the grain of bodies and landscape. It is an exploration of the power of language, not only as it seeps into bodies and shapes the very grain of them, but also as a powerful force

that individuals and collectives can use to retell lives against the grain . . .

(Davies, 2000a: 187)

This collaborative work, inspired as it is by our readings of both feminist and post-structuralist theories, 'stands both outside [of the Enlightenment project of emancipation and rational autonomy of the human subject] and deeply within its logics, trying to force a space for new questions about identity, humanity and agency' (Stronach and MacLure, 1997: 5).

In this chapter we have explored subjectification as it takes place inside the compulsory, public institution of schooling. In the next chapter we shift our gaze to a technology of subjectification taken up willingly and privately by schoolgirls once they have learned to read. We look at the work fiction served in our lives as a discursive strategy for taking us beyond the everyday into imaginary spaces. In the crevices of others' experiences we were exposed to the lives of other girls, each of them – like each of us – subjected to discourses of morality and seeking to become properly appropriate(d) girl subjects in their particular socio-historical and geographic contexts.

3

Reading fiction and the formation of feminine character[4]

In this chapter we focus on our readings of the girl heroes from three books written between the 1890s and the 1920s in Australia, the USA and Canada: *Seven Little Australians* (1894), *Pollyanna* (1913) and *Anne of Green Gables* (1925). Analysts of children's literature have long recognized that children's books, written by adults for child readers, operate as significant ideological tools with potentially powerful effects. Indeed, Stephens (1992) asserts that children are constituted by what they read. Texts are always historically, culturally and politically situated, as are their readers (Davies, 2005; Hunt, 2001). Thus there are traces in each of our chosen novels of the nation-building projects of developing distinctive Australian, American and Canadian post-colonial national identities. Discourses of Christianity and (white) racialized communities that are deeply rooted in their times are also evident in these novels. However, we read them many decades after their production in very different historical times and geographic locations. They came to us across space and time as part of a children's canon recognized by those adults who remembered them from their own childhoods – our grandmothers, mothers, aunts and teachers – who put them in our way. Although setting is important in each of these texts, much of the ideological work of novels is undertaken through the narrative codes of plot and character. The moral dilemmas that protagonists face, and the choices they make, extend the horizons of the moral universe for the child reader who locates herself in relation to characters that she comes to love. Thus fiction reading can be understood as a practice interested in, and provocative of, transformations. In this chapter our girlhood reading selves are remembered as they immersed themselves in the fictional lives of Judy, Pollyanna and Anne. We consider how particular feminine subjectivities are exemplified in these characters and the extent to which they were taken up and understood by our reading selves in our everyday lives.

The improving qualities of literature have been central to arguments that universal literacy is a civilizing practice conducive to moral order and good governance. Moral panics about the types of texts that contemporary children read often evoke nostalgia for canonical texts that supposedly promote unambiguous and 'traditional' social values. These values include appropriate gendered identities and behaviours for children. Thus the novels can be read as simple moralistic tales inviting obedient goodness from their girl readers, who cannot help but sympathize with the vulnerable heroines who struggle to be good and to be loved. In this reading they are elegant didactic tools for teaching the 'values and rules of action that are recommended to individuals through the intermediary of various prescriptive agencies such as the family (in one of its roles), educational institutions, churches, and so forth' (Foucault, 1985: 25). Yet during the collective biography discussed in this chapter we discovered that our struggles with the effects of the texts were more complex than mere absorption of the lessons for living embedded within them.

In this chapter we consider how the reading of 'improving' fiction by children can be understood as part of our repertoire of 'technologies of the self', those tools that:

> permit individuals to effect by their own means or with the help of others a certain number of operations on their own bodies and souls, thoughts, conduct, and way of being, so as to transform themselves in order to attain a certain state of happiness, purity, wisdom, perfection or immortality.
>
> (Foucault, 1988: 18)

The reading of children's stories, as in the work of becoming schoolgirls, involves the ambivalent constitution of the self as an active subject.

Although the novels we reread in this chapter are located at the heart of the children's canon, we brought them to the workshop in response to a general request to bring books that we had loved as children. We were surprised to find that several of us brought the same novels and that almost all of us, despite considerable age differences among us, were familiar with these three. We were interested in exploring the deep emotional engagement we had with these texts and that lingers into the present. Through the workshop we traced the slippage of these fictional characters, and what we learned from them, into our everyday lives and into our developing senses of self and of the moral universe. In our analyses we moved back and forth between close readings of key scenes in the texts to childhood memories that each of these moments evoked. We realized that although it is a truism that children's literature is concerned with moral questions, it is necessary to carefully unravel what 'morality' means and how it is materialized. As we interrogated extracts from the novel and our childhood memories, Foucault's work in differentiating between morality and ethics became central to understanding how our child selves were reading their ways into the transformative possibilities entailed in becoming moral and ethical subjects. We outline his moral schemata in the next section before moving on to the novels themselves and the memories generated though the collective biography on reading fiction.

Reading morality

It was in the final phases of his work, in the three volumes of *The History of Sexuality* (1978, 1985, 1986), that Foucault began to look explicitly at morality, particularly as he developed his ideas on technologies of the self (1997a). The rules and values of morality, he says, are sometimes 'plainly set forth in a coherent doctrine and an explicit teaching', like the biblical texts of which the adults in these novels are so fond. But they are also:

transmitted in a diffuse manner, so that, far from constituting a systematic ensemble, they form a complex interplay of elements that counterbalance and correct one another, and cancel each other out on certain points, thus providing for compromises or loopholes.

(Foucault, 1985: 25)

In our rereadings of these stories, we became interested in morality in terms of this interplay of elements as they are manifested in:

the real behaviour of individuals ... the manner in which they comply more or less fully with a standard of conduct, the manner in which they obey or resist an interdiction or a prescription; the manner in which they respect or disregard a set of values.

(Foucault, 1985: 25)

In this chapter we examine key scenes from each of the novels and in the memories they evoked in terms of the behaviour of individuals and the morality that is conveyed through that behaviour.

Foucault delineates two forms of morality, and both of these can be traced through the novels we have chosen to write about. The first form is 'obedience to a heteronomous code which we must accept, and to which we are bound by fear and guilt' (Rose, 1999: 97). Foucault classifies these responses to a 'prescriptive system that is explicitly or implicitly operative in [the] culture, and of which [everyone is] more or less aware', as the 'morality of behaviours' (1985: 26). In contrast, in the second form, 'morality is an exercise in ascetics, whereby through experimentation, exercise and permanent work on oneself one can make life into its own *telos*' (Rose, 1999: 97). In this morality, which recognizes that there are 'different ways for the acting individual to operate, not just as an agent, but as an ethical subject of this action', Foucault suggests that 'the contradictory movements of the soul – much more than the carrying out of the acts themselves – will be the prime material of moral practices' (1985: 26). This second form of morality he describes in a later interview as 'the kind of relationship you ought to have with yourself, *rapport à soi*, which I call ethics, and which determines how the individual is supposed to constitute himself as a moral subject of his own actions' (1997b: 263).

These two forms might be seen as exclusive, with the first, the 'quasi-juridical' (Foucault, 1985: 29), appearing to be more appropriate to 'less developed beings' such as children. Yet we find that both forms of morality are in constant tension with each other and that this tension creates particular problems for children. In both the novels and our own childhood memories this tension is vivid. Indeed, in tracing how these moralities entangle our characters and our child selves, we must also heed Foucault's warning that 'every morality, in the broad sense comprises the two elements . . . codes of behaviour and forms of subjectivation . . . they can never be entirely dissociated, though they may develop in relative independence from one another' (1985: 29).

The second form of morality – that concerned with ethics – is intimately connected with the 'biographical project of self-realization' (Rose, 1991: 12) that we are each assumed, even obliged, to be involved in. The children in our memories and our novels engage constantly in the project of 'self-reflection, self-knowledge, self-examination . . . the decipherment of the self by oneself . . . the transformations that one seeks to accomplish with oneself as object' (Foucault, 1985: 29). At the same time each of us/ them are obliged to be the kind of person who does not offend others in her community, and who is thus under considerable pressure to conform to its idea of the appropriate person. The girls are thus, also, caught up in the first form of morality. Foucault identifies both of these moralities, the 'ethic-oriented' and the 'code-oriented', as being important to Christianity (1985: 30), and unsurprisingly, Christianity is the overt moral code of these novels. We begin our exploration of the novels with outlines of each of their protagonists and the particular moral landscapes in which they are constituted by their authors.

The protagonists of the novels

In *Pollyanna* (Porter, [1913] 1994) and *Anne of Green Gables* (Montgomery, [1925] 1994), each of the girl heroes begins enmeshed in suffering from lack of love and homelessness, following the death of both parents. Both Pollyanna and Anne are faulty in the morality of good habits and politeness – the culturally recognizable codes of Foucault's first form of morality – that their new guardians want them to learn. Both long to be accepted in their new homes. They struggle to be good enough throughout the novels and each, at the end, is highly regarded and belongs securely in the familial and community landscapes that have become home. The resolution of their stories has each girl reconcile and achieve both forms of morality as she moves towards appropriate womanhood. In *Seven Little Australians* (Turner, [1894] 1983), Judy also loses her home and family not through the death of both parents but through her mother's death followed by her father's banishment of her to boarding school for her misdemeanours. Her struggle to return home ends in her death. In this chapter we will focus on the transformations in Pollyanna and Anne and the lack of transformation in Judy to see what kind of moral tales we might read these to be. We do so through linking our analysis of the texts with memories of ourselves as child readers.

Each of the girls in these stories finds herself abandoned, cut adrift from family and from home. Each one is somehow alien in the circumstances in which she finds herself. They look different, they behave differently and they think differently from the people around them. Anne, in particular, is concerned about her own ugliness and often appears naive, unsure how to behave in the new and foreign discursive/moral landscape in which she finds herself. She is at odds with, and struggles with, the moral code presented to her by her new guardian, Marilla, preferring instead her own ethics deriving from her own philosophical position. This is in contrast to her immediate love of, and ecstatic immersion in, the physical landscape of Prince Edward Island, where Marilla has her home. Pollyanna and Judy might also be read as loving the physical landscapes in which their stories are set, and they are also confident about their own philosophy and judgement. And their guardians (Pollyanna's aunt and Judy's father), like Marilla, are constantly offended by their charge's behaviour. The three girls are read by the central adults, who are responsible for them, as seriously in need of tuition and transformation. There is, at the same time, an implicit invitation to read each of them, against the grain of their guardians' readings, as deeply moral individuals, and as embodying Foucault's second sense of morality.

Pollyanna and Anne must make their new home in the alien moral landscape, and they must also transform themselves to become appropriate in that landscape. They each try to be, and eventually succeed in each becoming, the kind of person who can genuinely be cared for and for whom home becomes a safe haven. Their challenge might be said to be to create a new family and home out of the rather unpromising adults and communities they find themselves in. In contrast, Judy's challenge is to get back to her home, and to her brothers and sisters. She succeeds after a heroic journey, becomes very ill, and during her period of recovery, surrounded by loving brothers and sisters, dies in an act of loving self-sacrifice for her little brother. All three of the girl heroes face apparent conflict between rule-bound morality and morality as personal ethics. Their possibilities for belonging are contingent on their learning the first form of morality.

Unlike Anne and Pollyanna, Judy does not grow into a loved and admired young woman but is remembered for the priceless gift of her life that she gave her little brother:

> The General grew chubbier and more adorable every day he lived. It is no exaggeration to say that they all worshipped him now in his little kingly babyhood, for the dear life had been twice given, and the second time it was Judy's gift, and priceless therefore.
>
> (Turner, [1894] 1983: 192)[5]

Literary critics have struggled over Judy's death. Was it a failure of moral courage on the author's part to allow such a strong-willed and interesting young girl to become a woman? Is it a Christian story of self-sacrifice? Lois Keith (2001: 191) observes that the death is 'doubly shocking' since:

> Judy does not appear to be the sort of character who dies in novels. She is flawed and complex, but Turner does not seem to subscribe to the simplistic view that she is either 'too bad' and needs to be punished or 'too good' and destined to be one of God's children.

Indeed the narrator states at the outset of the novel that Australian children are never model children (Turner, [1894] 1983: 7). Keith believes Turner ultimately settled for convention, in which Judy's death plays the same part as the taming of characters in other novels. In Judy's death 'The author is spared the problem of what kind of woman Judy of the wild hair and wild spirit would have grown into' (Keith, 2001: 192–3).[6]

It is the two orphans, Anne and Pollyanna, who establish their moral right to belong to these social/emotional/geographic landscapes; while Judy – the only one of them to have parent, siblings and a home – loses her place in these landscapes and cannot reclaim it except in death.

Our own readings of these stories

So how did we read these stories as young girls? We were interested in how we did or did not take up as 'meaningful', and as life shaping, the fictions of these girls' lives. How is it that 'reading' takes place, we asked, such that we know at one and the same time that it is fiction, and at the same time read in it the possibilities of coming into a sense of our own positioning in the world? How do these fictions work on us and in us to produce the fictions that we recognize as the morality needed for our own lives?

As we have described, we began this collective biography by each choosing favourite novels from childhood and building the workshop sessions around them. The methodological innovation of this workshop involved a more complex multilayering of texts and memories than we had previously attempted. We read theory and fiction and memories, simultaneously, losing ourselves in the readings as we did as children and as we did at times in the writing of this chapter. During the week-long workshops we each reread the stories, examining the moral lessons they seemed to impart and reflexively searching, as we read, for the ways our moral selves seemed to be implicated in them. In each session we generated a particular focus for our memories from the discussion – about the texts, about our childhood selves and about the practice of reading as a technology of the self. Our topics became:

• the work that is done to bring the text to life
• shifting between the fantastic and the real in reading
• the body in reading
• virtue, or the desire for virtue
• learning to be appropriate, and appropriately recognized by others
• the work we do to enter into a heroic story or character.

Morality and the formation of feminine subjectivity crystallized as our theme through the course of the week.

In using the strategy of collective biography in the context of reading stories, we are breaking with the tradition in child literary studies where the major (and often only) focus is on the books themselves, and where the child reader is sometimes imagined, but rarely given a voice. Indeed we found, when we examined the papers in a book in which we might have expected to find children's voices, *Where Texts and Children Meet* (Bearne and Watson, 2000), an almost total absence of children's voices. Alongside this absence of children's voices, we find in such work a rather strange imagined child reader – one who is a rational, choosing child, who 'discriminates', who 'selects and rejects' and who is regarded as having failed 'if thinking and decision-making [are] not inherent in the reading process' (Daniels, 2000: 162). These children 'know exactly what they are doing when they choose to read popular fiction' (Watson, 2000a: 4). They do not 'ever lose sight of the fact that the books they are reading are produced by adults' (Watson, 2000b: 52).[7] This child sounds to us not so much like the child readers we know or remember, but more like an idealized reader who is not susceptible to the power of fiction to draw them in, who remains at all times, rational, autonomous, separate and reflexive.

Our memory stories suggest a reader who is not so perfectly in control of the separation between 'life' and 'fiction'. Not only did the children of our memories lose sight of the adult author (and certainly would not have known the difference between an author and a narrator), they could momentarily lose sight of the fictionality of the stories they read, and of the boundaries between themselves and the girl hero. One of us wrote, for example, of the moment in *Anne of Green Gables* when Anne first arrives at Green Gables and realizes that Marilla does not want her because she is a girl. The child who reads and the child who is read about do not exist in separate conceptual landscapes, nor are their embodied experiences able to be distinctly separated. Rather the reader moves in and out of the fictional landscape, and the world around her and the world in the novel overlap and merge:

> *Understanding came to Anne, not in a moment, not in a lightning strike, but more gradually. Matthew and Marilla don't want her! There's that strange wriggle in my skin again and my eyes want to turn to the back of my head and peer into the darkness of my skull, then they'll stop seeing me, those adults. All that's left of me is my ears, and they're invisible. All there is of me is hearing their voices saying, 'Go away!' They're thinking, 'She's not a boy.'*
>
> *Sounds are a lump in my throat, but Anne says, 'You don't want me.'*
>
> *They don't want me I think out loud in my head and I go ever so quietly outside to the cool under the house. It's a tall space, the under of my grand-mother's house where she made a grotto, plants and rocks with a wooden seat. I sit there with my book, the mozzies biting my legs and my arms and my face and my hands and my feet, but I am out of the way of the grownups.*
>
> *Anne wouldn't be sad in the east gable room if I were there too. She's crying, but I'm not. There are hands tight on my neck and my throat is full of my tongue but I'm not crying. I can see the long drive and the rosebushes out of the East Gable window. Diana isn't far away. Anne doesn't know Diana yet. I know, because I have read the story before. I know she will have a friend soon so I'm not sad about that. But I wish I were a boy because my parents always wanted a boy. My friend Diane is coming to stay with me soon. We'll climb down the steep cliff to the edge of our own Lake of Shining Water and jump across rocks, and we will run all the way to Sherwood Forest. The gum trees buzz with bees on white blossom. Is cherry blossom the same as gum flowers I wonder?*

The moment she describes when she writes *They don't want me I think out loud in my head and I go ever so quietly outside to the cool under the house* we can sense that her feeling of rejection both mirrors and imaginatively creates Anne's feeling. She can enter Anne's feeling because she knows something of it herself, and she can experience it afresh, as she reads, perhaps more vividly than she has done before. She can give words to it, through Anne's words, even though her own words stick in her throat. The girl reading feels Anne's anguish in her own body, but unlike Anne, she thinks she would have retreated into an interior, invisible space, away from adults, just as she has done now. She thinks about how she and her very own friend Diane draw on Anne's fantasies for their own, creating their own Lake of Shining Waters, though they do not have cherry blossoms and must make do with eucalypts.

Rather than the rational/analytic child, we find a child intensely involved in the story, surprised at what the characters can say, knowing herself both in contrast and sameness, taking a 'profound pleasure in literature – [where] there isn't one reality only . . . [but] several . . . enriching [her] capacity to think' (Byatt and Sodré, 1995: 245), *and* her capacity to speak out loud in her head, the unspeakable and the unspoken.

We found in Anne in particular, but also in Pollyanna, a fear of not being *good enough*. We use this term *good enough* with a double meaning – one of being sufficiently virtuous, and the other of being judged as passable – 'good enough', good enough in this case, to be cared for. In contemplating Pollyanna and Anne's struggles to be *good enough* we also found in our own stories the same fear of not being good enough. While our own stories were not of being orphans, we knew precisely the fear and anxiety attached to our own insufficiencies. And connected to these moments of fear we found a euphoric relief at finding ourselves recognized as both good enough and cared for. One of us wrote, for example, about her fear of doing badly in an examination:

> *The Year 10 public exams loom and I am sick with anxiety, my stomach a hard knot, my brain a swirl of confusion and panic. I get no help from the teachers – they only seem to have just read the textbook the night before, as I have. I have always come first in my class but now a sour taste of defeat is beginning to rise into my mouth. My mother's words after previous successes only add to my despair: 'Well, it's only what we expect of you!'*
>
> *I can already feel the coldness of her disapproval at my failure – no words, but a tight mouth and hard eyes that freeze my bones. Perhaps I really have been lazy, perhaps I should have done more homework, then I might have been able to understand the textbooks.*
>
> *I sit beside my father as he drives me to school, head bent desperately over the Chemistry book, his presence solid but not bringing the usual cheerfulness. 'So, how do you think you'll go in your exams?' he asks, casually. My fears burst out of my body in uncontrolled weeping, huge sobs hurt my throat; I cannot speak for trembling and search for my hankie to wipe up the tears that will not stop. He gently pats my knee as he continues to drive and when we arrive at the school he find the words to let me know that he knows I am not bad, that I have tried hard. He says, 'You know your mother and I only expect you to do your best.'*
>
> *That afternoon, returning home, I see Mum and Dad sitting together on the front verandah; they don't look angry, only concerned. The weight on my back shifts – he has told her and they know that I'm good and I can't be expected to do any better. I can trust my father to recognize me.*

The relief that we feel at the father's action and words (*He gently pats my knee as he continues to drive and when we arrive at the school he find the words to let me know that he knows I am not bad, that I have tried hard. He says, 'You know your mother and I only expect you to do your best'*) are capable, still, of bringing tears to our eyes. The fear of not being good enough to be cared for and the relief experienced at genuine, tender care, to our surprise, runs deep for all of us. Though this girl has not lost her parents and home as the fictional girls had, she experiences the same dynamic that is set up by that loss in the novels, of a desperate and prolonged struggle to be good enough. Like every other girl, as we saw in the last chapter, she is not able to produce herself as perfect, since at some point her struggles will not be sufficient. Like Anne and Pollyanna and Judy the adults have let her down – this time the teachers have been too incompetent to teach her. Her mother's dismissive words, *it's only what we expect of you* make the fear of failure unbearable. Effort alone is not enough; achievement is also necessary. She is saved in the end by her father's capacity to recognize her efforts and his equation of effort with goodness: *he knows I am not bad, that I have tried hard*. Her 'best' on this occasion will be good enough. The girl who breaks down with fear at not being good enough can enter into the emotional worlds of Pollyanna and Anne and Judy because she both recognizes *and* discovers herself there. In entering into our own stories, triggered by rereading these novels, we find that the struggle to be good enough is more familiar than any analysis of the characters' circumstances or the story plots might have suggested.

The formation of character

These stories can very easily be read as moral treatises for girls, in which the girl readers might learn from the mistakes of the girl characters and take to heart the lessons they learn about correct behaviour. In such a reading, the novels are about the breaking in of these girls, about their taming, about the absolute necessity of learning to be part of civil society through learning the correct feminine manners of that society. Such learning, though superficial in terms of morality, has been seen by moral philosophers as the first step needed for children to become acceptable human beings who can behave appropriately in the social landscapes in which they find themselves. Comte-Sponville, for example, drawing on Kant, in a formulation akin to Foucault's two forms of morality, suggests that politeness must precede morality, and that children must thus be educated in correct forms. At the same time he admits that there is an unavoidable contradiction in this reasoning, since all that politeness teaches them is the 'small change' or 'paper money' of morality (external rules), which should not be mistaken for the 'gold', which is fundamentally connected to intentions or ethics. But neither should it be discarded, he says, 'while the gold is a matter of the soul, the paper money is a matter of the body, which cannot be ignored' (Comte-Sponville, 2002: 10).

Pollyanna and Anne and, to a lesser extent, Judy, struggle (and it is a real struggle) to be obedient to the mores of the adults with whom they must form a relationship. The reading that places emphasis on their 'taming' suggests the agency is in the adults. But these girls each have a strong will to be appropriate, combined with a strong will to be free to critique the terms of their appropriation. What makes them fascinating is precisely their agency in both taking up the small change that allows them to belong and at the same time questioning the terms of their belonging. They long to belong, and eventually they do belong, happily, having questioned the moral order of the adults and, in Anne and Pollyanna's cases, transformed it. We see this tension between forms of morality in the adults themselves. The female guardians, Aunt Polly and Marilla, struggle to become (and eventually succeed in becoming) appropriately caring adults, largely through accessing maternal qualities. Judy's father, in contrast, is depicted as a brutal, typically Victorian man, who banishes his daughter from home. Believing she suffers from lack of appropriate discipline, he does not see reason to transform himself to become an appropriate caregiver. His new young wife is incapable of filling the gap, so he finds someone else to teach her to become appropriate: 'It was an excellent school he had chosen for her; the ladies who kept it were kind but very firm, and Judy was being ruined for want of a firm hand. Which, indeed, was in a measure true' (Turner, [1894] 1983: 50). Even the narrator gives her consent to the view that discipline, the paper money of goodness – which could be characterized as the explicit application of Foucault's first form of morality to young people – is necessary in Judy's life, as it was in Anne's and Pollyanna's.

Comte-Sponville says of goodwill, citing Kant, that it is the fundamental ingredient of goodness and of character (Kant, 1964: 61, cited in Comte-Sponville, 2002). The central adults in these stories have, at the outset, limited goodwill, and a fundamental lack of other qualities, such as a capacity for joy or for generosity. Judy's father spends money lavishly on his fine horses, but is loathe to spend any money on a holiday for Judy during her convalescence. His concern for his children is manifested in beating them or in banishing them. He blames his very young wife, the children's stepmother, for not caring for them. Aunt Polly takes Pollyanna in out of a sense of mean-spirited duty, housing her in a small airless attic room separate from her own opulent living spaces. Pollyanna, having previously lived in poverty, guesses that her aunt must be glad to have so much money. She is amazed and delighted when she first sees her Aunt's beautiful house. Her delight spills out into naive speech:

'Oh, Aunt Polly, Aunt Polly,' breathed the little girl rapturously: what a perfectly lovely, lovely house! How awfully glad you must be you're so rich!'

'Poll*anna*!' ejaculated her aunt, turning sharply about as she reached the head of the stairs. 'I'm surprised at you – making a speech like that to me.'

'Why, Aunt Polly, *aren't* you?' queried Pollyanna, in frank wonder.

'Certainly not, Pollyanna. I hope I could not so far forget myself as to be sinfully proud of any gift the Lord has seen fit to bestow upon me,' declared the lady; 'certainly not of *riches*!'

(Porter, [1913] 1994: 25)

Aunt Polly does not hear the way in which Pollyanna is talking of being glad, nor can she appreciate Pollyanna's delight. She replies as if Pollyanna were talking about a shameful kind of pride – thus revealing her own joylessness and narrow-mindedness. Later, Pollyanna even learns to love the small attic room she is confined to and to overcome her desire for something else, though she still struggles to keep her tongue completely under control, to only say what her aunt approves of. She tries to tell her aunt that she now loves her room, but accidentally mentions that she had wanted more:

'And of course *now* I just love this room, even if it hasn't got the carpets and curtains and pictures that I'd been want-.' With a painful blush Pollyanna stopped short. She was plunging into an entirely different sentence when her aunt interrupted her sharply.

'What's that, Pollyanna?'

'Nothing, Aunt Polly, truly. I didn't mean to say it.'

'Probably not,' returned Miss Polly coldly; 'but you did say it, so suppose we have the rest of it.'

(Ibid.: 88)

Aunt Polly is sure that her position is the correct and moral one, and that Pollyanna is faulty; but, as readers, we see her narrow mean-spiritedness in marked contrast to Pollyanna's honesty, openness and joyfulness. We see politeness as insufficient if not accompanied by goodness.

Marilla and Aunt Polly, both childless spinsters, are, at the outset of the stories, fundamentally lacking, particularly in maternal qualities associated with appropriate feminine morality. Marilla had been looking for a boy to adopt to help her ageing brother with work on the farm. Like Aunt Polly she adopts Anne out of a sense of duty, reasoning that she should do so since other adults have severely neglected her moral training. She says to her brother, a kinder person who believes they should adopt Anne for the good they can do her rather than the good she can do them: 'I suppose I'm willing – or have to be. I've been thinking over the idea until I've got kind of used to it. It seems a sort of duty' (Montgomery, [1925] 1994: 57), and later, 'it's about time somebody adopted that girl and taught her something. She's next door to a perfect heathen. Will you believe she never said a prayer in her life till tonight?' (ibid.: 63). Children are alien to Marilla and Aunt Polly and somewhat horrifying in their inability to behave as appropriate(d) subjects. Resolute, conscientious, constant, they impose their ideas of morality on these children who have come into their care. They set out to educate, to teach good habits. The deep contrast between the energy and delight in life taken by the children, and the lack of it in these adult women, creates a tension between the goodness that comes from the children's own joyful life force and goodwill, and the tedious manners and politeness that are the outer form required by others.

But Marilla and Aunt Polly, narrow and unloving as they may be at the outset, do each try to do what they believe is right by the child who has come into their care. Judy's father, Captain Woolcott, in contrast, feels 'bitterness of spirit' about his children (Turner, [1894] 1983: 13) and Judy actually exclaims on one occasion, 'What's the use of fathers in the world, I'd like to know!' (ibid.: 35) and it is her belief that her father should take some responsibility for his small son that is her undoing: 'It's a pretty thing if a father can't mind his own son for two hours' (ibid.: 42) she says before depositing her small brother, the General, in his father's rooms at the Barracks.

The narrator of Judy's story reminds us on multiple occasions that the seven children are suffering from lack of care. Of another of Judy's small brothers, Bunty, she observes for example: 'If ever a little lad was in need of a wise, loving motherly mother it was this same dirty faced, heavy hearted one' (Turner, [1894] 1983: 91). Esther the young stepmother is aware that she is not caring for them, and pleads her extreme youth as an excuse. And the author has dedicated the book to her mother. There is thus a chorus in this book of author, narrator, young wife and Judy, drawing attention to the lack of proper motherly care.

One might almost begin to imagine that the persons in need of moral instruction are the adults themselves: see what happens if you do not take good enough care of your children. Nor is such a reading incompatible with our memory of the year 10 public examination, where there is acute longing for, and relief at finding, care from the father in the face of the mother's lack of understanding. Perhaps these authors also had in mind the adults who might read these novels and who might learn to be more aware of and sympathetic towards the dilemmas of childhood.

One of the dilemmas of childhood comes about from the reading by adults of young children as having unformed characters, and from the assumption that it is the adult's will that forms the child through inducing such emotions as fear and guilt, invoking Foucault's first form of morality.

The adults in these stories certainly read the children, at least initially, in this way. But the narrators do not. They allow us to glimpse the reasoning of these girls, and reveal it to be in some fundamental ways superior to the moral position of the adults. While the adults may have the knowledge the children need to become recognized as civil members of the community in which they live, they do not understand either the extent of the children's will to behave appropriately, nor the importance of the questions they ask about the particular civil society of which they are becoming part.

In our own childhood stories we found a great deal of distress at adults' inability to support or comprehend our actions. Sometimes our actions were innocent explorations of the world and its wonders. In the following memory, for example, we find a combination of scientific experimentation and an extension of our capacity for fantasy through literary and biological knowledges. But this exploration met no sympathy from the child's mother:

> *Catriona MacKenzie and I collected all the leftover streamers from the hall. We took them to her house and made a potion in the backyard ... She brought out a big boiler and a kettle of hot water and we set up our cauldron on the lawn at the back. We shredded all the green streamers and poured the hot water over them and stirred and stirred it round as we dropped in imaginary toads and eels and made our special transformation spells. After it had cooled a little we took our clothes off, except for our underpants, and took turns to paint ourselves all over with the potion. We were evil witches, and mermaids stranded far from the sea, and lizards basking in the sun, and people from a far off planet.*
>
> *Before I went home I tried to wash it all off under the hose but the colour wouldn't come out. 'What have you done?' said Mum. She scrubbed my skin until it was red raw in the bath but it still stayed green through the red. I cried but she just whacked me with the scrubbing brush and made me go to school still green on Monday morning.*

The child knows the innocence and joy (and risk) of her play, *and* the misery of adult anger and rejection. She is unable to explain to them, having neither the words nor the position from which to speak the truth of innocence in ways that make it acceptable and understandable to the adult. Instead she is read as morally unformed, in need of induction into correct behaviour through fear and guilt. Just so, Anne's imagination is seen by Marilla to make her morally faulty – while we, as readers, are invited to see Anne's imagination as fundamentally spiritual, aesthetic and deeply philosophical. When Anne is reprimanded for not returning immediately with the prayer she is to learn by heart, we find that she has been gazing at a picture of Christ Blessing Little Children, and imagining herself small and lonely, like the girl on the edge of the picture, edging closer to Christ and then she imagines 'He would look at her and put his hand on her hair and oh, such a thrill of joy would run over her!' At the same time as she experiences this moment of spiritual joy, Anne also engages in critique. She is disappointed with the artist for making Christ so sorrowful. Marilla, of course, is scandalized. Anne's words are irreverent and should be stopped, though Anne is sure that her experience has been reverent. And we, as readers, find ourselves again implicitly invited to see the child as occupying the superior moral position.

While our own moralities may not have been as well developed and articulated as Anne's and Pollyanna's, and while we may not have been able to engage in the moral critique that they engaged in, we do have intense and distressing memories of our moral understandings being ignored and overruled by adults in their anger at our inappropriateness. One of us told a story of having come to believe that honesty was the most important definer of a moral being, and that her joyful experimentation could be tolerated as long as she was honest. Instead she finds her cousin's dishonesty rewarded:

She had heard the story of the little man and his axe many times. Every night her father would tuck her into bed and every night she begged him to tell the story. Sometimes he would tell it twice and she would drift off to sleep with his soft, gentle voice engulfing her. The little man in the story was rewarded for telling the truth and she believed she should tell the truth whatever the circumstances.

She was thinking about this as she lay sobbing under the bed in her grandparent's spare bedroom. Her mother had yanked her away from the paint tin, lifted her bodily in her arms and rushed her up the passage. When they arrived in the bedroom she had been thrown on the bed and been hit repeatedly while her mother yelled 'You naughty, naughty girl, get under the bed and stay there.'

She wasn't really sure what had gone wrong and why she had been treated so harshly. Her whole body was hurting and she felt as if the lump in her stomach would never go away. She sobbed uncontrollably for a long time but as the sobs subsided and she knew that she wasn't going to choke she tried to remember exactly what had happened.

She'd been playing on the verandah with her cousin Margaret. There was a large tin of red paint standing open near the front door. Margaret had said 'Wouldn't it be fun to put our plaits in the paint and pretend they are paintbrushes?' 'What a great idea', she thought. 'You go first,' said Margaret. 'Your plaits are thicker than mine, they'll make a better paintbrush.' She had gingerly put one thick, blond plait down towards the paint tin and then into the oily, red liquid. This was fun, she stirred the paint round and round with the plait. 'I've got a good idea,' said Margaret excitedly. 'Why not paint a picture on the wallpaper inside the front door.' The idea was perfect. She moved into the hall and started painting.

Margaret disappeared and then reappeared with her mother. 'Margaret said you were here, I can't believe it, you naughty girl, destroying your grandmother's wall.' She tried to tell her the truth but her mother wouldn't listen. As she was bundled up from the floor, she looked sideways. Margaret was smiling.

These novels explore the conflict between forms of morality in minute and careful detail through allowing the intentions and reasoning of the child to be fully visible, at least to the reader. This makes them both interesting and informative, especially for children who have run the gauntlet of adult rage, and who have experienced being positioned as wrong without any chance of (or words for) stating their case. The novels are also comforting – in so far as they reveal that there are other adults who do not hear and cannot see 'the gold', but more important still, that those adults are not only wrong, but that they can be changed – at least in the case of Marilla and Aunt Polly.

Both Aunt Polly and Marilla are obsessed with the small change and, at first, are totally incapable of seeing the character, or gold, of the girls. Marilla's task throughout *Anne of Green Gables* is to teach Anne to be respectable, to perform appropriately as a polite social being. Anne is afraid she will be sent back to the asylum if she fails to meet Marilla's exacting standards. When Marilla reprimands her for putting wild flowers on her hat on the way to church, Anne exclaims 'I'm afraid I'm going to be a dreadful trial to you. Maybe you had better send me back to the asylum' (Montgomery, [1925] 1994: 100), but Marilla tells her she doesn't want to send her back: 'All I want is that you should behave like other little girls and not make yourself ridiculous' (ibid.: 100). The narrator quotes Browning in observing Anne:

All 'spirit and fire and dew', as she was, the pleasures and pains of life came to her with trebled intensity. Marilla felt this and was vaguely troubled over it, realizing that the ups and downs of existence would probably bear hardly on this impulsive soul and not sufficiently understanding that the equally great capacity for delight might more than compensate. Therefore Marilla conceived it her duty to drill Anne into a tranquil uniformity of disposition as impossible and alien to her as a dancing sunbeam in one of the brook shallows.

(Ibid.: 214–15)

Marilla eventually succeeds in her training: 'she's real steady and reliable now. I used to be afraid she'd never get over her feather-brained ways, but she has and I wouldn't be afraid to trust her in anything now' (ibid.: 299). Yet we as readers are invited to know, by the narrator, that the 'feather-brained ways' that Marilla tries to train Anne out of are the real gold in Anne's moral character. They give her a capacity for a joyful spirituality that Marilla cannot, at first, recognize. When she first tells Anne to kneel and pray, Anne asks:

Why must people kneel to pray? If I really wanted to pray, I'll tell you what I'd do. I'd go out into a great big field all alone or into the deep, deep woods, and I'd look up into the sky – up – up – up – into that lovely blue sky that looks as if there were no end to its blueness. And then I'd just feel *a prayer.*

(Ibid.: 61)

This capacity for experience of beauty – of god in nature – is a long way from Marilla's own distrust of pleasure – even the pleasure Anne gives her: 'Marilla permitted the "chatter" until she found herself becoming too interested in it, whereupon she always promptly quenched Anne by a curt command to hold her tongue' (ibid.: 75). But gradually Anne transforms Marilla, without Marilla even realizing it: 'The spring was abroad in the land and Marilla's sober middle-aged step was lighter and swifter because of its deep primal gladness' (ibid.: 256).

The moral trajectory of Pollyanna's story has this same dual quality. Pollyanna bestows an expressive love on her aunt who is unable at first to return it:

Down the attic stairs sped Pollyanna, leaving both doors wide open. Through the hall, down the next flight, then bang through the front screened door and around to the garden she ran.

Aunt Polly, with the bent old man, was leaning over a rose-bush when Pollyanna, gurgling with delight, flung herself upon her.

'Oh, Aunt Polly, Aunt Polly, I reckon I am glad this morning just to be alive!'

'Pollyanna!' remonstrated the lady sternly, pulling herself as erect as she could with a dragging weight of ninety pounds hanging about her neck. 'Is this the usual way you say good morning?'

The little girl dropped to her toes, and danced lightly up and down.

'No, only when I love folks so I just can't help it! I saw you from my window, Aunt Polly, and I got to thinking how you weren't *a Ladies' Aider, and you were my really true aunt; and you looked so good I just had to come down and hug you!'*

(Porter, [1913] 1994: 41)

The spontaneous emotion and fundamental goodness of Pollyanna disarms this hard woman who begins to learn something about human kindness from her: 'Miss Polly opened her lips and tried to speak; but in vain. The curious helpless feeling that had been hers so often since Pollyanna's arrival, had her now fast in its grip' (ibid.: 94–95). She begins to realize she has lost something that is of value, that something being the kindness and goodwill that Pollyanna has in abundance. She realizes this

when the orphan Jimmy Bean tells her that Pollyanna had told him she
was kind, but that this is not true:

In the sitting-room window at that moment, Miss Polly, who had been watch-
ing the two children, followed the boy with sober eyes until a bend of the road
hid him from sight. Then she sighed, turned, and walked listlessly upstairs –
and Miss Polly did not usually move listlessly. In her ears still was the boy's
scornful 'you was so good and kind'. In her heart was a curious sense of
desolation – as of something lost.

(Ibid.: 104–105)

Miss Polly, too, wants to be good enough, and is found wanting.

While the most obvious moral trajectory of these novels might be of
Anne and Pollyanna learning more of the small change, the second moral
trajectory is of their guardians, Marilla and Aunt Polly, learning the gold.
Transformation is effected by our girl heroes on those adults around them.
Quite early on, Marilla begins to recognize the value of the innocent
truths that Anne speaks, and so stays her reproving tongue:

Marilla felt helplessly that all of this should have been sternly reproved, but
she was hampered by the undeniable fact that some of the things Anne had
said . . . were what she herself had really thought deep down, but had never
given expression to . . .

(Montgomery, [1925] 1994: 98)

The usually harsh, judgemental Marilla begins to see that there is another
way to view the world, a way that contains love. When Mrs Barry forbids
Anne from seeing her dearest friend, Diana, Anne tries to persuade her to
change her mind, and fails miserably. She says to Marilla:

'. . . There is nothing more to do except to pray and I haven't much hope that
that'll do much good because, Marilla, I do not believe that God Himself can
do very much with such an obstinate person as Mrs Barry.'

'Anne, you shouldn't say such things,' rebuked Marilla, striving to over-
come that unholy tendency to laughter which she was dismayed to find grow-
ing upon her. And indeed, when she told the whole story to Matthew that
night, she did laugh heartily over Anne's tribulations.

But when she slipped into the east gable before going to bed and found
that Anne had cried herself to sleep an unaccustomed softness crept into her
face.

'Poor little soul,' she murmured, lifting a loose curl of hair from the child's
tear-stained face. Then she bent down and kissed the flushed cheek on the
pillow.

(Ibid.: 157)

Both Anne and Pollyanna agree to learn the forms of habit and politeness that their guardians want, but they do not lose their joy in life, and in this sense can be read as powerful in their capacity to effect good deeds. They eventually enable the adults around them to take pleasure in life that they had previously denied themselves, that pleasure including a new-found capacity to love the strange, alien children who have come into their lives.

This tension between the 'gold' and the 'small change' was one that we found in abundance in our memories. We struggled to become autonomous beings whose character was defined in relation to our own wills, our own knowledges. At the same time we dreaded the moments of being inappropriate, of finding ourselves alien. While as adult readers we might be impatient with the hardness of, and lack of sympathy in, Marilla, when she is outraged at the wild flowers on Anne's hat, we found in our own stories a particular kind of grief when the adult women in our lives had not provided us with the knowledge and the means to become appropriate:

She entered the church dressed in a pink tutu and deep red high heel shoes. She gripped her toes into the top of the shoes as she performed a dramatic spin upon passing the holy water basin at the entrance. Her younger sister, who was wearing a white tutu and bright red lipstick, copied her twirl and let out a shriek of delight at having mastered her technique. This shriek, coupled with the clacking of both sets of shoes caused many of the people in the back row to glare at the two of them with a look of disdain. She noticed a man shaking his head and maintaining eye contact with her until she shifted her focus to the floor. Their mother didn't turn back to scold them. She simply continued walking down the aisle scanning the pews for a space for the three of them to sit. The two little ones hung their heads on the long walk, trying to slide in the shoes so as not to make too much noise. It was difficult to walk briskly enough to keep up with their mother and manage shoes that were twice the size of their feet. Fortunately, they squashed into the end of a pew close to the front. She was able to hide from the faces on the other side by virtue of the aisle end of the pew. When the congregation began to line up to receive the Eucharist she again felt their burning stares from above as they passed over their pew. She felt angry now. Why had her mother said it would be all right to dress up when these people's eyes were telling her it wasn't?

Like Judy, this small girl finds herself without the kind of guidance that would enable her to know how to conduct herself appropriately. She, like Anne and Pollyanna and Judy, must find the ways to belong, to shape herself as a person who has a right to belong. At the same time she must maintain her own sense of integrity, her own capacity to make sense of the world and to find joy in it. As girl readers, then, we see the importance of adult care – and in particular, of appropriate forms of care. We also learn the importance, even the potential power, of our own judgement and the danger inherent in not learning how to enact our decisions appropriately.

Longing and (be)longing: Anne and Pollyanna

What is it that each of these girl heroes longs for? Anne longs for the beauty of the Island, and the chance to live in such a beautiful landscape; to be good enough to be able to belong in both family and community; and not to be ugly. Pollyanna longs to belong in Aunt Polly's family, in particular to have Aunt Polly want her; and she longs to be free to live by the principles of joy that her father taught her. The adults too, in these stories, experience longing, which stems generally from some failure to find pleasure in life. The stories imply that this lack prevents them from seeing beyond a narrow set of principles. For Marilla and Aunt Polly part of this lack is having missed out on the rewards associated with mothering. Their lives are rule-bound because, as non-mothers, they are not seen to have become self-realized adult women. They are typical 'spinsters', needing the love for/of children to bring them fulfilment.

For the children, these longings are often in conflict with each other. Pollyanna's glad game, which her father taught her, is a game based on the rejoicing texts in the Bible. Aunt Polly refuses to allow Pollyanna to talk about her father, and so Pollyanna can neither teach Aunt Polly the glad game, nor enable Aunt Polly to appreciate her own deep moral principles. She successfully teaches it to others, however, thus transforming their lives. She has rather unsuccessfully tried to teach it to Mr Pendleton, a very wealthy but grumpy old isolate with whom she has struck up a friendship. Mr Pendleton's isolation dates from his unrequited love for Pollyanna's mother. Mr Pendleton develops an extraordinary longing for Pollyanna, whom he sees as a cure for his misery. He begs her to come and live with him, explaining that it is only from a child or a woman that a home can be created and, that now he has learned the glad game, he has changed. Pollyanna tells him he does not yet play it properly.

> The man's face suddenly grew very grave.
> 'That's why I want you little girl – to help me play it – will you come?'
> Pollyanna turned in surprise.
> 'Mr Pendleton, you don't really mean – that?'
> 'But I do. I want you. Will you come?
> Pollyanna looked distressed.
> 'Why Mr Pendleton, I can't – you know I can't. Why, I'm – Aunt Polly's!'
> (Porter, [1913] 1994: 170)

Mr Pendleton refuses to accept Pollyanna's refusal, begging her to come and live with him. She finally agrees, sadly, to ask Aunt Polly. But, on her way home, Nancy, Aunt Polly's servant, comes to meet her with an umbrella to shelter her from the rain, saying Aunt Polly is worried about her. Nancy explains that this worry means a big change has come over Aunt Polly, who has begun to care about her:

> *'Oh Nancy, I'm so glad – glad – glad! You don't know how glad I am that Aunt Polly – wants me!'*
>
> *'As if I'd leave her now!' thought Pollyanna, as she climbed the stairs to her room a little later. 'I always knew I wanted to live with Aunt Polly – but I reckon I didn't know how much I wanted Aunt Polly – to want to live with me!'*

(Ibid.: 185)

This theme of longing and belonging in Pollyanna has a fugue like quality and is as relevant to many of the male characters as it is to the female characters (Barthes, 1977a: 103). As well as Pollyanna's search for a home, there is the orphaned Jimmy Bean's search for a home. Pollyanna brings Jimmy Bean into the miserable Mr Pendleton's life so they can make a home together. Aunt Polly and her lost love, the unhappy doctor, are also, finally, brought together.

Judy's story

Let us turn then to look more closely at Judy's story. In *Seven Little Australians* the children are all a little naughty and neglected. The narrator tells us right at the beginning that we should not read on if we want good children since:

> *Australian children never are. . . . It may be that the miasmas of naughtiness develop best in the sunny brilliance of our atmosphere. It may be that the land and the people are young-hearted together, and the children's spirits not crushed and saddened by the shadow of long years' sorrowful history.*
>
> *There is a lurking sparkle of joyousness and rebellion and mischief in nature here, and therefore in children.*

(Turner, [1894] 1983: 7)

Spirited children, she tells us, will 'advance Australia' (ibid.: 8). The reader is thus invited to enjoy the naughtiness of the children, and to see it as patriotic. In its time this novel sat alongside a range of other texts associated with a rising nationalistic fervour culminating in the formation of the nation in 1901. The narrator evokes the second form of morality – still resonant in debates about national identity – which suggests that true members of the Australian landscape are motivated by a free spirit and a sense of rebellion against conformity and narrow-mindedness. At the same time, as we pointed out earlier, it is made clear – particularly because she is a girl – that it is a problem that no one teaches Judy the rules of politeness and obedience that Anne and Pollyanna are taught.[8] Like Pollyanna and Anne, Judy has her own moral integrity, a strong capacity for critique and is full of life and joyfulness. She, too, has a great capacity to love. Like them, she is different from other children. Her mother, before she died, had worried about the consequences of Judy's spiritedness:

> *That restless fire of hers shone out of her dancing eyes, and glowed scarlet on her cheeks in excitement, and lent amazing energy and activity to her young, lithe body, would either make a noble, daring, brilliant woman of her, or else she would be shipwrecked on rocks the others would never come to, and it would flame up higher and higher and consume her.*

> (Ibid.: 21–22)

Like Anne and Pollyanna, Judy is not one who can easily be contained or constrained, nor is she beautiful like a traditional heroine:

> *Judy, I think, was never seen to walk, and seldom looked picturesque. If she did not dash madly to the place she wished to get to, she would progress by a series of jumps, bounds, and odd little skips. She was very thin, as people generally are who have quicksilver instead of blood in their veins. She had a small, eager, freckled face, with very bright dark eyes, a small, determined mouth, and a mane of untidy, curly dark hair that was the trial of her life.*

> (Ibid.: 5)

Judy's father, like Marilla and Aunt Polly, at the beginning of their stories, is lacking in any kind of joy, or appreciation of young children, or appropriate parenting skills. Unlike Anne and Pollyanna, Judy has no capacity to transform her father. While he does recognize the gold in her, admitting, for example, that he knows she would never lie, he does not relent in his opposition to her spiritedness until he sees that she might die of the illness she has contracted in her long journey home from boarding school. Like Anne, Judy has had experience looking after small children and is good at it. She helps her young stepmother out by looking after the baby – the General. Although her wilfulness might be seen to disbar her from appropriate femininity, it is clear that Judy has maternal qualities that are lacking in the adult women of all three of the novels: her own stepmother, Aunt Polly and Marilla. As readers we have every reason, then, to expect that Judy belongs appropriately, and that she will go on doing so. So what goes wrong? How is it that Judy's longing does not transform into belonging?

When Judy and her brother Pip have an unexpected chance for a special adventure – a trip to the Bondi Aquarium – Judy's care of the General is in conflict with the outing. Pip harangues her for being a hopeless girl with a baby in tow, spoiling their adventure. She has the bright idea of leaving the baby in their father's rooms at the Barracks, reasoning that it is after all his baby so he should share some responsibility for it. But the plan backfires badly. When they return to the Barracks after their visit to the Aquarium, the father has departed for home in a rage, with the baby. The other men stand around gossiping and laughing at him behind his back. Judy, like Anne and Pollyanna, faulty but with character and a capacity to speak the unspeakable, immediately steps forward to defend his honour:

> *'It is my father you are speaking of,' she said, her head very high, her tone haughty, 'and I cannot tell where your amusement is. . . . I am afraid I must have put my father to some inconvenience,' she said quietly. 'It was I who left the Gen- my brother here, because I didn't know what to do with him for an hour or two. But I quite meant to take him home myself. Has he been gone long?'*

> (Turner, [1894] 1983: 37)

Judy thus claims responsibility for her actions and so shames the men who were humiliating her father. But her father selfishly sees only her fault. He asks himself: 'Was she always to be a disturber of his peace? Was she always to thwart him like this?' (ibid.: 112). In his outrage he banishes her from the family home, not even allowing her to return for holidays or when there is a life-threatening epidemic at the boarding school where he has sent her. Judy escapes the boarding school and walks most of the long, long journey home, sleeping out at night. When she reaches home she hides in a shed, where her siblings find her, ill and starving. They take care of her but, when her father discovers her, he is even more outraged. He is about to send her back when she coughs up blood. Only then, realizing her life is in danger, does he relent. The doctor recommends a holiday and Judy and the rest of the family go to stay on the farm belonging to the young wife's parents, where they are lovingly cared for.

In this idyllic setting they go on a picnic far into the bush. Judy, as usual, is looking after the General in her loving way: 'She kisses him fifty times. It almost hurts her sometimes, the feeling of love for this little, fat, dirty boy' (Turner, [1894] 1983: 164). Then one of the towering eucalypts falls towards the little boy as he toddles off into the bushes. One of us remembers her first reading of that moment:

> *I was unaware of where I was, unaware even of the act of reading. Tired eyes running over the print half awake, half asleep. Not sure even, if I knew what I read or not. To slide into the world of the words, be awake enough to read, yet open to the vivid dream-like images of the story, flowing on and on – late at night in bed when I was supposed to be asleep. Mostly the only thing that*

*interrupted was the lines of print curling and sliding off the page and the fall
into sleep and dreams. But once I found the dream on the page so horrible
that I could not believe I'd read it – like waking yourself up out of a bad
dream. Maybe I'd read it wrong. The print on the page became something to
be carefully examined.*

*' "You rogue!" Judy called, pretending to run very quickly. Then the whole
world seemed to rise up before her.'*

' "Judy" Pip said in a voice of beseeching agony.'

*How was this possible? Only minutes before the baby was eating fistfuls of
dirt, then squeezing a banana in his chubby little fingers 'gleefully watching
it come up between his wee fingers in little worm like morsels' then smearing
it over his face. It couldn't be right that on one page there was the squishy
banana and on the next the tree falling on her – it couldn't be right that she
didn't get him out in time and save both him and herself. I turned the pages
back and re-read, but it was the same, the tree falls and hits her. But does it?
Is she dead? The words on the page hold a gap inside of which the impact of
the tree on Judy is wrapped in silence – a silence filled with the anguished cry
of her brother. I read on to the end, my breath coming in short quick bursts,
that go only to my mouth, my lungs shut down.*

*She dies surrounded by those who love her. I read and re-read the scene of
her death with tears filling my eyes so I have to wipe them quickly away so I
can still see the words, see the scene of Judy, lying on the old door that was
ripped off the hut to make a stretcher for her. I press my lips together and
breathe quick breaths to stop myself from crying.*

Finally I put the book down.

*Why didn't she push him out of the way of the tree and then save herself?
Why didn't she run faster? I can see exactly how she could have pushed him
in a flying leap that takes her and him out of the path of the tree. I see her
propelled out of the tree's path and hear the loud cracking as it crashes to the
ground behind her. But I can also see her little grave, out there on the hillside,
by the old tree, and I imagine myself there, under the earth, in that perfect
setting, loved and remembered for having given the gift of life to the small
loved boy. At that moment, and only then am I unequivocally good enough to
be loved.*

In this novel the father fails tragically in his parental duty. Because we
know Judy is honest and has integrity, and we know the father is selfish
and ignorant, we cannot possibly see the failure as Judy's. The love that
she inspires in her siblings is intense and deep, but her father's incapacity
for joy and his inability to recognize and value Judy means that he loses
her. He is reminded of his failure by Judy's memory that lingers on in the
General as a constant reminder of her goodness, of her sacrifice. The second moral trajectory that we found in the other two novels, which focuses
on the adults and the necessity of their coming to learn the gold, is also

present in this one, though here the father fails to transform and so suffers an unfathomable loss.

And so . . .

The girl heroes of these novels are at one and the same time, and through the same processes, engaging in the two forms of morality identified by Foucault: the first being 'obedience to a heteronomous code which we must accept, and to which we are bound by fear and guilt' (Rose, 1999: 97) and the second being 'an exercise in ascetics, whereby through experimentation, exercise and permanent work on oneself one can make life into its own *telos*' (Rose, 1999: 97). This second form recognizes that there are 'different ways for the acting individual to operate, not just as an agent, but as an ethical subject of this action' (Foucault, 1985: 26). This second form of morality is 'the kind of relationship you ought to have with yourself, *rapport à soi*, which I call ethics, and which determines how the individual is supposed to constitute himself as a moral subject of his own actions' (Foucault, 1997b: 263). Pollyanna and Anne do bend themselves to conform, and at the same time are always engaged in becoming that ethical subject of their own actions. In this sense the two moralities are not necessarily incompatible with each other, though they may have apparently different driving forces, the first seeming to be outside the self and the latter being in relation to the self. The mechanism that brings these forces together can be defined in terms of longing and belonging. The girls long to belong – to become the appropriate(d) subject of the moral/emotional landscapes in which they find themselves. The complex task that each girl engages in is to become one who belongs and, at the same time, one who does not forgo her own ethical relationship with herself and others. Judy, in contrast, begins in the relative safety of her family and is cut adrift with no one to help her regain her footing. This highlights the fundamentally social nature of subjectification. Marilla and Aunt Polly are at first inadequate, but they become adequate as the girls move towards their own appropriate(d)ness. Neither Judy's father, nor her stepmother, nor, apparently, her teachers, move towards her and with her. Her ethical nature is not in question – she is a legitimate hero, an 'ethical subject of her own actions' – yet she is cut adrift and then sacrificed. The landscape in which she belongs is not adequate to sustain her.

The moral reasoning of these novels allows the girl reader to see that she will not, as she probably already knew, become fully human through the simple process of mimicry of the surface rules. She can see that some adults do not know this and are committed only to the rules, but that while one must learn these rules there is something more that is of greater value and power. She can also relate to the desire of the child for safety, and a place in which she belongs. She can relate to the fear of losing this place, this love, if she does not conform to the surface politeness that adults place such store in. Yet the moral reasoning of the novels tells her that even though she may still be only a vulnerable child who is sometimes naughty, and sometimes makes mistakes, her real chance of becoming a person in her own right will reside in knowing for herself what is good, based on her own *rapport à soi*. And that relationship is not incompatible with making mistakes and with adults being angry with you. This might be understood as the emergence within our heroines of traces of the rational humanist subject that we explore in later chapters of this book. It might be understood as marking a transformation from childhood into a more autonomous subjectivity as an adult. Although these novels were produced in places and times far removed from contemporary readers and from our own childhood selves, and although they are infused with discourses particular to their times, we suggest that the engagements we made with the moral landscapes of these characters may account in part for our own stubborn love of them.

Unlike the children reading romance stories (Walkerdine, 1991) who learn that being vulnerable is the necessary and even desirable (and sufficient) prelude to safety and love from the prince, who installs you in a home of your own, the girls we were as we read these stories learned that the way out of vulnerability and isolation is not a matter of simple obedience or submission. One must submit – we learned and continue to learn – but one must also struggle with the social world in such a way that it becomes able to encompass one as an ethical being. Transformation of both ourselves and those around us, and critical engagement with the discursive frameworks within which we understand and live, remain central to the project of becoming ethical subjects.

So how do these girls who struggle to become ethical subjects cope with their workplaces as adults. What happens to the Judys who rebel? How do the new neo-liberal practices affect and effect the women who find themselves under surveillance and never able to be good enough, by definition, within the new systems of control? In the next two chapters we move into the present, to find how the stories and the theorizing we have done so far enable us to think about ourselves subjected within our workplaces.

4

Embodied women at work in neo-liberal times and places[9]

In this chapter we explore our embodiment as women engaged in academic work with a particular focus on how our working bodies are constituted in neo-liberal workplaces and through neo-liberal discourses and relations of power.[10] To this end we gathered ourselves together to engage in a week-long collective biography workshop where we produced written memories of ourselves in our workplaces, and related memories of our embodied selves as students and as small children.

Ziarek (2001: 3) observes a tendency in those who analyse the relations between discourse, power and embodiment to lose sight of the embodied subject as agent, and as a site of revolt and of ethical responsibility:

> Certainly one of the most significant challenges to the imperialism of the autonomous, 'unencumbered' modern subjectivity has been issued by the historical examination of the constitution of bodies in the matrix of power/discourse. Yet, such an analysis all too frequently shifts the emphasis from the subjective to the disciplinary, institutional mechanisms of control and thus fails to interpret the embodiment as a possible locus of revolt or ethical responsibility.

In the analysis that follows we work to hold both these directions open – to make visible the constitutive power of neo-liberal discourse, and to explore both our take-up of this discourse as our own, to work with, *and* as a force to be worked against in ethically responsible (and sometimes surprising) ways. If the directions are held in binary opposition, we will suggest, sense cannot be made of this double directionality.

Neo-liberalism in the workplace

Neo-liberalism is characterized by the removal of the locus of power from the knowledge of practising professionals to auditors, policy-makers and statisticians, who need not know anything about the profession in question (Rose, 1999). As Hammersley (2001: 9) points out: '[D]emands for "transparent" accountability' (along with many other of managerialism's terms), are made into imperatives that are in turn justified as a response to severely limited financial resources. Neo-liberalism is characterized by the 'death of society' and the rise of 'individuals' who are in need of a new kind of management, surveillance and control. To this end universities have been 're-structured', old patterns of work and of knowledge broken up and managers allocated far greater powers and financial rewards for their part in overseeing the breakdown of old structures, knowledges and loyalties.

The new panopticism in new managerialist worksites works more or less invisibly through *multiple eyes* at every level – eyes whose gazes are finely tuned to the inflow and outflow of funding and to the multitude of mechanisms that have been generated to manipulate those flows. This *multiplied gaze* (which includes our own) works in such a way that it seems natural and makes us blind to its effects (Schmelzer, 1993).

Within the terms of the new system, individuals are presented with an (often overwhelming) range of pressing choices and administrative tasks for which they are responsible and, having learned to be one of the pairs of eyes that watches and calculates value in terms of the budget, we 'responsibly' gaze on our own acts and the acts of others. And we shape ourselves (or try to) as the ones who do have (monetary) value to the organizations we work in. At the same time any questioning of the system itself is silenced or trivialized (Davies and Petersen, 2005a). The system is, at the same time, and as part of that trivialization, characterized as both natural and inevitable (Fairclough, 2000).

Winefield et al. (2002: 9) have found in a survey of academic staff that 'approximately 50% of the Australian university staff taking part in the study were at risk of psychological illness, compared with only 19% of the Australian population overall'. The study of 8732 university staff found that:

> Most academic staff were dissatisfied with five aspects of their job: university management, hours of work, industrial relations, chance of promotion, rate of pay.
>
> At the individual level, the organisational factors that best predicted psychological strain were job insecurity and work demands. The best predictors of job satisfaction were procedural fairness, trust in heads, trust in senior management, and autonomy.

Trust in senior management and perceptions of procedural fairness, (both predictors of job satisfaction) were both low.

(Winefield et al., 2002: 9)

Although Winefield et al. do not discuss neo-liberalism as such, the problems with intensification of work, weakened unions, reduced autonomy, increased vulnerability and alienation from management, are all hallmarks of neo-liberal forms of organization.

Chiasma

We draw on the concept of chiasma in this chapter to explore the multiple and continuing crossings over between being constituted and being constitutive, between embodiment and discourse, between one discourse and another. The concept of chiasma, or crossing over, is drawn from a biological process that may occur during meiosis, when two chromosomes of a homologous pair, one being of maternal origin and the other of paternal origin, cross over, and in that process exchange equivalent segments with each other, each thus becoming, in part, the other.

Our focus, then, on the embodied subject, is similar to that which Ziarek (2001: 5) describes, when she points out that the chiasma, or crossing over, of 'the constituted and the constituting character of the "living flesh" means that embodiment cannot be confused with the biological body'. Drawing on the work of Levinas and Fanon, Ziarek (2001: 5) elaborates this crossing over of constituting and constituted bodies using the concept of chiasma:

> The ambiguity and anachronism of constitution cannot be resolved into the classical oppositions of nature and history, body and language, passivity and activity, matter and form . . . but makes both sides of these oppositions undecidable. Instead of privileging one set of binaries over the other, Levinas and Fanon elaborate their chiasmic reversibility: the obverse side of the linguistic constitution of the body is the incarnation of language, which renders this constitution incomplete, indeterminate, and thus not only open to transformation but also exposed to radical exteriority.

It is that exposure to radical exteriority, in part, that makes us vulnerable to taking up aspects of new workplace discourses such as neo-liberalism, even when we regard them as monstrous, laughable and, at times, antithetical to ethical practice. But we are not idle victims here, nor are we confined to only one discourse, even when that discourse has become dominant and capable of diminishing and dismissing critical and contrary discourses (Davies and Petersen, 2005a).

In relation to bodies at work, Wallace (1999) suggests that gender and sexuality are embedded in organizations and inscribed on and lived through bodies. Organizations, she claims, permit certain 'styles of flesh' and banish others (Wallace, 1999: 43, as cited in Somerville and Bernoth, 2001). In the organization of our workshop we made possible a 'style of flesh' that was different from our every-other-day working selves, that offered, as one of us wrote later, a *wellspring of life and energy with a primitive rhythm far beyond the time pressure recently experienced at work*. From that life-space, which was unequivocally also a workspace, we explored the tangled skeins of regulatory practices by which we are made (and make ourselves) docile bodies in workplaces suffused with the doctrines of neo-liberal managerialism. And parallel to this exploration, and crossing over with it, is the exploration of ourselves, in the workshop in particular, but also in other workspaces, as working to create an embodiment that might also be described as a responsible 'locus of revolt' (Ziarek, 2001: 3).

Another way of describing bodies that are formed out of these multiple crossings over is as assemblages. As Probyn (2000: 17–18) says: 'bodies are assemblages: bits of past and present practice, openings, attachments to parts of the social, closings and aversions to other parts'. Out of the possible discourses through which we might constitute and be constituted, we are, to use Probyn's image, most *open* and *attached* to post-structuralist and feminist theory for the feminine lines of flight they open up. As Gargett (2002: 36) writes in an exploration of Deleuze's contemplation of the feminine:

> Becoming-woman disengages the segments/constraints of the molar identity in order to reinvent and be able to use other particles, flows, speeds and intensities. Becoming-woman involves a series of processes/movements, outside/beyond the fixity of subjectivity and the structure of stable unities, it means going beyond identity and subjectivity, fragmenting and freeing up lines of flight, releasing multiple sexes that identity has subsumed under the One.

In stark contrast we do not find neo-liberalism opening up such creative lines of flight, though it does set its subjects in motion and claims to free them from old patterns of governance (Martin, 1997). The difference between creative lines of flight and constant motion, we will show, is not always possible to tease out, since they can cross over and become one another. Neo-liberal discourse is not as easy as one might think, to separate out from post-structuralist discourses. It would be possible, for example, to create a homologous text to the quote from Gargett above, but this time in neo-liberalese:

> In order to become an efficient worker *disengage* from old work habits and *identities*. Reinvent yourself as both flexible and responsible so

you can *move* with the new *flows, speeds and intensities* of the market. Become aware of and responsive to movements outside and *beyond* your old *fixed self* and the old *fixed structures* of thought . . .

In neo-liberal discourse primacy is given to the flexible individual who acts 'responsibly' in relation to, and who is valued in terms of, the market. The individual must respond to the market and also anticipate it, and must always be ready to be rejected as a relevant player if no longer of any (monetary) value. Though it is true that the narrative of neo-liberalism as external monster can (already) be read as a narrative in our text, in what follows we will avoid giving an innocent 'merely theoretical' role to post-structuralist and feminist discourses or situating neo-liberalism as entirely outside ourselves and as wholly malign and coercive. Though we are practised at separating out one discourse from another, part of our task in this chapter is to show the possible leakage of one discourse into another. Although it is easy to say one discourse is good and liberating and another bad and oppressive, our analysis shows this to be a fictional and misleading binary.

Percepts and concepts

Although our memory stories are not 'fictional' (in the sense that they are generated through memory rather than imagination), they tap into the art of fiction-writing to the extent that they attempt to work with *percepts* rather than *concepts*. Muecke distinguishes between these terms as fundamental to the traditional (and, he points out, no longer sustainable) difference between literary criticism and literature, literary criticism 'unmask[ing] the secrets of art' and literature 'always there re-enchanting the world by putting on the beautiful masks again and again' (Muecke, 2002: 108). He goes on:

> Criticism uses concepts and fiction percepts. Philosophy, according to Deleuze, is about the invention of new concepts which have the abstraction and flexibility to be taken up by others and used. Art, on the other hand, invents percepts, monumental perceptions if you like, which are just there, either they work or they don't. They can stand alone. You can use someone else's percept, but it will be an imitation. And percepts and concepts chase each other around successively masking and unmasking.
>
> (Muecke, 2002: 109)

We could describe our collective biography story-writing and subsequent analysis as just that, 'percepts and concepts chas[ing] each other around successively masking and unmasking'. Our remembered stories are attempts to create the enchantment, though not by an intentional masking, but by making them perceptually as true and as vivid as our memory and writing skill will allow. Yet to the extent that memory is flimsy, and lived experience impossibly complex, and to the extent that our stories do achieve that enchanting quality that simply draws the reader in uncritically, we are creating fictions of life through which we (and you as reader) can put 'on the beautiful masks again and again' (Muecke, 2002: 108). At the same time, our analytic writing is influenced by our memory-writing – we seek to tell a tale (as any good writers do) that you will be taken in by. Analytic and creative writing thus cross over with each other, and what is mask and what is reality cross imperceptibly, each taking on features of the other.

In our workshops we came together in the quite different space/time of a shared house on Magnetic Island in order to examine the bodies we had, in some sense, left behind in those workplaces in five different cities in Australia. During the week we relaxed, we laughed, we talked and we wrote – and we took care of our bodies. We took a break from the often lonely nature of academic work to face each other around the table as embodied women. We set out, in this process, to extend our understanding of post-structuralist concepts, using them in our talk with each other, to make sense *of* and *through* that talk, and to make sense of our written memories. We re-membered stories from that *other* kind of workplace – the official university – and of ourselves at home, alone, writing, and of ourselves as children and as students. But we were also and at the same time writing in and of that other workshop space, the possibilities of which crossed over with what it was we wanted to say about our every-other-day workplaces.

Across the five days of our workshop, each of us took responsibility for a discrete half-day session. This included selecting an aspect of embodiment at work to focus on, finding and circulating pre-readings, choosing the particular memory question to work on, designing and conducting the session, and participating in the collective writing that followed the workshop. These included: the bodies that we most want to be, and do not want to be, in the workplace (Bronwyn); the ideal teacher (Eileen); flexible bodies in neo-liberal organizations (Sue); the labour of producing stillness (Margaret); and time and embodiment in the workplace (Jenny). We each chose a specific strategy for drawing our own attention to our bodies in these sessions. These included: a guided yoga nidra, voice work, foot massage, and a guided visualization. While these strategies were initially conceived of as a way to take care of our bodies alongside our academic work, they also provided a way to keep the body in central focus *in* our academic work. Sometimes the body work was used in a direct sense to elicit memory stories such as a guided visualization through all the clocks we have known. Sometimes the body work provoked memory stories more tangentially, in that, for example, a feeling of relaxation after a massage highlighted the contrasting tensions we talked about in our bodies at our usual workplaces, or the body session on voice led to a flood of memories of highly politicized moments of speaking (or silence) at our workplaces. Other methods that we used to elicit stories included choosing and describing postcard images of bodies, drawing pictures of teachers, reading extracts from fiction and constructing a bricolage of found objects. In a session conducted for us by a visiting artist, discussed in more detail in the next chapter, we constructed images of childhood landscapes and made paper dolls that linked with our memory-work on embodied subjectivity, as did sharing food, wine, walking, swimming and working together on Magnetic Island.

The feminine body in social science

Prior to the last three decades the specific, enfleshed body was, academically speaking, the province of the biological sciences. Social scientists were more concerned with the social and political body, abstracted from its fleshy specificity – a fleshy specificity that could be, at least as far as academic work was concerned, both taken-for-granted and ignored. At the same time it was also constructed as: 'the primal possession of the subject. . . . [T]he ideals of the possession and the preservation of the body form[ing] the basis of the liberal notions of private property, social contract and moral philosophy' (Ziarek, 2001: 3). That imagined normative social/political body enabled social scientists to ignore bodily difference and specificity, and the white male body, by default, was constituted via liberal discourses 'as the invisible somatic norm of political power and moral value' (Ziarek, 2001: 3). The constitution of the embodied self through the ideas and ideals of (white, male) social and political scientists achieved (with very little reflexive awareness, and perhaps even without malicious intent) not only women's exclusion (from rationality, from political life, for example) but also a meaning structure in which rationality and citizenship themselves 'were defined against the feminine and traditional female roles' (Gatens, 1996: 60). Because the social and political body constituted through academic texts was an abstracted, generic, idealized collective body, its inherent masculinity and its reliance on the negation of the feminine to make sense of itself were not immediately recognized, even by the women some of us were back then in the 1970s, who worked with such (masculine) texts (Davies, 1987).

Inevitably, then, making the feminine body visible and relevant has been central to the feminist struggle. As Gargett (2002: 32) observes:

The body or the embodiment of the subject, is a key component in the feminist struggle for a redefinition of subjectivity; it is to be understood as neither a biological nor a sociological category, but rather a point of overlap between the physical, the symbolic and the material social conditions.

The tightrope of working life

In focusing on ourselves now, as embodied women at work, we found and were inspired by the trope of the 'tightrope walker' in a photograph of 'The Sky Boy' (reproduced in Wolkowitz, 2001: 99), and also as a metaphor in Martin's (1997) work on (immune) systems and contemporary work practices. In the 1931 photograph, a worker dressed in overalls balances on a line attached to the top of the Empire State Building. We see the worker putting his life on the line with no safety net. His body, silhouetted against the skyline of the city is taut and strong and in control of itself. He is suspended on a potentially lethal 'tightrope' but he also has a 'transcendent' look about him, and he is thus simultaneously, in Wolkowitz's words, 'almost a flying angel' (2001: 98).

Martin's tightrope is a metaphor she develops to explore the neo-liberal/ new managerialist demand for personal control of and responsibility for the self, which may seem liberating but is also dangerous, in that the self is compelled never to rest. The controlled self must always be flexible, propelling itself into the ever reinvented demands of the institution: 'to move gracefully as an agile, dancing, flexible worker/person/body feels like a liberation, even if one is moving across a tightrope' (Martin, 1997: 360). Martin's worker, like the Sky Boy, finds her apparent freedom exhilarating as she flexibly dances through the constantly changing spaces in which she works. Martin finds danger crossing over with apparent freedom in her image of the tightrope walker. She asks us to realize simultaneously 'that the new flexible bodies are also highly constrained' (Martin, 1997: 360). She points out that '[t]hey cannot stop moving, they cannot stabilize or rest, or they will fall off the "tightrope" of life and die' (Martin, 1997: 360). In our own experience the demand for constant work, constant movement, has also been dangerous. We have had, for example, repetitive strain injury related to stress, and crippling arthritis that is, also, apparently, related to stress. Yet we continue to push ourselves and demand more: '*At the end of last semester*' one of us wrote, for example:

> I can remember days starting at 4 am, trying to make time stretch because I cannot stand deadlines. Dead lines. Dead in a line. Wondering if I could do my teeth and shower and have a wee at the same time. Even simple body care erased in busy-ness.

She contrasts this with the work we did at the workshop:

Tapping into this other sense of time was part of the safe place of the work-shop, what each woman offered and the unfolding of the week. Making conversation, making memories and making stories, making dolls, connecting with landscapes. This making requires a totally different experience of time but also makes time different.

In that different space, and particularly in the art session, the usually difficult exposure of self became not so difficult, became even the thing that could, in a collective sense, be loved best:

I find it quite difficult to make anything with an audience because I feel conscious of censorship, both my own and others when working in a group. On the other hand, I loved best of all seeing the cut out dolls appear on the wall in a group and the sculptured dollies hanging on the veranda. The landscape panorama was fun because shining through the landscape of trees and bush was the same sort of golden light that I experienced being down in and under the bush as a kid. Especially as it was made from beer carton gold because it was a pretty scrappy, urban, 'lurky' place, our bush. I loved watching the dolls moving in the breeze because the thing I was trying to achieve with my doll was mobility. When the breeze came up she danced with her bits of lurid pink skirt fluttering and her red shoes dancing. She was dancing so much that I had trouble getting a photo of her.

There is a difference here between the worker in the too busy workplace who constrains herself in so many ways in order to be in constant motion, and the dollies dancing in the breeze, or the flying angel who is poised to soar into the unknown, in an emergent, unfolding, non-linear time. Yet these images can inhabit the same body, even in the same moment, or in the same thought. This complex dual image, organized around the Sky Boy, created a thread that ran through our workshop and brought us again and again to the twin themes of constraint and movement in our working bodies. In the trope of the Sky Boy there is a crossing over of the responsible neo-liberal worker with his/her eye on her own and others' (monetary) value and on linear time, with workers who yearn for the enchantment of the not yet known, for a flowing, unfolding sense of time, for the joy that comes from an increased capacity to act on work that we are passionate about.

Deleuze associates a diminution of the power to act with sadness (Muecke, 2002: 109). Our stories contain both sadness and joy: 'Sadness will be any passion whatsoever which involves a diminution of my power of acting, and joy will be any passion involving an increase in my power of acting' (Deleuze on Spinoza in his 1978 lecture, cited in Muecke, 2002: 109).

What we find when we examine our stories, however, is that it is not so easy to separate out sadness from joy, or (too much) movement from flight. Our following story is clearly one of sadness, and yet the sadness is associated with too much movement, too much will to act. The story gives us the percept of a weeping body, a body that has stretched itself beyond its own limits to meet the demands of work – her own demands of her work. The worker remembers, in this moment of sadness, herself as a helpless child who could not move her body appropriately according to the linear time everyone else was working to:

> *The students are struggling. The system hurts them. They organise a dinner and I am tired but I go because I know they want to be connected to someone who helps it make sense. I go because my body needs them to make my work make sense. We share food, wine, stories, meet partners. This morning as I type, I cry. The students are not sad, but I am. I wonder if I will be sorry at the end that this is what I did. I am remembering the busy dailyness of my childhood, the impossibility of being ready on time to get in the car so the car could meet the bus. I remember Dad chasing the school bus, furious at me, again, because I can't be ready on time. How is it that I feel like I am chasing the bus now?*

She tells us here that she freely chose to go to dinner with her students. She governed her body to do what she believed was good for her students, and for her – to make her work make sense. The job is flexible – she can choose to go out with her students or not. She goes because she conducts her own conduct according to a specific set of values that require her to go, not because it has (monetary) value to the university, but because she is committed to her own and her students' struggle to understand. Now, as she types, she weeps from exhaustion, and she wonders about the value of what she does. She remembers, as a child, being inappropriate – not yet adequately appropriated within her family. And that is how she feels now, unable to be the appropriate subject required by her workplace. Her sadness suggests a diminution of the power to act, at the same time as she goes on compelling her body to work.

As Butler (1997a: 116) points out in her analysis of Althusser's thought, the more we master the dominant ideologies or discourses, their rules and laws, 'the more fully subjection is achieved. Submission and mastery take place simultaneously, and this paradoxical simultaneity constitutes the ambivalence of subjection'. There is a particular satisfaction to be had, perhaps particularly for academic women, who have been so recently excluded from academic discourse, to becoming appropriate subjects and in doing so to experience the deep satisfaction of belonging (Davies, 2000a). In the case of neo-liberal forms of organization, we drive ourselves to produce the embodied self who produces what that dominant ideology, that discourse, requires of it, and at the same time attempt to find in its interstices and in among the constant movement, moments of joy, moments so pleasurable that we will *intensify* our subjection in neo-liberal terms, in order to clear the spaces in which those unpredictable moments of joy will be possible. We illustrate this with a story one of us wrote about a staff meeting in her new workplace. Fearless at first she defines her new workplace as enabling thought, as one in which she can take pleasure in critique, in an ethical act of revolt. But her colleagues' (non-)reaction makes her fearful. Just remembering the moment makes her nauseous:

Queasy stomach – I remember.
Sitting in a group – all of us talking about the infiltration of new managerialist discourses into our documents, our programs, our talk.
Others arrive, and the official meeting begins. A colleague presents a document on changes to our programs. When questions and comments are invited I speak.
I point out the new managerialist discourses in the document, point to this document as evidence of our earlier conversation. I am amused by the overtness, the extremeness of the visibility of these discourses.
Others in the group join me while others are silent.
The chair steers the talk onto safer ground – away from critique towards praise of our colleague's hard work.
All weekend I replay this meeting – remembering unseen glances between colleagues, averted eyes.
On Monday I meet a 'mentor'.
I ask her: Did I embarrass myself?
*   Was I too critical?*
She says: Be careful
*   Remember you're new*
*   Remember others here don't know you*
*   Remember to think about where you are and who is there when*
*   you speak*
*   Be careful*
I ask: Have I crossed the line?
*   Not yet, she says*
*   But be careful.*

As Martin points out, there are many 'disturbing implications' in the new flexible change-oriented workplaces, notably what she describes as 'the propensity to extol harmony within the system and reliance on the group, while paradoxically (and distractingly) allotting individuals a dynamic, ever-changing, flexible role' (1997: 93). The role of this new 'knowledge-industry' worker is not, as she might have anticipated, to apply the critical intelligence that may have secured her the position in the first place in her new workplace. Her critical intelligence must be put on hold until some unspecified future – it must find its own (appropriate and appropriated) spaces. In contrast, the silencing of dissent is fundamental to the adoption and infusion of new managerialism into our workplaces. The 'flexibility' of new work practices depends upon it.

When we imagined the person we would most like to be in the workplace, choosing among pictures of bodies to facilitate that imagining, our ideals were redolent with images of flying. Describing the images we chose of our ideal selves at work one of us wrote of the image she chose:

> *He is strong, his body is perfect, muscular, balanced, poised. He is still, but about to take flight. He is grounded – but his wings are raised for flight – he is about to take off into the not-yet-known – to go where his wings will carry him – he can enter a new medium – he is not trapped in the already known. He stands at the liminal space of sea and land and gazes up and out.*

Another of us wrote of the image she chose:

> *She's on a flying carpet ride, exhilarated, holding on to her hat, her mouth wide open with joy and surprise. She doesn't know where the ride is taking her but she trusts it will be fantastic and the feeling will stay with her. She's not alone on her flight. She's experiencing all this with someone else who's with her, who trusts her and who she can trust and who also trusts the benevolence of the journey, and there may be more of them all on their own fantastic adventure but together at the same time. She's flying over the mundane landscape that she knows well and that was her life and when she lands even if it's in the same place it will be transformed for her because she is. She's open to everything and though perhaps she should be scared she's not. She's clever and she's lucky. She's elegant, neat and professional and bodily competent but she's still able to fly.*

Neither of these exhilarating (imagined) flights has a particular destination. They are both flights of discovery, of surprise, of adventure. They are, in that sense, *becoming-woman* stories: 'Becoming-woman . . . means going beyond identity and subjectivity, fragmenting and freeing up lines of flight' (Gargett, 2002: 36). In these images and the memory stories that we wrote in relation to them, flying represents the desired sense of embodied academic self. This desired moment of working selves takes place in places other than institutional workplaces, in home spaces, which are coterminous with the surrounding landscapes. Our writing-flying bodies are in a productive synergy with sunbirds, blue butterflies, bougainvillea and the sea:

> *Sitting in my study at the computer, looking out to the veranda and to the sea, shifting the boundaries of myself/my thought, as I contemplate the sunbird building its house on my veranda. Reading the words of others, writing and rewriting, a line of flight, experiencing my body in connection*

with the veranda, the sea, and the sunbird – powerful, beautiful words on the page.

Flying, when I'm working well and the words flow out like a thread that I'm just hanging on to and following. I'm high in my treehouse and looking at blue butterflies, bougainvillea and birds. I don't know where I'm going, where these words are taking me but I know I'd rather be here, hanging on and flying, than anywhere else.

Time is irrelevant here, as is the (monetary) value of what we write. We are unequivocally in a state of joy, even bliss – our capacity to act is intensified and the possibility of going beyond the already known lures us on. Given the intense pleasure we perceived in our moments of flight, how is it that we cross over, seamlessly, into the stressed-out bodies we so often are at work? The writer who gazed out at the verandah and the sunbird, tells of such a crossing over – not as an imposition or an act of choice, but as a shift in desire to another set of competencies. The long morning of pleasure in her work is broken into by the realization that she is running out of the time that she has allocated to the task. The days and weeks that stretch ahead already have other tasks allocated to them. She desires completion. She has set herself a time limit, and so she crosses over to becoming an efficient worker:

She wanted so much to get to the point of completion that she had looked forward to. She began to work fast, pressing herself to go quickly, no longer savouring the sentences, no longer fully attending to their meaning, relying on gut instinct to know what to cut and what to change. Her back and neck were in tight spasms, her breathing was shallow, her face screwed up with anxiety and concentration. She watched the clock with one eye, pacing herself, dividing up the task according to the time left, becoming more stressed as the time grew shorter.

Our story of crossing over from one kind of writing to another encapsulates the chiasma of our bodies at work. It is *writing* – which can cause our muscles to spasm and our faces to grimace – that is both the source of our greatest pleasure in academic writing and the source of this pain. At first the writer had been writing with pleasure. Then she turns her eye to the clock – not because someone tells her to, but because she desires the pleasure of the end point being achieved before the other tasks begin. She is no longer in flight, no longer on the liminal edge between the known and the unknown, but a tightly constrained machine. Her will governs her body to work to the clock – she makes it work for her and does not register its increasing pain. In mastering academic work she takes as her own the desire to complete (yet another) paper. Her body both will and will not do what she wants of it. Our bodies carry the marks of the diverse constraints within which we labour, and they also contribute to the misery of work through their very corporeal, enfleshed materiality, *and* through their susceptibility to desiring marks of achievement and to meeting goals.

How is it that we enter so readily into the self-punitive time-driven destruction of the pleasure of our writing? In the assembling of our embodied selves, is it not possible to choose to be the body in flight and to stay there, exploring as long as we can the new spaces (and times) that we have entered? How is it that we take on as our own the measurement of linear time and the eye that controls accordingly? The writer of this story says that she hates these controlling eyes, especially when they are her own, and she rejects them. But they lurk at the edge of consciousness. Time, we found, cannot be so simply cast as an external master that should be resisted. In our first story of sadness, the small child had not yet mastered time. We found when we examined childhood stories of clocks that our relation to clocks and time was integral to a sense of connectedness to and competence in the world. Subjection and mastery constitute the subject in the same act (Butler, 1997a: 116). In one memory story the earliest remembered clock is located as a deeply embodied pleasurable connectedness to her grandmother's presence:

> the first clock she can remember, she travels down a long passage to the dark warmth of her grandmother's house. She is only six months old. She cannot get a picture of her grandmother's clock but she can feel the chimes in the place in her chest where she would feel a heart beating when she was held close against someone who loved her. Then she can feel her grandmother's skin against her cheek. Soft like crinkled silk. The smell is her grandmother's smell but permeating the dark of the room is the smell of coke burning in the old Kosi stove and the red glow of its warmth.

Another remembers, as a small child, mastering time by actively lodging the knowledge of it in her body, thus making herself competent and connected in the familiar space of her mother's kitchen:

> The electric clock in the kitchen, up high on the cupboard, had a large round white face with small ornate black hands, and a long thin second hand. Its surround was painted green – kitchen green, the same as the kitchen. She loved to sit at the wooden table and watch the second hand sweeping around the clock in its series of small perfectly regular movements from one second to the rest. She taught herself to count seconds by feeling in her body the rhythm and speed of its movement from one small black line to the next. Four small lines between each number, the fifth being the new number. She practiced with her eyes open, watching the movement, listening to the faint sound, then with her eyes shut. She could count five perfectly, then ten, and eventually a whole minute. She could feel the seconds in her body with her eyes shut as she

counted from one to sixty, opening her eyes quickly as she reached 'sixty' to find the long thin black hand sweeping onto the twelve.

Later she enjoyed the fact that she could keep her eye on this clock and know precisely at what point she had to run downstairs and jump on her bike to get to school on time. This pleasure in acquiring competence and efficiency in relation to time stays with us. It is integral to our subjection. It is also a source of inordinate anxiety as the work expands in such a way that it simply cannot fit inside the linear hours and days and weeks and years of our working lives. It seems with linear time that we can enjoy having competence in relation to it, *and* feel totally oppressed by it. Our attempts to master it put at risk the kinds of open spaces and creative possibilities opened up in the workshop or in the spaces we set aside for writing, or in the pleasurable critique and revolt against it.

Crossing over with the linear time, then, is that time that is associated with the angel's line of flight, a time that expands and is expansive, and that holds a strong sense of embodiment rather than denial and disciplining of the body. We cannot separate out, entirely, linear time from those moments of creative flight. One of us, working against a very tight time line for the completion of her PhD during the process of writing this chapter, caught perfectly the crossing over of flight and the intense pressure of linear time when she wrote in an email:

My nose is bleeding from the grindstone I have it pushed against. How do I make sure they're the right words? Let me tell you it doesn't feel like flying right at the moment but I'm near. . . . Love to you all and hope you're having FUN (I am actually).

But perhaps we have gone too far in this play of chiasmas. The demands and limitations of neo-liberalism must be critiqued, and revolt against it could be said to be the only possible ethical line of action. We must hold the tension between the chiasma of our neo-liberal selves and ourselves engaged in creative flight, outside its controls, at the same time as we make visible what this dominant discourse is and how it works on us and through us to push our bodies to the limits. Our critique of it is, in this analysis, accompanied by an analysis of the ways in which we are drawn into it and seduced by it. The pressures it creates in linear time, for example, make us particularly susceptible to rationalities of efficiency. Increases in efficiency are seductive. They are experienced as desirable, even pleasurable, at the same time as they are harmful to our embodied and emotional selves, catapulting us into a loss of joy and loss of capacity to act on the very work we are passionate about.

One of the rationalities we have used to justify the growing dominance of technology in our professional lives, for example, is the pleasurable increase in efficiency that it can afford us. We can communicate, using email, with so many more people in any one day, we can write so many more papers now we have computers, and we can communicate with people at a distance. It is seductive precisely because it taps into already embodied commitments, desires and competencies. But technology, like time, can also dominate in ways that are harmful, its seductive efficiencies can lead us to put our hard-working bodies into the background – even inviting them to disappear. As Guertin (1999: 5) observes: '[t]he rhetoric surrounding virtual reality . . . argues not for the disappearance of technology, but for a disappearance of the body in favour of existence as a state of pure information'. 'Flexible learning' as a substitute for real bodies in real spaces is everywhere in academic teaching. Increasingly, units of study are being designed as modules that can be packaged and delivered 'online' with what seems to be very little involvement (or investment in) teaching. There has been, as McWilliam elaborates, 'a bifurcation of teaching into "design and delivery" wherein the "embodied teacher" is unnecessary, even problematic' (1999: 128). Yet the embodied teacher, as the following story shows, experiences this in her body despite the removal of her students and of her own body from more conventional teaching–learning contexts. Her body almost disappears from the story itself, even though we know she suffers intense pain from repetitive strain injury. In this course competence in information and communication technology is one of the generic skills on 'the list' of what students must be taught. In order to 'tick off' this skill, the lecturer for whom the story teller is tutoring, shifts the usual, on-campus, enfleshed tutorials 'online' for approximately one-third of each semester. Not only is it a generic skill, but the university is committed to 'flexible delivery' because it reaches more students, and because it is cheaper. 'Flexibility' is the new ideal when the pace of change is so rapid. But as Martin says, flexibility is achieved through an impossible combination of fearlessness and docility. Workers must be 'able to risk the unknown and tolerate fear, willing to explore unknown territories, adrift in space, but simultaneously able to accept their dependence on the help and support of their co-workers' (Martin, 1997: 83). In our story this 'flexibility' becomes an (in)flexibility written on the body of the teacher (and of the students):

> *The virtual tutorial took much more time and energy than the real tutorial had and her hands hurt after working through hundreds of entries across two subjects. Several students contacted her about problems they had with the technology. They asked if they could come in to her for a special face-to-face session with her instead but she felt that this would let down the groups more as some of them were quite small to begin with. She spoke to the lecturer about the problems students were having and the flatness of the discussions online but he said it was just too bad. They have to learn to be more flexible, he said.*

The students must embody the new workplace rhetoric and so must she. They must make it their own, no matter that it might be counterproductive in terms of learning or in terms of the stresses on their bodies. She must take risks, move fearlessly towards the unknown. However successfully we disappear our bodies, or become flexible, fearless bodies, heedless of what the new order might be, we still are bodies and we go home exhausted, agonizing about how to make ourselves strong enough or competent enough or clever enough or healthy enough to do this job well. We demand (because our workplaces demand) that our bodies be flexible enough to accommodate the new time pressures, the discourses of flexible learning, marking moderation, teaching evaluation, generic skills, accountability and funding constraints. Our material bodies produce the effect that is our performing selves and they produce, collaboratively, the contexts we inhabit. And they are, at the same time, effected, or brought into being, in these performances, in these contexts, as specific individual bodies – not automata, not bodies that simply carry the meanings of the institutions we work in (though they do this too). Each individual works in an ongoing way to be able to be, and to continue to materialize herself as, the appropriate body/subject within her workplace, and in doing so achieves a recognizable identity. But more than that, she works to achieve the body that is passionate about its work, which is also the body that can act strongly and is full of joyful energy. As Butler says:

> The body is not a self-identical or merely factic materiality; it is a materiality that bears meaning, if nothing else, and the manner of this bearing is fundamentally dramatic. By dramatic I mean only that the body is not merely matter but a continual and incessant *materializing* of possibilities. One is not simply a body, but, in some very key sense, one does one's body and, indeed, one does one's body differently from one's contemporaries and from one's embodied predecessors or successors as well.
>
> (1997b: 404, original emphasis)

And so . . .

What we have explored here is the crossing over that occurs in the discursively constituted and constituting body that means that what it is that materializes is not the result of a rational choice to engage now one discourse and now another. The discourses and related practices cross over in such a way that they are lived as something new, something that is not one or the other, something that is linked with multiple desires formed in relation to being an appropriate and appropriated worker, to being one who survives and is safe, to being one who is fluid and in movement, to being one who goes dangerously and pleasurably beyond the already known. These desires cannot easily be separated out, nor clearly attached to one discourse and set of practices or another. The discourses themselves cross over, they mutate, form new possibilities, carry with them burdens from other forms they have crossed with. We find ourselves again and again seduced by the discourse and practices of neo-liberalism, caught up in and approving of newly appropriate patterns of desire, struggling to keep open the spaces of revolt and of flight, by becoming, ironically, ever more appropriate(d) subjects of neo-liberal discourses – discourses that can also be read as anti-intellectual, exploitative and controlling.

The next chapter is one in which we visit again the work we did together on embodiment and work, asking ourselves how, in the face of what we have written in this chapter, we might return to the question of power and agency to ask in what ways we have worked against our sense of frustration and of being subjected in neo-liberal regimes. In part our answer lies in the practices of collective biography themselves, and in part it lies in the strategies we have developed for making visible the discourses through which we are subjected.

5

'Truly wild things': interruptions to the disciplinary regimes of neo-liberalism in (female) academic work[11]

She is truly a wild thing though I didn't know she would be right until the end.

In this chapter we extend our expression of concern with the regulatory discourses and practices of neo-liberalism in academic workplaces, and we generate strategies for interrupting them and *decomposing* them. Barthes proposes 'decomposition', rather than destruction: 'In order to destroy' he says 'we must be able to *overleap*. But overleap where? Into what language? Into which site of good conscience and bad faith?' (Barthes, 1977b: 63, original emphasis). Like Barthes, we 'scrape, catch and drag' in our neo-liberal institutions, but we also find some moments of wild exhilaration in the processes of our own decomposition and the decomposition of our workplaces.

We find ourselves, as we showed in the last chapter, simultaneously thwarted, exhausted, terrified and seduced by our neo-liberal workplaces. In this chapter we describe some of the ways we have found to interrupt the disciplinary regimes of those workplaces through the practices of collective biography themselves. In the 'body at work' workshop we developed a range of innovative bodily practices to facilitate our focus on embodied beings in the workplace. In the workshop out of which these two chapters were produced, we attended particularly to the body, our bodies, which are generally made irrelevant in neo-liberal workplaces, except as the (un)reliable machines that go on (and on) working and which need restorative care outside work. Further, we chose our 'bodies at work' as our topic, in part because this is a particular research interest of several of us (Browne, 2000; Davies and Petersen, 2005a, 2005b; Gannon, 2003; Somerville and Bernoth, 2001), and because we are academic workers in Australian universities at a time when neo-liberal discursive regimes generate highly stressed bodies that seem barely able to accomplish what is asked of them.

In collective biography we recall the tastes, smells and feelings of past memories. We perceive (and thus constitute) our bodies as alive with layers of inscriptions. Foucault describes the body as 'the inscribed surface of events (traced by language and dissolved by ideas)' (1998a: 377). In post-structuralist theory there is 'no clear distinction between the body and its inscription; the text *on* the body becomes the text that is the body' (Brush, 1998: 29, original emphasis). Those inscriptions can be read as biological, emotional, moral, intellectual and political. They are mobile, volatile and unstable. They provide us with the tools for reading our bodies, and at the same time constitute our bodies as texts to be read. The memories unfolded in collective biography enable us to begin to read these inscriptions. The work of imagination and of connection that we undertook in this workshop also enabled us to begin to generate multiple readings of how our bodies might be at work.

In each collective biography workshop we have experimented with productive variations in our research practices that complement the particular topic under investigation. We theorize this particular collective biography as rhizomatic research, and we focus on the opening of unexpected linkages and lines of flight through our embodied and unorthodox practices. This rhizomatic research practice led us to reread the collective biography on our bodies at work in search of the joy that Deleuze identified as inhering in any 'increase in my power of acting' (Deleuze, cited in Muecke, 2002: 109). In this chapter we explore how innovative collective work might invigorate our imaginations, enabling the possibility of taking up new ways to re-member and think about our work, surprising and sustaining us with glimpses of the 'truly wild things' that we might be and become.

What did we and can we do, then, to interrupt the embodiment of ourselves as the over-regulated neo-liberal subjects that we see ourselves to be in our workplaces, to generate another way of working in the space of the workshop and in the gaps and crevices of our usual workplaces? For this workshop, as we have described in the previous chapter, we brought our bodies together in a site far removed from our usual workplaces. One of us wrote, after this week together:

> *In our intensely focussed practice of collective biography, there were moments when one woman seized a word uttered by another and spun a tale that drifted over our collective group, and draped over our collective shoulders. In these moments we found ourselves uttering collective sighs of understanding, of appreciation, of sadness, of pleasure, of anguish, as we sat under a veil of storying that we had all collectively spun.*

This is not to say that the work of interruption that we were doing to our usual practices did not also create moments of extreme anxiety and doubt about what we did and how we were doing it. Interrupting usual ways of seeing and being is both exhilarating and confronting.

Our strategies, then, confronted usual work practices including the usual practice of collective biography. It was important that this was more than time out, more than a break from usual practices or a time to restore ourselves. Our theoretical work, too, had to work towards the possibility of a certain decomposition of our usual workplaces, and of ourselves within them. In our discussions about what we were doing in our practice of collective biography we used the metaphor of rhizomes (Deleuze and Guattari, 1987) to focus on the 'possibility of a certain resignifying process' (Butler, 1992: 13). Rhizomatic analysis emphasizes the unexpected and invites thought to move in non-linear ways. The rhizome anticipates movement that is not predictable, linear and contained. Instead, it focuses attention on process and on the accumulation of allied possibilities in such a way that sedimented identities might be uprooted:

> A rhizome has no beginning or end; it is always in the middle, between things, interbeing, intermezzo. The tree is filiation, but the rhizome is alliance, uniquely alliance. The tree imposes the verb 'to be', but the fabric of the rhizome is the conjunction, 'and . . . and . . . and . . .'. This conjunction carries enough force to shake and uproot the verb 'to be'.
>
> (Deleuze and Guattari, 1987: 25)

We found the rhizomatic practices of the workshop with its accumulation of possibilities in the woven fabric of the stories that were generated in the intermezzo spaces, its 'and . . . and . . . and . . .', its non-beginning and non-ending, productive of an openness to unexpected lines of flight.

Post-structuralist theory is interested in the folding and unfolding of history, in the movement from one configuration to another, in the lines of flight that make new realities. The configurations of our academic work include: the divergent discourses of post-enlightenment ideas and ideals of expanding the boundaries of knowledge; the egalitarian ideas and ideals of inclusion; and more recently the neo-liberal regulation and auditing of academic work. The distress experienced in relation to these neo-liberal regimes suggests it is time to begin to begin work on a new configuration. A particular configuration 'makes history by unmaking preceding realities and significations, constituting hundreds of points of emergence or creativity, unexpected conjunctions or improbable continuums. It doubles history with a sense of continual evolution' (Deleuze, 1988: 35).

That theoretical work needs to be accompanied by practices that are sympathetic to the work of reconfiguration. In our storying we produced lines of flight that we followed, traversed and mapped in the spaces we made together. As one woman told a memory, another woman caught part of the story and took flight, following a particular line that connected quite unexpected memories. These linkages occurred within sessions but also across different sessions during that week, connecting memories to images we created with paint and artistic assemblages, to the sounds and movements of our bodies. In the weeks and months after the workshop, when we had scattered to our far-flung places of work and living, the lines of flight continued to provoke new stories and reflections. We envisaged our workplaces as a rhizomatic (cyber)space in which there might be a series of escapes, of small slides, of plays, of crossings, of flights, that open (an other, slippery) understanding (Derrida, in Cixous and Derrida, 2001).

Individual bodies are contingent and unstable assemblages, created through connection: '[t]here is no finality, end or order that would govern the assemblage as a whole; the law of any assemblage is created from its connections' (Colebrook, 2002: xx). In collective biography, the lived episodes we recall and re-member in our telling, and writing, are moments of 'articulation' (Probyn, 2000: 16) – demonstrating for us how we constitute ourselves, and are constituted, within our social, embodied and political contexts and histories, with the aim of de-normalizing and to de-naturalizing those moments – making them visible as historically specific practice. In doing so, we de-individualize those practices, seeing struggles for survival and desperation over work, not as our own individual products, but as products of neo-liberal regimes of regulation. In making the constituted body available for inspection in this way, we open ourselves to a certain decomposition. We see at the same time that we cannot replace the disciplinary regimes in which we work, nor can we destroy them. We are already part of them – constituted by them and constituting them with our own embodied practices. We therefore work within them, subjected by them, to decompose them.

In our first readings of our bodies at work, presented in the previous chapter, we found almost nothing but the effects of neo-liberalism variously inscribed on our bodies. In this chapter we want to juxtapose such readings with stories of how bodies might be lived otherwise, against the grain of neo-liberal imperatives. When looking for such stories, they are extraordinarily difficult to find.

In terms of organizational and institutional practices of (worker) subjectification, and the technologies of the self that sustain them, Foucault's genealogical work on 'docile bodies' has been important to feminist theorists. Bordo, for example, describes how her work on female bodies and femininity has been informed by Foucault's notion that:

> [n]ot directly through ideology, but through the organization and regulation of the time, space and movements of our daily lives, our

bodies are trained, shaped and impressed with the stamp of prevailing historical forms of selfhood, desire, masculinity and femininity.

(Bordo, 1997: 91)

This training, shaping and impressing of bodies, of inscribing them with structure and language is not a final process like, for example, engraving, which takes place on superficial and hardened surfaces. The inscription and sedimentation takes place on the deep, enfleshed, enfolded surfaces which are at the same time active in the process of inscription (Davies, 2000a). In the ongoing palimpsest of meaning-making, in which both the meaning of that which is to be inscribed and the body are implicated, neither the meaning nor the body is solely active or passive. While the repeated, minute accretions of everyday practices achieve in one's body the sediment of social structure, that sediment is itself always potentially in motion. Corporeal (enfleshed) instability is characteristic of post-structural thinking about the body: the subject strives towards stability and unity and is also in a state of 'perpetual disintegration' (Foucault, 1998a: 377).

The artistic and creative practices that we took up in the workshop involved imagined spaces that we may already and may not (yet) have bodily inhabited. These practices encouraged us to explore different ways of thinking, of reinventing and reassembling our bodies. In response to a large collection of photos of fleshy beings, for example, we chose, and told stories about, our ideal embodied selves at work and of the embodied beings we did not want to be at work. This led to talk of what we love about our work, what inspires and rejuvenates us and keeps our bodies labouring, as well as what we hate about it, what we find debilitating, even lethal, and how this manifests in our labouring bodies.

Truly wild things

In planning to attend to our bodies during the workshop, we did not imagine that the image of the truly wild thing was what we might find. As we massaged each others' feet with essential oils, as we listened to another's voice guiding us through the process of attending to each part of our body in a yoga nidra, and as we listened to our own and each others' voices singing in the garden, we anticipated 'relaxation', 'care', 'well-being' and 'pleasure'. In adopting these bodily practices and the innovative artistic and imaginative strategies of working with photographs and art, we found possibilities for movement, and for new ways of envisaging our selves at work. With surprise, we reminded ourselves that we were 'at work' at the workshop even though we were, for the most part, relaxed and enjoying ourselves, and were engaging in lines of flight that were not governed by neo-liberal systems of thought.

The characters in the photographs that we chose to represent our ideal images of ourselves at work were expansive, unrestrained and mobile. One of us chose an image of a voluptuous naked woman she called 'laughing woman and her shadow':

> *She is alive, fleshy, exuberant, full of new ideas and in a way, careless. Her shadow is big, larger than life. She is her shadow. She makes it and yet it is not her, nor is she it. There is so much to do/be/see/feel/understand. She is filled with anticipation, laughing, not panicking. She delights in the large, moving image behind her on the wall.*

As well as these and the figures of the angel and the flying carpet ride described in the previous chapter, the images that we chose included a thrilling roller-coaster ride, and a suited woman with a briefcase walking briskly through a city, impervious to the stares of the men. These images opened up a visual sense of what it was we longed for, and what it was we already knew to be possible in the slips and slides away from surveillance, auditing and management. We also chose pictures of and told stories about the person we did not want to be at work, and in doing so gained some distance between ourselves and the bodily inscriptions at work in our neo-liberal workplaces that we would like to erase. One of us wrote of her self-to-erase:

> *He has disappeared into the wallpaper and the furniture. Even his genitals are painted over so as to become part of the furniture. Yet he stands crouched over, arms out in a gesture of despair – a perfect member of the corporation. He has been made to fit in perfectly so that even his despair is not visible. His face is stressed and worried, but it's easy to look away – to not even notice his existence. The context is grotesque, absurd, and so is he. He could be replaced by anyone else willing to be totally appropriated.*

In another session that began with drawing, we remembered teachers who had inspired us. Our ideas of flight into the unknown, of gaining power to shrug off some of the embodied knowledge of current work practices, of laughing rather than crying, were invigorated by stories of wild women, wild women who could exist within and in spite of their institutional location. One of us, for example, drew and wrote of a teacher–nun who was tough and yet eschewed convention:

> *She was different from the others. She walked really fast, with long strides, like a man. She was tough and funny. She gave them six cuts of the cane for 'forgetting' their sewing and then sent them, the three farmers' daughters, best friends, out to garden for the afternoon.*
>
> *She was the principal as well as the full time year six teacher so she was really busy. But sometimes she would pull her tall stool up close to their desks and sit near them, her sleeves rolled up, her habit hitched up out of her way,*

her feet wide apart. She talked about stuff no other teacher ever talked about: war, famine, politics, justice. She treated them like they could think. They loved her.

We remembered that we loved, in ourselves and in each other, our own willingness to hitch up our 'habits' and speak of what matters. The wild figures that we might be(come) took on new substance in a session where we worked with an artist/sculptor, Gay Hawkes, herself a woman with wild red curls and a wonderful presence, who guided us on an adventure that was far from our usual research practice. We tore out paper figures, constructed and painted landscapes of memory and shaped elaborate dolls from newspapers coloured paper and paint. The possibilities that emerged in our paper dolls were in direct contrast to the figures we felt ourselves to be in our stories of constraint at work. Some of our dolls were vigorous and vibrant, mobile and vocal, forces to be reckoned with, and defiantly, distinctively female:

The paper doll I tore out deliberately had both her arms thrown up in the air and her feet steadily planted on the ground. My can can dancer newspaper doll . . . made herself into what she is because the legs were so insistent on kicking up into the air. After I had lined her skirts with green and red petticoats her legs looked so silly as newspaper that I painted them red too (but said that it was blood).

Another of us describes her doll, and the unexpected joy and surprise of her creation:

I worked like one obsessed on my doll with no idea of what she would turn out to be. She is truly a wild thing though I didn't know she would be right until the end. Her original face was a blanked out face (small pixilated squares) then right at the end I added Hugh Grant's blue eyes and then a large shouting mouth with bright red lips. She has an ornate indigenous style headdress (reminiscent of New Guinea men), huge hands, one hand holding a magical indigenous style musical instrument and the other in a fist as large as her head. On her back she has a blue cape made out of a map of Australia and on her front she has an ornate apron beginning with a Rubenesque painting (near her genitals) and then flowing blue and gold and orange skirts and a red band around her waist. I am amazed at her. She is so powerful she is almost scary. The shouting mouth could also be read as a laughing mouth or even a singing mouth but the huge fist and the headdress makes that reading unlikely. I was amazed and delighted by her, and still find her surprising whenever I look at her. She seems to represent the creative forces of the unexpected and the unknown. She represents what I love about my work and also expresses the rage I feel . . .

And so our work during the workshop was itself a form of mobility.

We worked against the grain of our usual workplaces, literally and in imagination, leaving them in order to do our work. We let our imaginations and our bodies free in the safe spaces of a different kind of collective work. Each of us was challenged or confronted at some point by our unorthodox research practices, provoked by art or by the need to sing out aloud, yet the space within which we took risks to think differently was a safe space that ultimately enabled us to begin to think about and see our working lives differently. As we worked together we looked back at our embodied selves in our usual workplaces with amazement and horror, and some growing comprehension of the mechanisms and discourses through which we were caught there. We wrote first about those discourses in the preceding chapter and then turned to the story of how we dwelt on and revived and imagined and created images of wild women who can and do work differently, who can and do produce their flesh differently. We utilized 'play' and 'pleasure' in the space of our collective biography as strategies to productively 'unsettle what it means for women to behave properly in the academy' (McWilliam, 2000: 176). Our painful stories of the neo-liberal panopticon and its absurdities and violence became, in the retelling, not just futile evidence of the oppressive nature of these regimes, but also stories of necessary intransigence in becoming and remaining the women we love to be and love and want each other to be. It is to the both/and of these stories that we turn to discover that we are *both* working in an oppressive regime that often silences us *and* we are the wild women who will laugh at it and name its absurdity and violence.

And so . . .

In following this line of flight through our memories of work in academic workplaces, our care-full attention to our bodies, and our imaginative artistic experiments, we found ourselves as wild women. Our flesh is mobile, flexible, malleable but at the same time at risk and creatively and intellectually constrained. What we must do, despite (and within) neo-liberal workplaces, is to become also the points of articulation of discourses that are productive of other ways of thinking and being in these workplaces, discourses that do not negate or erase bodies but which use them as theoretical and creative sites of production. We found that incorporating focused acts of imagination and of body work into our practice of collective biography enabled us to begin to bring to life some possibilities for retaining a sense of ourselves as truly wild things, as women who might act and speak powerfully and independently, at least some of the time, despite (or because of) the neo-liberal discursive regimes that we have begun to decompose. Decomposition is not destruction, it is a mutual recognition and reworking of possibilities. Freedom is taken in tight and constrained places. Lines of flight that open up the possibility of other space/times may not be able to be taken up by colleagues locked into neo-liberal discourses. As one of us wrote afterwards:

> *The other day amidst a fight about teaching hours . . . someone said that if you run a course on line, it is 'worth' two hours a week. (!) There are so many replies to that aren't there? (Including just 'Fuck off!') However, I said, 'when you count my time as two hours, do so knowing that you are doing both me and my students a grave injustice'. Like this chapter, my words don't change the system . . . but the person did at least look embarrassed and I felt better than if I said nothing and was left to feel guilty about being inefficient.*

The subjects we are and might become are not isolated beings independent of others, but beings constituted *in concert* with others, through discourses that may be imposed and/or actively taken up. With others we might begin the work of decomposing (in the doubled sense of undoing the active composition, and of material rotting) and we must be embodied within that decomposition, since there is no outside place where such work can be done. At the same time we can open up lines of flight towards spaces and times and modes of being that stir the imagination, that lead to laughter and bliss, that work against the grain of the weighty world-as-usual, the world that busily goes on speaking itself and each of us, separately and collectively, into existence as docile and afraid neo-liberal subjects.

In the next chapter we focus on the reflexive processes through which we turn our gaze on our own consciousness, and on the discourses through which it is constituted. Qualitative research generally, and collective biography in particular, assumes a subject who can engage in reflexive practices, who can open up discursively constructed subjectivities to inspection and, not only to critique, but to reinvention. While the previous chapters have engaged in a reflexive and retrospective analysis of memories, in the next chapter we interrogate reflexivity directly. We ask just what is the process through which we cast our reflexive gaze on ourselves as subjects in process? Who is it that gazes, and upon whom? How are the doubled mo(ve)ments of immersion in any moment and gazing at that moment possible?

6

The ambivalent practices of reflexivity[12]

Sketching out the problem to be examined

Reflexivity is an everyday and inevitable aspect of language use – we must know *that* we use language and to some extent *how* we use it, and with what effect, in order to use it at all. In the development of forms of social scientific thought that have deconstructed and gone beyond positivism over at least the last four decades, anthropologists, literary theorists, historians, psychologists, philosophers and sociologists alike have written about the social construction of reality in history, literature, culture and daily life as an unavoidable and necessary aspect of any investigation (Barthes, 1985; Berger and Luckmann, 1966; Harré and Secord, 1972; Mills, 1959; Novick, 1988; Sartre, 1963; Wax, 1971). A further extension, often drawing on post-structuralist thought, involves turning one's reflexive gaze on discourse – turning language back upon itself to see the work it does in constituting the world. It entails the development of a kind of 'critical literacy' in which the researchers understand that they too are caught up in processes of subjectification, and must see simultaneously the objects/subjects of their gaze *and* the means by which those objects/subjects (which may include the researcher as subject) are being constituted. In this model researchers come to see what is achieved through particular discursive acts as well as the constitutive means by which the particular act was made possible and interpretable-as-this-act-in-particular. Researchers see meaningful actions in the world, analysing them both in their own terms, and, at the same time, as the result of the constitutive acts engaged in and made visible by the researchers themselves.

As we have moved towards more experimental and self-consciously reflexive writing in the social sciences, we find some of that writing being dismissed as self-indulgent, or narcissistic, or lacking in method or validity, or too literary and not theoretical enough – as creating no more than an illusion of intimacy and verisimilitude, or of making false claims about authenticity and objectivity (Denzin, 1997; Pinch and Pinch, 1988). Also, the consciousness of self that reflexive writing requires may be seen to imply the very self (a very real self) that contradicts the focus on the constitutive power of discourse and on the necessarily shifting and fragmented nature of the (always) discursively constituted subject (Davies, 2000b). The practice of reflexivity may be used in a (tacitly) realist fashion, as Denzin (1997) observes, where the researchers use their own experience of being subjects, becoming the legitimate ground of exploration, as well as the legitimate explorers of that ground, striving for a kind of 'authentic' account of some aspect of everyday life (see, for example, Behar, 1993; Ellis, 2004; Stanley and Wise, 1983). But, as Lather points out, while reflexivity might be regarded as the new canon there are deep tensions in the practice of it:

> [T]here are few guidelines for how one goes about the *doing* of it, especially in a way that both is reflexive and, yet, notes the limits of self-reflexivity. To attempt to deconstruct one's own work is to risk buying into the faith in the powers of critical reflection that places emancipatory efforts in such a contradictory position with the post-structuralist foregrounding of the limits of consciousness.
>
> (Lather 1993: 685, original emphasis)

Such foregrounding of the limits of consciousness usually leads reflexive researchers to eschew anything smacking of realism and to interpret their task as making visible at all times the discursive constitutive work that is always at play in any act of observing or reporting or analysing. At this end of the spectrum of reflexive work, the subject is deconstructed in such a way that it can no longer be read as a fixed object to be read, nor as a superior transcendental consciousness that can engage in objective readings. But such a position can be a slippery one to maintain since researchers are (always already) subjects who engage in readings, and in analysis, and who draw on their own experience of being in the world to make sense of it. And because of the rejection of the so-called objective all-seeing eye/I of positivist research, it is not acceptable to write as if the author were not present at each stage of the discursive constitutive work of research. These two ends of the spectrum of reflexive research, of authentic, realist self-narratives and discursive textual analysis that foregrounds the limits of consciousness (Lather, 1993: 685), may appear to coexist in the same text, the former often being seen to undermine and erode the latter. The existence of the subject in reflexive writing has thus become a contested field (see, for example, Davies, 1997; Jones, 1997): the subject both does and does not exist in reflexive social scientific writing. It is the slippage between these two ends of the spectrum of reflexivity that we take up as our site of exploration in this chapter.

The problem we face is much greater than the old puzzle of how we might be both the gazer and the object gazed at in the same moment. If the gaze is understood as constitutive, and if we are foregrounding the 'insufficiencies of language and the production of meaning-effects, produc[ing] truth as a problem' (Lather, 1993: 685) then the object gazed at (oneself as subject, and oneself as the conductor of the reflexive gaze) is a slippery object indeed. In post-positivist/post-structuralist research practice there are no secure foundations. Practice is not based on reliable 'methods' that produce validity. Rather, practice is a site of innovation. And in such research, 'Reflexivity', writes Denzin (1997: 223), 'is not an option'.

Given the slippery theoretical ground that this takes us into, reflexivity turns out to be much more complex and demanding than we had at first thought. Not only must we engage in such an apparently fraught practice as reflexivity, but we must, in our engagement with research, invent our own methods of meaning-making as we go, *and* catch ourselves in the act of engaging in old practices and modes of meaning-making that we are in process of deconstructing and moving beyond.

Drawing on the writing of Hartsock and Spivak, Lather (1993: 674) observes that innovatory practices entail:

> a reflexivity that attends to the politics of what is and is not done at a practical level in order to learn 'to "read out" the epistemologies in our various practices' (Hartsock, 1987: 206). Yet, as Spivak writes, 'The field of practice is a broken and uneven place, heavily inscribed with habit and sedimented understandings' (1991: 177).

Those habits and sedimented understandings may lead researchers to incorporate themselves into their research as if they were 'some meta-linguistic substance or identity, some pure cogito of self-presence [rather than a being who] is always inscribed in language' (Derrida, in Kearney, 1994: 125). And when they do manage to resist those habits and sedimentations, to make the constitutive force of discourse visible, and revisable, they will nonetheless find themselves caught in multiple layers of ambivalence around the existence of the subject.

Post-structuralist theories of the subject and experimental writing

In attempting to make some sense of this slippery, ambivalent ground we will draw in particular on post-structuralist theories of the subject. The subject, according to Derrida, is an *effect* of subjectivity. Derrida's interest, he says, is in re-situating the subject, in moving from the assumption of a supposed liberal humanist, essentialized, unified identity that has substance independent of language, to the *subject inscribed in language*:

I have never said that the subject should be dispensed with. Only that it should be deconstructed. To deconstruct the subject does not mean to deny its existence. There are subjects, 'operations' or 'effects' (*effets*) of subjectivity. This is an incontrovertible fact. To acknowledge this does not mean, however, that the subject is what it says it is. The subject is not some meta-linguistic substance or identity, some pure cogito of self-presence; it is always inscribed in language. My work does not, therefore, destroy the subject; it simply tries to resituate it.

(Derrida, in Kearney, 1994: 125)

As Butler (1992: 4) comments, refusing the subject as a theoretical starting point does not mean we can dispense with it altogether:

To refuse to assume . . . a notion of the subject from the start is not the same as negating or dispensing with such a notion altogether; on the contrary, it is to ask after the process of its construction and the political meaning and consequentiality of taking the subject as a requirement or presupposition of theory.

What the encounter with post-structuralism does is to enable the subject to see itself in all its shifting, contradictory multiplicity and fragility, and also to see the ongoing and constitutive force of the multiple discourses and practices through which it takes up its existence. It is through making that constitutive force visible that the subject can see its 'self' *as* discursive process, rather than as a unique relatively fixed personal invention.

The self who carries out research and the self who is the subject of the researcher's gaze is thus not denied in this model, but neither is it made central or separate: it is there, *as an effect of discourse*, and it is an important presence in any research (and thus important too that it be acknowledged). As Foucault reflects:

Every time I have tried to do a piece of theoretical work it has been on the basis of elements of my own experience: always in connection with processes I saw unfolding around me. It was always because I thought I identified cracks, silent tremors, and dysfunctions in things I saw, institutions I was dealing with, or my relations with others, that I set out to do a piece of work, and each time was partly a fragment of autobiography.

(Foucault, 2000a: 458)

Those authors who argue for the constitutive discourse analytic version of reflexivity, which foregrounds the limits of consciousness, are generally interested in its power to move us beyond the certainties of what is already known. This entails a certain serious play with language, a play that recognizes its deadly force, its capacity to contain and restrain thought as well as its productive possibilities. Laurel Richardson writes: '[t]hrough concrete, self-reflexive analyses of specific projects we might come to recognize our own and other's social positionings as both constructed and constructing of knowledge' (1997: 108). Through such strategies reflexivity opens new ways of addressing old long-standing questions of how and what we can legitimately take ourselves to know, and what the limitations of our knowledge are.

Good reflexive work, Denzin (1997) suggests, following Marcus (1994), can be found in what he calls 'messy texts'. These are 'texts that are aware of their own narrative apparatuses, that are sensitive to how reality is socially constructed, and that understand that writing is a way of "framing" reality' (Denzin, 1997: 224–225). As Lather (1993: 675) says of such framing: 'It is not a matter of looking harder or more closely, but of seeing what frames our seeing-spaces of constructed visibility and incitements to see which constitute power/knowledge'. Lather (1993: 675) defines reflexivity, or 'seeing what frames our seeing', as a process of establishing a dialogue with readers about which discursive policy is being followed, which regimes of truth the work is located within, which masks of methodology are assumed. Legitimation depends, she says, quoting Bennett, on:

> a researcher's ability to explore the resources of different contemporary inquiry problematics and, perhaps, even contribute to 'an "unjamming" effect in relation to the closed truths of the past, thereby framing up the present for new forms of thought and practice'.
>
> (Lather, 1993: 676, quoting Bennett, 1990: 277)

Such innovative, generative 'messy texts' are also responsible texts, according to Denzin. They are:

> many sited, intertextual, always open ended, and resistant to theoretical holism, but always committed to cultural criticism ... A responsible reflexive text announces its politics and ceaselessly interrogates the realities it invokes while folding the teller's story into the multivoiced history that is written.
>
> (Denzin, 1997: 224)

In relation to writing what Denzin calls messy texts, Barthes argues that we are always present in our texts, even when we write in so-called objective ways, attempting to obliterate ourselves altogether. Objectivity, he says, 'is an image-repertoire like any other' (Barthes, 1989: 8). So is a text that claims there is no such thing as the author or the subject. He suggests that we take as our primary research focus the text that is written, rather than the (real) person who writes it. In privileging the texts of our writing,

Barthes enjoins us to *give birth to ourselves* in our writing, that is, to know ourselves as *coincidental* with our writing, and in this way to write ourselves as multiple in the multiple texts that we write. The self need not be produced as a fixed (fictional) describable entity existing independent of the text, but rather these selves should be born in the same moment as the texts we write (Gannon, 2006). The texts are thus oneselves, and oneselves are there, embodied in the texts – able to be written and read in multiple ways. Through such texts, in which self and writing do not exist as independent projects, we open the possibility, Barthes says, of moving from pleasurable repetition of that which is already known, to the moment of bliss where that pleasurable surface is punctured with another way of knowing. The writer of such texts, he says, is:

> born *at the same time* as his text; he is not furnished with a being which precedes or exceeds his writing, he is not the subject of which his book would be the predicate; there is no time other than that of the speech-act, and every text is written eternally *here* and *now*.
>
> (Barthes, 1989: 52, original emphasis)

But although it might be thought that Barthes can only take up this position because his major interest is in literary texts rather than in the social condition, he also, like Foucault, talks about himself as subject – that subject being the legitimate ground he draws on in the development of his thinking. His focus on literary texts does not preclude, or obviate the necessity of, the embodied subject(s). Rather he presents an example of how the literary and the social cannot be separated. He constitutes his own body as a text to be read, though the act of reading is inextricable from the speaking or writing in which that self is being constituted. In an interview about his book *A Lover's Discourse* (1977c), for example, Barthes talks in terms of and about reading the text of himself as relevant to his writing, and as shaping what it is he chooses to write about:

> *So then the lover who speaks is really you, Roland Barthes?*
>
> My answer may seem to be a pirouette, but it is not. The subject that I am is not unified. This is something I feel profoundly. To then say 'It's I!' would be to postulate a unity of self that I do not recognize in myself.
>
> *Allow me to rephrase my question: For each figure in the book, one after the other, do you say: 'There I am'?*
>
> Well! . . . When I conducted a research seminar on this same topic, I took into account figures that I had not experienced myself, figures taken from books . . . But, obviously, that's what was cut from my book. Yes, I definitely have a personal relation to all the figures in the book.
>
> (Barthes, 1985: 305)

Himself as a unified subject is not something *he can recognize* when he gazes at himself as subject. In his book *he can recognize himself* in the figures he has created.

Collective biography requires a strategy of reading the meanings inscribed on the body very similar to what Barthes talks about. There is a sense in which we create texts inside which we are simultaneously born. Collective biography involves locating the traces of language as they mark and shape the body, and as the body marks and shapes the text. In this strategy, the embodied self becomes a text to be read and written, not as an object separate from our thinking analytic selves, but as the material substance integral to ourselves and to the texts we create. As Trinh writes:

> we do not *have* bodies, we *are* our bodies . . . We write – think and feel – (with) our entire bodies rather than only (with) our minds and hearts. It is a perversion to consider thought the product of one specialised organ, the brain, and feeling, that of the heart.
>
> (Trinh, 1989: 36)

Cixous, too, writes about how her body is a text, inscribed with language, to be read:

> Life becomes text starting out from my body. I am already text. History, love, violence, time, work, desire inscribe it on my body, I go where the 'fundamental language' is spoken, the body language into which all the tongues of things, acts, and beings translate themselves, in my own breast, the whole of reality worked upon in my flesh, intercepted by my nerves, by my senses, by the labor of all my cells, projected, analyzed, recomposed into a book.
>
> (Cixous, 1991: 52)

In contrast, in realist self-narratives, Denzin observes that what he calls self-reflexivity has 'an epistemology of experience based on the standpoint of the self-reflexive individual in the world' (1997: 221). Citing Clough (1994), he observes: 'A generic model of the person as a unified, gendered subject with agency and self-identity organizes this framework' (Denzin, 1997: 221). There is a risk in such realist texts that they will claim an unwarranted authenticity in an attempt to guarantee objective, or at least valid, forms of truth (Lather, 2000). In contrast, at the critical, post-structuralist edge, queer theory, and what Clough (1994) calls feminist materialist reflexivity, insist that 'experience is always mediated by language, ideology and desire', that 'the concept of an autonomous gendered self with agency is a fiction', that 'subjective reflexivity may be a trap that too easily reproduces normative conceptions of self, agency, gender, desire, and sexuality' (Denzin, 1997: 221–222). While Denzin is critical of these slippages into realism, he nonetheless claims that these various forms of reflexivity 'cannot be pulled apart; every text exhibits features of each' (Denzin, 1997: 223) such that the self both is *and* is not a fiction, is unified and transcendent *and* fragmented and always in process of being constituted, can be spoken of in realist ways *and* it cannot, its voice can be claimed as authentic *and* there is no guarantee of authenticity.

Denzin's point here has much in common with Derrida's claim that we must put the subject *sous rature* (Derrida, 1976). When we place the concept of the subject under erasure, we maintain the concept of the subject because we cannot do without it, at the same time subjecting it to the kind of critique that constitutes the subject as something other than it thinks it is or intends itself to be when it constitutes itself as the unified, rational subject. Denzin's point appears to be slightly different from Derrida's, however, as it poses a theoretical conundrum in which the subject as it is constituted in liberal humanist forms of realism, of which we are critical when we find it in our own and others' writing, is nevertheless inevitably present in the reflexive writing that attempts to deconstruct and go beyond that subject. When we evoke the constituted and constitutive subject in our writing, can we conceptualize it differently from the subject that is evoked in realist texts? Is it possible to write of research selves/ subjects as if they exist in the ways Foucault, Barthes and Cixous do, and yet not invoke the narrative self of realist accounts? How might we go about doing this? This chapter is a partial attempt to address this problem.

In the context of the queer and feminist materialist theories, Denzin describes ethnopoetic and narratives-of-self ethnographies as examples of reflexive texts that:

> are not just subjective accounts of experience; they attempt to reflexively map the multiple discourses that occur in a given social space. Hence they are always multivoiced. No interpretation is privileged. These texts resist the principles of realist ethnographic narrative that make claims to both textual autonomy and epistemological validity.
>
> (Denzin, 1997: 225)

At the same time, he says, they:

> always return to the writerly self – a self that spills over into the world being inscribed. This is a writerly self with a particular hubris that is neither insolent nor arrogant. The poetic self is simply willing to put itself on the line and to take risks.
>
> (Ibid.: 225)

There is, in this account, in relation to the writerly self and the self that is taken as the ground of experience to be drawn on, a deep ambivalence. The writer moves among descriptions, interpretations and voices in an attempt to re-create 'a social world as a site at which identities and local cultures are negotiated and given meaning' (ibid.: 225). In doing so, writers are both 'modernist observers telling realist tales, deploying a parallax view, and [are] recording a constantly changing internal and external world' (ibid.: 202). They must ideally avoid realist claims and the reproduction of narrow and oppressive frames that hold social categories in place *at the same time* as they search their own and others' embodied selves that exist in relation to particular social worlds, that come into existence, and go on coming into existence, actively using (and at the same time being determined by) the discursive tools already available to them (Butler, 1997a). It is in looking at what is found when one gazes at oneself as constituted subject *and* the means of its constitution, that the details may be found that enable researchers to recognize and (at least momentarily) break out of the oppressive determinate structures and practices through which those selves are constituted and made real.

During this collective biography workshop we read our embodied selves in order to catch ourselves engaged in reflexivity in order to examine reflexivity more closely. Reflexivity entailed the act of analysing with(in) and against those discourses through which we are constituted (including, and perhaps especially in, the reflexive moment), and also entailed the possibility of seeing that it might have been otherwise. It allowed us to transgress, in moments of bliss (Barthes, 1975), the determinate discourses that might otherwise hold us captive. In this sense, reflexivity entailed turning the gaze of language upon itself, both seeing and producing its constitutive force; and seeing ourselves seeing and producing it, and opening up the possibility of critique and change. We were, in our workshop, embodied beings who wrote, who listened to the texts we created, who were born, in Barthes's sense, in the texts we produced, and who were always potentially caught up in discourses that we could not be said in any sense to have chosen.

Post-structuralist discourse entails a move from the self as a noun (and thus stable and relatively fixed) to the self as a verb, always in process, taking its shape in and through the discursive possibilities through which selves are made (Davies, 2000b). Who is it then, we asked, that engages in the reflexive act? Who is the subject of the reflexive gaze? How are we to conduct our reflexive work if the one who gazes and the one who is sometimes gazed at are themselves being constituted in the very moment of the act of gazing, by the discursive and political and contextual features constituting the moment of reflexivity?

In preparation for the workshop we surveyed some of the existing literature, attending to different conceptualizations of reflexivity and different ways of 'doing' reflexivity as part of the research act. Also, we had emailed to each other some of our early thoughts on the topic, and Bronwyn had developed a list of memory topics that emerged during this preparatory stage, which we would use to turn our gaze on our remembered experiences of being reflexive. These included:

- the first memory of reversing the gaze of language upon itself
- the first memory of turning a reflexive gaze upon writing itself – of seeing writing as a way of coming to know
- the first memory of knowing being located in biographical situatedness as an embodied being
- the first memory of going beyond the limits of those discourses that held us captive.

One early decision that we had to make was whether to focus on our earliest memories, as we usually do, or on our more recent memories of our adult researcher selves. Some of us felt that the researcher memories might be too difficult to retrieve. Since the emphasis on earliest memories had, in previous workshops, never ceased to surprise us with its productiveness, we decided to continue with that strategy. But we decided, as well, to add a further reflexive loop, by watching ourselves at work during the workshop. In this way we hoped the process of reflexivity at work in research might be made visible and analysable.

When we told our stories and began our usual process of questioning, our reflexive gaze fell over this work of questioning and answering. Our discussions were similar to the discussion Haug and her colleagues described in relation to the first draft of their written stories. Here, they say:

> spontaneous discussion of any story began with an implicit comparison, in which one experience was pitted against another. This was an initial corrective focusing discussion on the credibility of the situation as well as its typicality . . . Comparison demands of memory exactitude and plausibility.
>
> (Haug et al., 1987: 56)

Out of their discussions of the first draft, when they came upon resistances to the meanings others were finding in their writing, Haug et al. would sometimes flesh out each others' writing with their own. Our own strategy was, in contrast, to pursue these conversations around each others' stories during the initial telling of them. It was then the responsibility of the originator of the story to pursue the detail in the writing that satisfied the criteria that the story now make sense to, and be readily able to be imagined by, those listening to it.

The words 'pitted' and 'pursue' are chosen carefully here. This process is not a warm fuzzy pursuit of empathy in which we assume a union of two or more selves in a mirroring relationship (Lather, 2000: 19). The questioning and challenging of each others' stories can take on a ruthless quality as we pursue the detail that might otherwise be obscured by the clichéd phrases that announce: 'this is what anyone would know and recognize'. This sometimes brutal process is aimed at breaking open platitudes with which anyone could empathize and a pursuit of the detail that makes it possible for something else to take its place. 'To argue against empathy,' as Lather (2000: 19) says, 'is to trouble the possibilities of understanding, as premised on structures that all people share.'

The writing does not thus seek merely to document what we said when we first told our story (as if that telling captured some kind of authentic truth about our own individuality), but to tell the story in such a way that it is vividly imaginable by others, such that those others can extend their own imaginable experience of being in the world through knowing the particularity of another. This imaginability comes not out of the repetition of predictable or familiar storylines but out of the detailed attention to embodied detail that brings a new and unexpected view of what happened to light.

This searching of the embodied self for detail might be read as denying the fictionality of identities. But we regard it as the reverse. The fiction of the self is created when detailed embodied memories are only made relevant to the extent that they fit an essentialized unified (fictional) version of self that fits within and makes sense within hegemonic forms of meaning-making about individuals in the social world. By searching out the multiple embodied details, and doing so collectively, those fictions can be realized in all their superficiality as generating a self that is abstracted from and prior to discursive imperatives. In place of that fictional self one discovers not a 'real' self, but the discursive imperatives at play (in the past, and in the present) along with their multiple inscriptions of desire, emotion and modes of understanding on the body. We are thus not writing about why we think the things we remember happened, or what judgements we want to make about their meanings. We are struggling to articulate the concrete detail that is usually obscured with abstract clichés, and forgotten or made irrelevant inside the regimes of truth through which the stories might otherwise be told (Davies, 1994). In a sense this means treating your own story as if it were experienced by a stranger – all the embodied detail becomes relevant, when usually that detail is assumed, or taken for granted, or obscured or silenced in usual ways of speaking and writing. To this end we sometimes also adopted the strategy of writing in the third person. The writing thus becomes, itself, a self-conscious, reflexive and innovative act that seeks to avoid the repetition of well-practised ways of knowing and includes, instead, detailed, embodied memories.

We read our written and rewritten stories out loud. This reading out loud is, for us, important, as it heightens attention to the embodied and emotional aspects of the memory. The vibrations of vocal cords, of tongue and lips and ear drums remind us of bodies, and of selves as bodies, as we attempt to shed the discursive constructions that all too easily leave bodies out, and that essentialize the abstracted persons that we might inadvertently constitute as lying behind our texts. In this sense we followed Barthes (1989: 52) in giving birth to ourselves in our texts, in which we exist wholly in the present moment of the text. In reading out loud the texts we created, we sometimes discovered whole wells of emotion that we had not known were attached, or attachable, to the words we had written on the page or screen. Those emotions, both in readers and listeners, helped attune us to the fleshiness of the remembered moment, to its capacity to be relived and re-evoked through the particular intonation, the feel and sound of the words out loud.

Each evening we wrote our reflections on the day's work, asking: 'what were the moments of insight, and how have I thought about thought?' We included this exercise of turning our reflexive gaze upon each day's work in order to practise thinking about the act of thinking *as researchers*, and to be as close to the research act as possible. The reflexive writing we engaged in each night became a body of data along with the collective biography stories. When we met the next day we began by reading our reflections out loud to each other, thus hearing them and voicing them as well as writing them. Those written reflections evoked conceptual, methodological and 'processual' discussions as well as further personal reflections. In a way, we tried to install a doubled, or even trebled, attention to reflexivity – pondering on its meaning/practice, remembering it as we have lived it, doing it, both in writing and talking about memories and in installing this further reflexive loop of night-time writing and then reading and discussion of that night-time writing each morning.

Reflexively examining ourselves at work

Despite our unquestioned enthusiasm for reflexive work, many of the reflections we wrote, after the long and intensive workshop days, were about feelings of exhaustion, about minds that went 'blank' at the overactivity, or even paralysis, at not being able (any more) to engage in this process of reflexivity:

> *Still struck by paralysis. Words dying on her tongue the minute they are thought and not yet spoken, killed by the controlling reflecting gaze she suddenly puts on her language and thoughts. A glimpse of a singing voice within her: 'Thoughts are free, they cannot be caught by anyone, they pass flying like shadows of the night'. Yet this is about reflecting upon yourself/your self, reflective arcs, back and forth – and you are you and your language, you and your thinking, you and your working of brain and tongue. Think right here and speak right here, now! Comforted by the song of her childhood – relieved to read (a reliable source) that paralysis might be a consequence of reflexivity.*

There is a certain skill, we found, in catching oneself in the act of thinking, feeling, knowing – catching oneself, and in the very act, not killing or distorting the thing that is caught. The original moment seems to exist only to the extent that it is let go free – free, that is, of a self-conscious gaze that asks, 'how might I describe what it is I am thinking, doing, saying, right now, for the purposes of reporting it later, in a quite separate act from the one I am now engaged in?' or, later, while writing, 'what might I say about what I have thought and done during the day that does not in some sense recreate the day as something other than the thing we took it to be at the time?' Sometimes our night-time reflections produced observations about aspects of the day that we had not reflexively, consciously attended to during the day. These nightly reflections produced both constructive changes in our daily practices and an underbelly of our method – moments of resistance and dissatisfaction that might otherwise have gone unspoken. One of us recorded, for example, feelings of resistance to the method of discussing and analysing the stories, since she felt that we were insufficiently reflexively aware of the constitutive and methodic work we were engaged in when remembering and discussing and analysing. As a way of provoking us to look at that constitutive work, she wrote that the stories seemed true enough in their 'original' form – and of the analysis and subsequent rewriting killing the stories dead. She drew our attention to the way our talk could be read as 'evaluation' or judgement, rather than the (intended) process we were trying to engage in of recognizing the reflexive strategies through which selves are made. While our attention was primarily on the constitutive work that was done then, when we were the subjects of our memories, she wanted to jolt us into the present to look at the constitutive work we were doing now. She wrote, angrily:

> Realise that I don't have a clue on what ground we evaluate each other's written memories. What does it mean, this question we ask: 'does it work'? Feel uncomfortable, feel I don't know what I ought to know, that there is a hidden agreement that I'm not in on. Because I'm new to the method? Because I'm apprehensive and not open-minded enough? Why is it that you want the stories stripped of 'explanations' and 'clichés'? When we tell them to each other they seem to make sense only because we place them into a narrative form that entails explanations, well-known story-lines, plots, beginnings and ends. You say you only want the 'embodied' moment. What does that mean? Can it be separated from the 'intellectual work' we employ when we tell it . . . Does it 'work' when it gives us goose bumps or makes us want to cry? Is that what you mean when you say 'powerful'?

This reflection provided an opportunity for the group to make explicit and discuss the criteria contained in the question we asked of each written story: 'does it work?' After analysing what we meant by the question, and the problems being experienced, we changed the question to 'were you with me?' in order to transform it from being read as an objective truth-evaluation, to an inter-subjective, collective reading and listening. This reflection also evoked a discussion about what the concept 'collective' (in collective biography) meant to the participants in the group. We explored afresh the idea that our individual biographical moments can be used to explore not some essential self locked in our individualistic memories, but the common, collective discursive threads out of which we all have constituted ourselves and been, and go on being, constituted. Thus the meaning of the word 'collective' was collectively re-addressed, renegotiated and reconstructed through the very same act in which we expressed our different reactions to the processes we were engaged in.

In that way, the reflexive arc on the process did more than dampen down and paralyse. It occasioned opportunity to develop new ways of thinking and acting. Even so, one of us, who had participated several times in these workshops, worried away at the critical gaze brought to the written stories, expressing anxiety about her (in)capacity to write without clichés and explanations:

> *I can't seem to get it (my stories) 'right' yet even though I've done it many times before. . . . Though I think I am an OK writer usually this context seems to block me. . . . Sometimes I resist/argue against. The fears I wrote about in the poem my very first time seem to overhang me in these workshops. Tendency to explain, over-elaborate, justify.*

The skill of writing from the body, in detail and without clichés and value-laden explanations is one that has to be struggled with every time we engage with this form of writing, because it is so different from the usual ways we tell our stories – those usual ways being the ways the familiar, rational, unified subject is created as an effect of discourse. Another thread in our nightly reflections, also loaded with anxiety, had to do with our individual contribution to, or position in, the group, in relation to the others, revealing an unwelcome sense of paranoia:

> *Uneasiness – what do the others think she is? A kind of spy? Does Bronwyn regret having invited her? Does she belong to the ones that regard this as not real work? . . .*
> *I still worry about my contribution to the group. Have thought a lot about my position in the team. What is it I can offer a group like this? Funny how your position, your strengths and weaknesses, change in every new group. Sometimes the entrepreneur, sometimes the water boy.*

When, in a further reflexive arc, we cast our reflexive gaze on our night-time reflections/reflexions we were also, at first, surprised at the unwelcome self-governing force that was portrayed in them. We had caught ourselves, it seemed, self-consciously conducting our own conduct – producing the selves on which we were gazing (Rose, 1999: 5). We were, almost in spite of ourselves, engaging in a narrowing moral judgement over the 'I'; our own eye acting as an uninvited self-disciplining force. As one of us wrote in her night-time reflections, that governing force was not what she wanted to find when she engaged in 'reflexivity':

> *Reflexively analysing, or even just noting, what I'm doing takes extra energy and maybe in some ways damps me down. The reflexive eye/I as I am experiencing it right now is maybe a little too close to Pinnochio's Jiminy Cricket eye/I – the small conscience sitting on his shoulder . . .*
>
> *The gaze that judges already narrows what is possible before it happens, trusses the body and mind like a turkey ready for baking – you will stay neat and orderly – in this pre-ordained state – a state which we know to be better – or else you will be found lacking. The judgemental eye/I is, for me, potentially always switched on, gazing at and containing my actions. The reflexive eye/I in contrast, ideally, gazes without judgement, and, like a good novelist, finds the unexpected, the surprising – the contradictions, the 'good' and the 'bad' in all its detail – not with a mind to censor, but to say with fascination 'oh so that's how it is!'*

The moral gaze restricts, binds one's thoughts, defers and refers constantly to the discourses of respectability, of morality, of discipline, of method. The unwanted guest at our table was unequivocally there, however. The surveilling, governing eye of one of us makes an appeal to the 'I' of experience and writes and rewrites, struggling to find the words that will be recognizably authentic, that will meet all the requirements of validity. Even though she knows post-structuralist writers have put that term under erasure, she worries about it when she thinks of journal editors and readers:

> *She puts her stories into order, connects them to the days and the questions asked each day, goes over them again and again, rewrites under the surveilling eye that a publication might require, her reflections reflected by the computer's screen, rewritten again, attempts to gain validity by asking herself 'is that what she felt?'*

Is it possible to divide off the governing eye, we asked, from the eye/I that records? Can we both acknowledge the presence of this containing force and yet also find some method of bypassing it, even if only momentarily? Perhaps we can switch organs, as Irigaray suggests, and listen with 'another ear', such that we *listen* to the texts of our stories and reflections with that other ear, without judgement:

> One would have to listen with another ear, as if hearing an 'other meaning' always in the process of weaving itself, of embracing itself with words, but also of getting rid of words in order not to become fixed, congealed in them.
>
> (Irigaray, 1985: 29)

The negativity of these writings took us by surprise. We thought we were enjoying what we were doing, yet this is what we wrote. In discussing this surprise, we decided that these stories had become the 'news' that needed to be written, since we had all assumed that we could and should easily engage in this thing called reflexivity – whatever it was. In a further discussion, we decided that the nature of the group and its work also needed to be articulated as the body underneath which this underbelly could be constituted. We talked about the way we perceived ourselves (constituted ourselves) as having established and sustained the ideals and relations of a network, a peer group, a place to find both support and productive challenges. We talked about the workshop as a place to think and breathe, laugh and cry with professional/personal (soul)mates. It was, we said, a feminist space in which our desire to think constructively 'with' instead of destructively 'against' each other could be indulged. We talked about an ethos that more or less invisibly governed the interaction, the ideas and ideals of the workshop, that was anti-hierarchical, non-competitive and non-confronting. We thus articulated a set of tacit principles (in)forming what we did, and in doing so, reconstituted it as the thing we talked about. We also articulated/constituted, in our talk both the ways we faltered and confounded those ideals, and the fears and anxieties that drove those comments, and about the way that our self-conscious engagement in reflexive work required that we see (and thus constitute) both the ideal of what we practised and the disruptions to that ideal.

There are in this reflexive examination of ourselves at work, two deep sites of ambivalence:

- between reflexivity as necessary for language and thought, *and* reflexivity as dampening down and obscuring thought
- between reflexivity as a mode of controlling and making oneself appropriate to the culture or context, *and* reflexivity as liberating oneself from the determining force of discourse and culture.

We will now leave this partial and situated account of 'what we did' and what rationalities we found at play in conducting ourselves as researchers, and move on to the stories we told in the workshop about being reflexive subjects in our remembered stories. The analysis of these stories will help us make sense further of the questions about who it is that 'does' reflexivity, and with what constitutive effect.

Re-membered stories

We hyphenate *re-membered* here to signal both the work of remembering and the fact that we are, inevitably, in those acts or remembering, constructing and reconstructing ourselves as subjects – making ourselves as members anew in the acts of re-membering. We begin, here, with stories that allow us to look at and listen again to Foucault's (1982: 220–221) analysis of the conduct of conduct. In order to examine the *conduct of conduct*, and the power of one group over another, Foucault argues for an examination of the rationalities that are involved. He suggests that, rather than rail against powers of particular groups in society, we look at the forms of rationality through which particular relations are constituted and maintained:

> What has to be questioned is the form of rationality at stake. The criticism of power wielded over the mentally sick or mad cannot be restricted to psychiatric institutions; nor can those questioning the power to punish be content with denouncing prisons as total institutions. The question is: how are such relations of power rationalized?
>
> (Foucault, 1981: 254)

Rose puts this point slightly differently, referring to thought rather than rationality. What it is possible to think, and, in turn, what we take to be true, are fundamental to the conduct of conduct and the practices whereby subjectivities are governed and made governable:

> the activity of government is inextricably bound up with the activity of thought. It is thus both made possible by and constrained by what can be thought at any particular moment in our history. To analyze the history of government, then, requires attention to the conditions under which it becomes possible to consider certain things to be true – and hence to say and do certain things – about human beings and their interrelations as they produce, consume, reproduce, act, infract, live, sicken, die.
>
> (Rose, 1999: 8)

Here, in our stories, we find one of us, as a small girl, reading her self, reading the context, and managing her self within the context of hospital to produce what she reads as appropriate for the rationalities at play in that context. She has been run over by a truck on Christmas day:

> *She is three years old and in hospital. The blue and white patterned cover over the steel hoop hiding her crushed foot. The cover smooth – tucked in at the sides holding her still. She sees far down the row of beds her teddy bear. It was one of the many Christmas presents she had been going to get but the truck running her over got in the way. Too many presents for one little girl. The nurse gave some of her presents to other children. She wanted that Teddy back. It's hers. Be still. Don't cry. Lie straight. Don't let them say she is greedy.*

Her Christmas teddy bear, has been given away, without her knowledge or permission, to another child in the ward. It is an outrage. But she hears the nurse's rationality 'too many presents for one little girl' and she instructs herself to contain her emotions, to be still and straight. She successfully constitutes herself as not greedy. Foucault (1997a: 224) asks: 'What must one know about oneself in order to be willing to renounce anything?' The little girl renounces ownership of the teddy bear in order to know herself, and be known, as 'not-greedy'. She also renounces the desire to cry and to make a fuss about losing something she had been so excited to receive. She knows already that this is necessary, and she knows, to answer Foucault's question, that she can do it. She also knows, and over this she has no control, that it is better to be read as not-greedy, and that this reading must override her desire for her new teddy. In this story the small girl reveals her early knowledge of how to conduct her own conduct, even in the face of formidable odds. The moralizing I/eye is already visibly at work in the constitution of self.

In seeking to listen to ourselves with another ear, not to judge the self, but to find the detail, we encounter selves whose judgemental eye/I is already well trained, dominated by discourses that dictate what sort of girl she *should* be. Within an(y) institution, Foucault argues, 'power reaches into the very grain of individuals, touches their bodies and inserts itself into their actions and attitudes, their discourses, learning processes and everyday lives' (Foucault, 1980b: 39). The reflexive eye, in this story, is integral to that insertion: the child reads the situation and knows how others read it, and how they will read her. She inserts herself into the everyday lives and meaning-worlds of others and of herself by distancing herself from one set of emotions and disciplining herself to align herself with another set. This story of the three-year-old girl in hospital vividly evokes the judgemental controlling eye of reflexivity, revealing its centrality in the process of achieving ourselves as appropriate and appropriated subjects.

Let us move, then, to stories that do not submit, that run against the grain of dominant discourses. Derrida (1976: 162) argues the:

> necessity of 'departure' as part of the deconstructive act . . . [It is] 'exorbitant' – an attempt to get out of the orbit, to 'reach the point of a certain exteriority' in relation to the space that is protected, closed off by disciplinary institutions.

That exteriority, however, is always accompanied by a certain necessary ambivalence, since we are always both caught inside discourses at the same time as we struggle against them. Our stories demonstrate that once we had felt the pleasure of winning against our own frightened, dominated selves, as well as against the selves of others, achieving a certain exteriority to dominant discourses, that moment of 'getting out of orbit' became a principle of the soul to be sought over and over again. At the same time, as we show in the last part of the chapter, it is also true that we agonized about belonging, about being good enough, casting a narrow, controlling, moralizing constitutive gaze on ourselves in spite of our intention to, or belief that we should, look with unbiased eyes.

We thus find ourselves caught in the sticky web of discourse, *at the same time* as we reached out for that 'point of a certain exteriority', both enmeshed in and resisting the power of determinate discourses. Reflexivity implies a critical consciousness of the discourses that hold us in place, that is, a capacity to distance ourselves from them, at the same time as we are being constituted by them; a capacity to see the work they do and to question their effects at the same time as we live those effects. This does not mean that one is outside of language, or floating free of discourse. It means, rather, that the possibility exists of reflexively turning the gaze of language upon itself.

One of us remembers when she was six years old:

The other kids call her a hippie. Danger, danger. What do you mean? Your mum pushes wheelbarrows in the nude. The sense of exposure almost swallows her. Must react, must react now. Tomorrow the word will be even bigger. Struggling to keep calm, to be matter-of-fact: Well, she is not exactly nude, she just takes off her top when it's hot, pushing wheelbarrows makes you hot, it helps taking off your top. Thinking, thinking. Remove the danger, make it go away. 'Difference is good' she says fixating confidently on the staring eyes. Had she pushed it too far? No, she succeeded. The word will be all right tomorrow.

Here the girl uses one discourse against another. She mobilizes the discourse of 'difference is good', using body language that suggests this is legitimate knowledge, and that her mother's actions can be spoken about openly and without fear. She defuses the potential that the other children have to use 'hippie' and 'nude' to constitute her as someone to be marginalized and teased. The girl offers to the children another rationality – that difference is good – and successfully recasts herself as legitimate, as not someone against whom such power moves can be made. She makes the world right again. In this instance, reflexivity works to assess the power and potential of one discourse and in that assessment sees the need for a counter-discourse. At the same time it involves a careful reflexive gaze on herself, instructing herself and monitoring her capacity to follow her own instructions, at the same time as she watches the others to see how it is that they take up the constitutive effects of the counter-discourse. Reflexive awareness as it is experienced here requires multiple layers of attention and is potentially powerful in its capacity to turn one discursive frame into another at the same time as it judges and controls.

We also turned our reflexive gaze on writing, on seeing writing as a way of coming to know. Writing is a significant everyday practice in the lives of all the women in our group, all academic workers. We write in our professional lives and in our personal lives, each of which bleed into one another in our writing, as they do in our living. Yet despite our high levels of literacy and comfort with writing practices, the stories we recalled about self-writing did not celebrate this practice or suggest that it was easy or readily accessible. Although several of us have written about writing as *jouissance*, in these memories of reflexivity we did not remember writing as finding '(o)urselves in writing like fish in the water, like meanings in our tongues' (Cixous, 1991: 58). Rather we found ourselves writing of drowning, spewing, poisoning, blockages: the words as abject, the practice of writing as a practice of abjecting ourselves. The words – out there in the world – become risky. The reflexive eye/I of writing – the eye/I that writes itself through the sinews and muscles of the shoulders, down the arm, through the hand and the fingers on keyboard/paper/notebook – is a vigilant and simultaneously an endangering/endangered eye/I. Care of oneself, in which writing and vigilance intertwine (Foucault 1997a: 232), is both a necessary and a dangerous practice.

One of our stories illustrates this danger and necessity intertwined. The girl writes in her diary. She is a teenager and her words are secret – her writing personal. But, 'find me, read me' is the subtext that the mother reads to the considerable outrage of the girl:

Writing for spewing
This is what I'm supposed to do
All girls keep diaries
They write in them about love and romance
So I sit up in bed
And start to write
About love and romance
But what comes out on the page
Is ugly
Angry and frustrated
Why doesn't he like me?
If I have sex with him will he like me?
If I let him stick his finger in my pants instead of on top of them
Will we fall in love?
Awful, horrible words and thoughts are there on the page
(but now I think why do those words seem so ugly?)
I close it up, lift up my mattress,
and shove it as far away as I can.
(But of course, naturally, Mum finds it anyway).

The girl uses the diary to record the details of her engagement in a certain 'truth game', in an obligatory 'technology of the self'. She knows that other girls record (spew out) their enmeshment in romance and love. They take up, and she tries to take up too, 'the duty to . . . try to know what is happening inside [her], to acknowledge faults, to recognize

temptations, to locate desires . . . to bear . . . witness against [her]self'
(Foucault, 1997a: 242). But instead of spewing forth the correct tale of
love and temptation, she unleashes something she remembers as ugly –
anger and frustration and puzzlement. She identifies crucial questions
about how bodies and emotions work in relation to each other. Do phys-
icality and emotionality relate in some causal way? Does the emotion of
liking or love spring from the body, or intimate fleshy contact with another's body? Engaging the technology of self she finds her questions horrible
– she has committed her abject self to the page. The girl writer is disgusted
with what she writes and pushes it under her bed, as far as it will go. But
her mother finds her words and reads them. The woman looking back is
'spewing' (i.e., furious, angry in Australian slang) that her mother found
(and read) her diary. Perhaps the mother assumed a right (even an obligation) to cast her eye over the writing in an act of surveillance – perhaps
she assumed the right, even obligation, to make moral judgements, to
guide her daughter along particular paths that must be followed if she is to
be the right sort of girl. The girl can be described as caught between the
liberal humanist directive to 'reveal' her true thoughts in a diary, and the
moralizing directive that she become the right sort of girl. The girl's questioning about how and whether emotion is triggered in the body trans-
gresses the romantic narrative in which she is supposed to write herself as
girl. It disrupts the hegemonic fiction about what girls should be. It is ugly
because it does not fit the romantic storyline: she speaks words that girls
are not supposed to speak; she seeks knowledge girls are not supposed to
want. Her words are dangerous and she shoves them away from her into a
secret place under the mattress, but the surveilling eye of her mother finds
them anyway.

Our fourth story picks up the theme of surveillance, and moves away
from childhood and into the workplace of schools. Surveillance, inducing
states of fear and guilt, is increasingly something we each live with in our
working lives as neo-liberal management strategies are put in place in our
educational settings. Some of those strategies can be deceptive, seeming at
first to be 'for our own good' or even something we believe in and desire
for ourselves. One of us found herself and the other teachers in her
school, for example, invited by their school principal to write a reflexive
journal about their work:

*Reflective dialogue journals – what a great idea! Every week before the staff
meeting they spend ten minutes reflecting on the week before. She writes freely
about how she feels about everything – kids she's worried about, classes that
have gone well (or badly), how she has behaved as a teacher and how she
could behave better. The principal collects them all up and writes brief and
quite personal comments back: suggestions, support, affirmations that it really
is getting better. She looks forward to reading her comments. What a great*

continuous professional development strategy she thinks. She was a great supporter of the idea when the principal first suggested it. She's excited to be part of such a progressive and reflective team. Until a distressed colleague comes to see her, in her role as union representative. The principal has just read sections of this woman's journal back to her as justification for refusing to renew her contract for another term. 'You don't belong in my school,' said the principal to the teacher. 'Listen to what you say here.' She reads the journal out loud and the woman sits hearing her own words, in another's voice, condemning her. As the woman retells her story, the union representative can do nothing but empathise (and worry about her own vulnerability).

Cixous says of her own writing: 'Writing is good: it's what never ends. The simplest, most secure other circulates inside me' (1991: 4). While we assent to this as an idea(l) that we imagine when we write, in our memories we also find that writing can be dangerous, even 'bad' in terms of the consequences. Writing is always writing in context, and each context (itself constructed) invites particular readings. Particular contexts can make the writing dangerous, no matter how good or true the impulse to write. Perhaps even especially when writing is as honest as one can make it, as reflexive and committed to 'truth' and self-examination as we can possibly make it, it can be dangerous. Its danger depends upon the discourses made relevant by those charged with surveillance over that which is written. Reflexive writing can be passionate and emotional. It can be writing in which the mind, heart and body are all engaged. Yet once those words are out there in the world, objects themselves of reflexion by others as well as ourselves, they can become weapons to turn against us.

In each case where spoken and written words become dangerous, we find that a humanist rationality is at work in the reader. It is assumed by the one who looks and judges that the words reveal a true self who exists independently of the text and yet who can be revealed by the text. That pre-discursive self can be interacted with in very real ways – that is, the reading of it as *existing* has very real consequences. The daughter is read by the mother as revealing something unacceptable about her real, essential self – a self that must be managed, that must learn to conduct appropriately its own sexual conduct. The teacher becomes one whose contract should not be renewed because of the words she has written on the page. The surveilling eyes do not see the words as discursive strategies, taken up, in this case, as the appropriate form of journal writing that the principal wanted. Rather the words are read as a kind of mirror held up to the soul of the writer: the self is both subject and object of the reflexive eye/I, and is pin-down-able, fixable and therefore remediable and punishable. The figure of the essential self who lurks behind or is 'revealed' by the text becomes the dominant image – the text is secondary – a transparent window on the soul.

This figure of the self who might be thought to exist independent of the text, has necessarily haunted this text. Its potential presence makes unsustainable and unstable the move to a reflexivity in which the focus is on 'the text which is, after all, the only "true" result of any research' (Barthes, 1989: 319). In the everyday worlds evoked by our stories, the humanist unified pre-discursive self can always, potentially, be read back in.

The task of turning the stories and reflexions into this text has involved the seven of us in multiple layers of complex reflexive work as we negotiate our way through what is to be written, whose experience and whose stories will be counted as relevant, and who it might be that we tell this story to. (An added layer of complexity was brought in when Babette translated this chapter into German and sought reviews from a journal in Germany that was taking reflexivity as a topic for a special issue. We had no way of knowing what they wanted until we found that they did not like what we had written.) Thus laid over (or is it under?) the story of 'what we did', in a palimpsest of meaning-making, we find ourselves carefully monitoring what kinds of knowledges about ourselves and our somewhere(s) find their way to these pages, what sort of knowledges (accounts and accountabilities) are made relevant and legitimate for this academic work (asking, which journal, which audience, which academic-hood). We ask: what is silenced and set aside? What governs these choices/readings, which rationalities and desires are at play? What kinds of 'somewheres' that we write to and from, do we (re)construct? What others do we not? How do we know ourselves as a collective and how as individuals? What is the multiply layered reflexive process we are engaged in?

And so . . .

Returning then to Denzin's observation, that these theoretically contradictory forms of reflexivity – self-reflexive realist texts and discourse analytic texts which claim that there is no pre-discursive (real or essential) self that floats free of discourse – 'cannot be pulled apart; every text exhibits features of each' (1997: 223). From this position we must accept that the self both is *and* is not a fiction; is unified and transcendent *and* fragmented and always in process of being constituted; can be spoken of in realist ways *and* cannot; its voice can be claimed as authentic *and* there is no guarantee of authenticity. Do our explorations make any difference to how we are to make sense of the slippery and difficult theoretical ground on which we work?

First we would like to discuss the claim that the subject is not removed from the second approach – it is there *as an effect* of discourse. In this approach the subject is under erasure, it is not the source of itself, nor is there an authentic account it can give of itself. It cannot be either an all-knowing all-seeing eye, or a unified whole that can be accounted for. What we hope to have moved (partially) towards is the evocation of a subject who, as an effect of multiple discourses, can both examine and be examined without the (tacit) evocation of a real unified pre-discursive self. At the same time it is important to note that that self can always be read into our texts and judged with a narrow moralizing gaze. What we have shown with our children's stories, in particular, is that reflexivity is not a technology with which we might stand outside ourselves, or outside discourse, turning an impartial unsituated gaze upon our ourselves-in-process. It is a technology of selves that is integral to the very kinds of selves made possible in the discourses through which selves are constituted and through which they constitute themselves. As children and also as researchers, we were engaged in constituting ourselves as particular kinds of people, not through descriptions of ourselves as being one kind of person or another, but through what it was we made describable *and* the rationalities and discourses through which we came to see that that was what it was we wanted to make relevant and salient.

Casting our reflexive gaze on our own work as researchers, and our memories as children, we found reflexivity to be integral to the process of conducting our own conduct – a (sometimes) unwelcome coercive, controlling judgemental gaze, present in our childhood stories and in our reflexive work as researchers, and at the same time the very (life-giving) means by which we became persons. While we did not welcome the moralistic gaze that narrows and traps, as reflexive researchers, mapping the ground of the selves we gazed at, and examining the detail whether we liked it or not, we had no choice but to acknowledge its presence. While we preferred a judgement that sees that being trapped in some specific ways is not acceptable – a judgment that seeks to open up possibilities, and that experiments and innovates, we must observe that the former is always present shaping what we see and do, even though its roots are, we suspect, deeply mired in the liberal humanist conception of the prediscursive, unified, 'real' self.

How then are we to conceptualize the doer behind the deed? Butler writes of the relation between subjects and discourse:

> [I]f the subject is a reworking of the very discursive processes by which it is worked, then 'agency' is to be found in the possibilities of resignification opened up by discourse. In this sense, discourse is the horizon of agency, but also performativity is to be rethought as resignification. There is no 'bidding farewell' to the *doer* 'beyond' or 'behind' the deed. For the deed will be itself and the legacy of conventions which it reengages, but also the future possibilities it opens up;

the 'doer' will be the uncertain working of the discursive possibilities by which it itself is worked.

(Butler, 1995c: 135, emphasis added)

The threads that might be impossible to separate, then, are the discourses through which we are constituted as, and constitute ourselves as, agentic beings (a sense of ourselves we cannot do without as persons or as researchers). We cannot disentangle ourselves from or float free of discourse. In order to engage in reflexivity we must hone our skills of critical literacy – becoming literate subjects both knowing well and using competently the discourses through which we constitute ourselves and are constituted as selves *and at the same time*, bringing a critical consciousness to those processes, seeing their effects (seeing their effects *as* effects) and seeing that they might be otherwise. We must therefore occupy an ambivalent position of competent agent and transgressive critic.

The reflexive researcher must find a way to write that:

- makes visible the technologies of self and of researcher–selves that are engaged in analysis and writing
- reveals the limits of our knowledge, particularly in the research act
- makes clear the political orientation driving our work
- reveals what discursive and textual framing shapes our work both in practice and in writing
- opens up the possibilities of thinking other-wise once old interpretive certainties are made visible, and finally
- acknowledges that at some points it is necessary to get on with the story, in which the effects of discourse are made visible, since otherwise there would be nothing on which to cast our reflexive gaze.

The reflexive process is, thus, like being held within a hall of mirrors – the hall of mirrors that enthrals us in sideshow alleys at fairs and amusement parks. Standing in front of one mirror, our reflection is caught in another, and that other reflects yet another image, in a ceaseless infinite regression. For the researcher, the boundaries between 'illusion' and 'reality' may be broken, just as they are broken when one enters an amusement park, itself a place of border transgressions. Yet the infinite regression captured in such a hall of mirrors draws attention to the backward looking of reflexivity, as if the process is always a return, a turning back. Yet the act of reflexivity creates new thoughts and ideas at the same time as going back over old thoughts and ideas. And is not going back in fact a new process in itself? If reflexivity is a process, a back and forth process, then the act of catching the moment, the doing of the reflexive gaze, and of listening with the reflexive ear, must change the thinking that is being thought. That reflexive process is elusive and exhausting, and often threatens to disrupt the very thing it sets out to observe. Yet it is necessary for finding both how that constitutive work is done and how it might (on occasion and perhaps temporarily) be done otherwise.

In this last sense, reflexivity is itself a form of power and a form of knowledge. It enables thought to be worked with and worked on. In chapter 8 we delve into the complex Foucauldian terrain of power and knowledge to grasp its ambivalence, its doubled motion of acting upon us and enabling us to act.

So far we have talked about the workshops as the primary site in which collective biography is done. We have made mention of the fact that the process, afterwards, of collaborative writing can be difficult and painful, and in the past we have left it at that. Occasionally among the collective there was a suggestion that we should look at the process of collaborative writing more closely. In the next chapter Sue and Bronwyn, in consultation with the others, gingerly approach the too-hardness of the topic of collaborative writing and its attendant struggles to see if we can tell what it is that happens to make it seem so hard, sometimes, that it makes us angry and fragile. Instead of a memory workshop, Sue and Bronwyn have written letters to each other on the topic, and then sent those letters out to all the others for their comment and engagement.

7

A conversation about the struggles of collaborative writing[13]

Hi Sue,
I thought I would begin this conversation on the struggle of our collaborative writing by reflecting on writing and on my own approach to writing, since I know that at least some of the struggles have come from my open ended attitude to writing. I will begin with some words from other writing about writing.

Cixous writes about how she doesn't know where she is going when she begins a book. That is how I write too – I have no idea at the outset where this particular writing might be taking me. I know that has been a source of stress, particularly for some of our Scandinavian collaborators. They wanted us to plan the paper before we began, and I found that idea incomprehensible, though I did finally succumb to planning meetings at the end of our workshops so we at least left with a writing plan, though I was never convinced that the plan would be what delivered the paper. I remember Hillevi saying she would never agree to participate in another one of our projects unless we agreed to plan the paper from the beginning of the writing. But as Cixous says of her writing:

> When I begin to write, it always starts from something unexplained, mysterious and concrete . . . It begins to search in me. And this questioning could be philosophical: but for me, right away it takes the poetic path. That is to say that it goes through scenes, moments, illustrations lived by myself or by others, and like all that belongs to the current of life, it crosses very many zones of our histories. I seize these moments still trembling, moist, creased, disfigured, stammering. When I write a book, the only thing that guides me at the beginning is an alarm. Not a tear [*larme*], but an alarm. The thing that alarmed me at once with its violence and its strangeness.
>
> (Cixous, in Cixous and Calle-Gruber, 1997: 43)

This is not an individualized searching of her individual soul but a searching in the current of life – her own and others – a search that will find the unexpected that will resonate with others.

> As for this weaving you [Mireille Calle-Gruber] spoke of a minute ago, here too there is nothing voluntary for me; I do not take an element *a* and an element *b* to connect them. This happens in my deepest depths. The signified and the signifier work together without my being able to say which one leads, because the one calls for the other. And vice versa. How? A kind of work takes place in this space that we do not know, that precedes writing, and that must be a sort of enormous region or territory where a memory has been collected, a memory composed of all sorts of signifying elements that have been kept or noted – or of events that time has transformed into signifiers, pearls and corals of the 'language' of the soul . . . There must be a sort of magnetic 'force' in me that collects, without my knowing it, jewels, materials of the earth, that are propitious for a future book. It is my memory of writing that does this. I say 'my memory of writing' because it is not the memory of life, or the memory of thought. It happens with sound elements, aesthetic elements, etc. Perhaps there is also a recording surface deep in me receiving micro-signs – it must guess that these signs are not solitary and lost, but emitters; in communication with other signs. An example: I had been struck, without realizing it, by the red geranium that lights up in *The Possessed* of Dostoevsky. It was as if, quite by chance, I had picked from the ground a key that opened a magic world. In the end, the geranium was absolutely not accidental, it was overdetermined. And it was not only my own mania or my own memory, but in effect a clue that functioned in more than one unconscious. Not only my own. Many others.

(Cixous, in Cixous and Calle-Gruber, 1997: 29)

I feel that our collective biography work opens up a collective searching not unlike what Cixous talks of here. In the collective biography workshop we search for those 'scenes, moments, illustrations' that take us to an unexpected and wonderful place of resonance and agreement, not just among ourselves, but with others who read what we finally write. Our stories hold moments that work like Dostoevsky's geranium. But here, immediately, we touch on the heart of the trauma of writing. If we are, as Cixous suggests, writing from the soul, trying to tap a collective soul, the freedom we have granted each other to overwrite each others' words in attempting to facilitate and collectivise that search may also be experienced as an obliteration of the individual's soul. Because we have gone back to each of our homes after the workshop, often very far from each other, we no longer inhabit the space where we can see/touch/hear the other embodied selves. Each one when it comes to her turn of writing struggles alone with the words on the page produced by others.

But what about collaborative writing – when more than one person is responsible for the words on the page. Today I came across Deleuze talking about his collaborative writing with Guattari – which is what sparked off my idea of writing to you. It is a recorded conversation between the two of them with Catherine Backes-Clément in 1972. She is interviewing them about their joint writing. Deleuze is deliciously rude about their collaboration, making no attempt to paper over what might have been difficult about it, but there is a tenderness, or affection, and a kind of humour in the way he does it that I wish we could find in talking of our own struggles:

> So Felix and I started to work together. It started off with letters. And then we began to meet from time to time to listen to what the other had to say. It was great fun. But it could be really tedious too. One of us always talked too much. Often one of us would put forward some notion, and the other just didn't see it, wouldn't be able to make anything of it until months later, in a different context. And then we read a lot, not whole books, but bits and pieces. Sometimes we found quite ridiculous things that confirmed for us the damage wrought by Oedipus and the awful misery of psychoanalysis. Sometimes we found things we thought were wonderful, that we wanted to use. And then we wrote a lot. Félix sees writing as a schizoid flow drawing on all sorts of things. I'm interested in the way a page of writing flies off in all directions and at the same time closes right up on itself like an egg. And in the reticences, the resonances, the lurches, and all the larvae you can find in a book. Then we really started writing together, it wasn't any problem. We took turns at rewriting things.
>
> (Deleuze, 1995: 14)

One of the things we have talked about as a difficulty is the letting go of our own individual egos as we launch into the collectivity of the writing. We were dismayed when words we might have struggled over disappeared in someone else's drafting. We felt obliterated. Writing is such a deeply personal expression of who we are and of what it is possible to think. We place our words into the collective space of the writing and someone else changes them or drops them out – because they don't understand them, or don't agree with them, or because they come up with something better – or worse. It is an emergent space in which the possibilities of our own subjectivities are struggled after, sometimes flowering into something new and collective and exciting, sometimes neglected and forgotten.

Foucault says of his writing that it is a process of becoming someone else. It is not only not something that can be planned, but it is more than words on the page, it is oneself emerging on the page. It is not only our egos that have been so delicately and indelicately trounced about in this process but our very emergent selves:

> I don't feel it is necessary to know exactly what I am. The main interest in life and work is to become someone else that you were not in the beginning. If you knew when you began a book what you would say at the end, do you think that you would have the courage to write it? What is true for writing and for a love relationship is true also for life. The game is worthwhile insofar as we don't know what will be the end.
>
> (Foucault, in Martin, 1988: 9)

Foucault talks of the courage that it took for him to unfold the ideas he wrote onto the pages of his work, and that part of the courage is the not-knowing where it will end. I think with our collective biography writing we not only didn't know what would be the end, we didn't know what the journey would be either – how bumpy or tearful the ride.

Dear Bronwyn,
How strange it is to move from the fusion of 'we' – the 'we' who wrote each of the collective papers, the 'we' who wrote a chapter on collective biography (Davies and Gannon, 2005) – back to our respective 'I's. You and I . . . The veil of the 'we' is lifted and 'I' am exposed.

The production of the 'we' in each of these texts fascinates me. In many ways the writing practices that we adopted were inimical to academic work where individuals are rewarded and competition encouraged. Writing alone is much easier – and more valued in our workplaces – than writing with others but we would not have been able to do this work, this particular thinking and writing, alone. Though something like this can be done. In your body/landscapes research (Davies, 2000a), for example, you did the subsequent writing around collectively generated memories. The workshop was a profound experience of immersion/emergence into a new collective discursive space for me. Back home, I tried to capture this poetically:

> . . .
> Once we start talking
> Stories spill out
> Lap over each other
> Wash us into other stories
> . . .
> *I don't quite understand 'embodiment'*, she worries
>
> Until the taste of nectar on her tongue

Blue bubblegum on pink flesh
Warm hot piss streaming through clenched thighs
Sour damp sheets
Heartbeats of fear
Mrs Snake
the (wicked)
Banksia men
Water and sand swirling me over and over
I'm out of control
the salt sting inside my eyelids
I'm drowning
Vomit in the back seat of a car
Please stop
I'm going to be sick
Cold knees
She's gone to London to visit the queen,
said Christopher Robin to Alice
The weight of soft ripe figs in my hand
My strong legs running
Now look at me! I can do it!
. . .

(Late Thursday night, alone, she shed as many clothes as she could and waded out into the cool water. She sat back on her heels, waves rippling around her shoulders, watching the patterns of refracted light on her skin, on the sand beneath her legs. Her skin tingled and quivered in the moonlight. She turned to water, to moon, to air.)

Other parts of this poem have already been used by you (Davies, 2000a: 46–47) but I indulge myself again here because the poem stresses two critical aspects of our collective writing process: our bodies together in a particular place and time. Binaries of self/other, inside/outside, body/landscape collapsed in the experiences I tried to represent in this poem. The group did not write together after that particular workshop, but for me, our collective writing in cyberspace after subsequent collective biographies has been sustained by the deeply embodied experience of these bodies together in that place.

You talk about excitement and yes, that was there, exhilaration at recognizing words and thoughts in a text that I might have laid down but that others had massaged and reshaped into something more and better than I could have myself. I thought better and harder and into new places through our struggle to write. Yet, sometimes, perhaps every time, the 'end point' also came when we were exhausted, when we had done as much as we could, when we might be too lost inside our text to see where next to go with it, when a dispassionate view (from above, from afar) seemed necessary. Our collective 'we' was fragile, fleeting, fluid, a fiction we co-created in each text. A necessary fiction. I could quote Barthes here, perhaps, to stress that I have not forgotten the author is (always) already a fiction:

> Writing is that neuter, that composite, that obliquity into which our subject flees, the black-and-white where all identity is lost, beginning with the very identity of the body that writes.
>
> (Barthes, 1989: 49)

Indeed. These collectively authored papers were textual spaces into which each 'I' disappeared into a new 'we'. This was frustrating, even dangerous, and in the process of each paper there were moments when it (almost) seemed too hard for all of us. Such a moment might have come in response to radical erasure (of stories or analysis), or insertion where some of us felt the shock of an abrupt turn (towards some new author or concept). Just when we hoped we might have a final version (after months of passing the paper around and around), the journey took off to a new place and the text we thought we were coming to understand flew away from us again. Though we knew that this would happen anyway. Yet despite our fears, despite Barthes, despite the tears and sweat, we moved through to an end point in each of the papers in this book.

Our struggle to write is well documented in the other layers of writing, particularly in the email messages we sent (or didn't send) to the group alias through which we wrote each paper. These included both finely detailed analytical responses to drafts in progress as well as more emotional responses that emerged in sticky patches:

> After many anxious moments, a lot of self-bashing, and frustration I have decided . . . that I need to send the paper on to the next person on the list . . . Being brought up with certain ideas about solidarity, commitment to the collective, the-chain-is-only-as-strong-as-its-weakest-link mantras etc. makes this a very integrity-challenging thing to do and I feel really really bad. (Eva)

> Dear everyone – it's so damn hard to get the right words to say what we mean (even to determine what we mean – speaking for myself of course?). I didn't mean to sound so haughty or precious or whatever either and I also realised I probably contradicted myself quite directly . . . (Sue)

When our 'we' is wavering, the messages are traces of the effort put into re-establishing our collective sense, finding a speaking position where we might reassemble the assemblage that is the 'we' who writes the text. In many of these messages we apologise for our inadequacies, for our insufficient understanding, for lack of time. We negate ourselves, at times, in favour of the collective 'we' that we desire to be. Another sort of crisis marked at some point in the email messages around each paper is silence, the absence of responses to a request for feedback, that void is itself read as a message: 'there has been so little feedback on the paper that I feel unable to move forward'. These are all crises in our struggle to write these papers (and ourselves in writing them). Perhaps we (I slip so easily into the seductive embrace of the imagined 'we') could reconfigure all of these as moments of aporia, of paralysis or impasse, seeing them as Derrida does, as 'not necessarily negative' but as situating us 'before a door, a threshold, a border, a line, or simply the edge or the approach of the other'. He says that at these moments what appears to:

> block our way or to separate us . . . where we are exposed, absolutely without protection, without problem, and without prosthesis, without possible substitution, singularly exposed in our absolute and absolutely naked uniqueness, that is to say, disarmed, delivered to the other, incapable even of sheltering ourselves behind what could still protect the interiority of a secret.
>
> (Derrida, 1993: 12)

There are points of aporia through which we must work ourselves in order to continue writing.

The point I wanted to make in this letter to you Bronwyn, circling right back around to the extracts from my poem, is that our struggle to write is sustained I believe through our embodied experience of the collective biography workshop that begins each process. More than any academic ambitions, it has been my desire to remain part of each of these embodied assemblages that has kept me writing, responding and caring about our 'we' and the text we struggle with. Another layer of the text we write of ourselves through the processes of collective biography is the embodied memories of our bodies there at those times. When I have struggled at times to make use of a new philosophical concept, it has not been intellectual curiosity that kept me committed to the writing and thinking. (This reads like a guilty confession.) It is my body remembering. When I read these papers later, and I read and worked on so many drafts of them over these years, my body remembers these things and why I love the women with whom (and for whom) I/we write. I remember fresh baked cinnamon scrolls one morning, a birthday feast, music on a verandah, singing Pasty Cline in a lush tropical garden, making a doll with blood on her legs. I remember walking and swimming and cooking and talking and playing together, sharing intimate spaces and thoughts outside of the work of the workshop. I remember sleeping in a room hidden behind a wardrobe door, listening to possums and curlews, knowing that in the next room was a woman who cared for me too, and in the next room another. I remember the night of the electric storms when nature went crazy and while we worried about two of us on the ferry between the lightning strikes, I lay in emergency full of drugs after an allergic reaction to an insect bite. It was you women who noticed that I was swelling up, dilating, fainting. All these as well as the intense emotions of our story-telling, of the work we've done with childhood memories. It has been these embodied memories of the intense collective spaces we lived together on Magnetic Island that sustained me through the struggle to write.

This is not a writing where the writer disappears (not yet anyway) but more the sort of writing that Cixous talks about, writing grounded in the body, our bodies. 'What sets me writing', she says, 'is that lava, that flesh, that blood, those tears, they are in all of us' (Cixous, in Cixous and Calle-Gruber, 1997: 12). She says elsewhere in the same book that:

> The origin of the material in writing can only be myself. I is not I of course because it is I with the others, coming from the others, putting me in the other's place, giving me the other's eyes. Which means there is something common.
> (Cixous, in Cixous and Calle-Gruber, 1997: 87)

The something (in) common is what we produce *before* the collective writing of a paper, in our collective biography workshops, but also in the spaces we used to create our collective 'we' outside any schedules; living, breathing, being together spaces, sustainable spaces. I pause here before I send this back to you Bronwyn and check myself. I sound like I'm spinning some sort of fictional feminist utopia which is not how it was either. But perhaps it is part of what it was and is to aspire to work this way.

Dear Sue,
Yes it does sound like that – a feminist utopia – made up out of an ethical practice of love. There was that wonderful sense of care for each other that we each experienced, and an openness to the new – to trying out new ways of being, new ways of being cared for, without the complex demands and assumptions of (hetero)sexual love. We could, for example, massage each others' feet in order to more fully imagine being relaxed in our bodies as part of a serious exploration of embodiment without finding that strange or seductive. Although I sometimes found myself propelled to the outer edge, positioned as the authority who knew and judged and was therefore not one of 'us', I also shared in the sense of collective expanding, of trust, of mutual support. Because my task also involved setting the initial agenda, choosing the readings and drafting the memory questions to come out of those readings, finding the funding for the house, keeping us on track according to the timetable I had invented, and taking responsibility for the final publishability of the collective paper, I was both inside and outside the group that engaged in these ethical practices of love. I don't

want to get sidetracked onto reminding you that that space also had some frictions and tensions and anxieties, because what I want to say is that our collective work and play at the workshop was not the only basis for the shared knowledge that we collectively pursued in the writing. The collective knowledge Cixous writes about, 'that lava, that flesh, that blood, those tears, they are in all of us' (Cixous, in Cixous and Calle-Gruber 1997: 12), is, I think by virtue of being human – it is 'all of us'.

But there is another clue here to the struggle of writing. Perhaps the idyllic quality of the workshops (or our wish to construct them as that, not focussing on the tensions and dissensions) gave rise to the sense of dystopia when things went wrong in the writing. We have talked of being shocked, traumatized, betrayed at times of crisis in the writing. Or more mildly, of extreme irritation. One irritation was participants' inability or unwillingness to cut out anyone else's writing, so that the paper grew in messy incoherence as ideas lay side by side with no flow or logic to them. It was irritating to have to sort out that incoherent mess – to be the one brave enough to cut. We (that is, you and I) encouraged people to be 'brave enough' to cut, to insist that as they added words, these words did not add to confusion, but to clarity. But then this encouragement backfired when words that had been laboured over for weeks suddenly disappeared. When that happened to my words in a first draft I had spent weeks labouring over, I was more traumatised than I could have predicted. When I read Deleuze's words: 'Often one of us would put forward some notion, and the other just didn't see it, wouldn't be able to make anything of it until months later, in a different context' I thought about that time, and the difference between the two situations. One in which either Deleuze or Guattari fails to understand the other, but assumes that what has been written does have an important sense in it to be found, so rather than deleting it, he circles back around to it in another context to finally come upon the significance of it. I yearned for that level of care. The obliteration of the words on the page felt like an obliteration of me. Jenny said I should 'get over it – it happens to all of us' and Lekkie, who'd cut my words, and had seen that not as cutting but as providing 'another take' on the ideas, was horrified that her creative engagement with the paper had caused such a negative reaction. Our busy lives, driven by neoliberal technologies, don't allow us to wait for months as Deleuze describes himself and Guattari doing. We each set aside a week or a day for our turn on the paper; we 'bravely' dive in, feeling moral pressure not to delay, since we have only a limited time to work on it and pass it on to the next drafter. So we add and cut, finding a way to make our contribution, to explore the ideas on the page, to fit our thinking in and around the words someone else has written. Being scattered around the country and the globe, there is little chance to sit around over coffee to refine our thinking, or check it out with the others. In haste, under pressure, we cut, and risk the dystopia that is filled with that sense of negation, of betrayal, outrage and despair. And email has turned out to be no substitute for the face-to-face work, sometimes sparking off more bad feeling. I remember Margaret saying heatedly on email, that email 'sucked' as a form of communication, when the body paper was stuck somewhere. I both agreed and felt wounded that she rejected the strategies we had developed over our years of collaborative work.

When I experienced my own words being cut I began to ask: is this act of collective writing, where we each take turns on drafting the paper, too brutal? Should we give it up? Yet I think what we have produced is some outstanding writing. I really love what we have written, but I am no longer sure whether the difficulties in the process of writing make it too hard to continue. Cath usually remained silent in the past on email during the emotional outbreaks around this collective writing. But she listened carefully. When I met up with her and talked to her once about the latest trauma, she reminded me that there was trauma every time. That I just forgot about it. She was intrigued by the conflict inherent in the process we had developed.

Hi Bronwyn,
I agree. There is trauma every time, and every time also there is love. Perhaps both are inherent in the process. Cixous says writing is always a practice of love: 'Because I write for, I write from, I start writing from: Love. I write out of love. Writing, loving: inseparable. Writing is a gesture of love. *The gesture.*' (Cixous, 1991: 42). It seems even more necessary in this process of writing, to hang on to that idea that our writing can be a practice of love. It's interesting how we're sliding now into particularities of selves, of the humanist individuals who made up our collectives: what x says or y, what we say to each other one to one around the edges of the collective. We move here away from the struggle of writing, from writing, to embodied individual selves, egos rampant and fragile. Hardly the post-structural subjectivities we eulogize, yet perfectly reflecting the tangled relationship we explore between post-structural subjects and humanist individuals in a later chapter of this book. The writing collective – although each grouping of individuals was different and the specific histories of each paper varied – seems to me now like a shifting body that in my thesis I named quite confidently, in the singular, the 'Magnetic Island Collective', even though I knew there were eighteen different individuals in those collectives.

Returning to our apparent veering away from writing in this correspondence, we could broaden our definition of writing and consider all of our work together to be a sort of writing. We might consider that writing is living, that the discursive space of writing encompasses far more than artefacts we produce and the technologies we use: documents, keyboard, pens and paper. Writing is also me tucked into my bed in the little room hidden behind the cupboard door, listening to the curlews cry in the dawn, and others listening to me muttering in my sleep. Writing is me (or you or any others of us) falling on to a text a few weeks after a workshop or a draft that seems to provide a pivot for the next leap forward. Finding a new text is not a matter of coincidence or even of deliberation but a consequence perhaps of remaining open, remaining still inside the text even though it might not be before me at that moment. It might not even be my turn, but I am still in the process of the text. The writing is still one of the layers of my ongoing daily life. Cixous, as always, comes to mind, talking about the collapse of writing into life: 'I don't "begin" by "writing": I don't write. Life becomes text starting out from my body. I am already text' (Cixous, 1991: 52). We are already, and continue to be, text.

What do you think? I feel like this writing in dialogue is taking me to new thoughts about our process. Although it is you and I who have begun this task I wonder if others might like some input too. Perhaps after we have said all we can we might invite our collective authors to write in response to what we have written. I'd like to come back for a moment, before I send this back to you, to the idea of utopia and feminist research practice. My desire for inclusivity must emerge from an ethics grounded in this ideal, in the peculiarly feminist version. There's a fragment of text that was lost and then found again in one of our papers in process that still haunts me as the ultimate expression of the utopian space we set out to make. It encapsulates all that I said in the previous message about embodiment, and also the rapture in which we (sometimes) came into being as a collective:

> [T]here are moments when one women can seize a word uttered by another and spin a tale that drifts over our collective group, and drapes over our collective shoulders. In these moments we find ourselves uttering collective sighs of appreciation, of sadness, of pleasure, of anguish, as we sit under a veil of storying that we have all collectively spun.

Does this make you sigh, or quiver with longing for these moments? Does this bring back the traces of the 'we' we made between us? Over to you . . .

Dear Sue,
I look forward to your letters. For me this space we have generated in our writing to each other is an easeful and productive space in which it is so easy to think and to engage. Ironic I suppose that in choosing the topic of the difficulties of collaborative writing, and in setting out to collaboratively write about it, I should find it so pleasurable to be talking to you in this way. It is not unlike the pleasure you remind me of, of the moment of

the collective sigh. But are we entering into a false binary here, where I try to delve into the difficulty of collaborative writing (our stated task) and you feel that by implication what was good and powerful about what we did is being negated? Is that why we have remained silent about the struggles – because of a lurking binary that says if we talk about the hard stuff we have denied all that was good? Do I really need to remind you how much I love that collective storying process, the work of listening that we do, the mode of telling and retelling that we do to arrive at that moment when we enter the world of the other and feel a profound satisfaction in the truthfulness of the words we have chosen to tell the specific remembered moments – to the whole complex task of being human, of becoming appropriate, of struggling to be and to know? I have put this collective biography writing ahead of all the other writing I have done in terms of its value and its pleasure. It breaks the loneliness of intellectual life and it generates energy amongst us, an energy for writing that is qualitatively different from the energy generated in working alone. I also treasure the supervisory space for that reason, not that I often write with my students (other than in these projects) but that it is two people together working towards understanding, rather than one solitary person struggling. In that solitary struggle I have always needed to find readers who will react to the words on the page, so I can find how they come to life in the eyes/ears/body of another. In thesis supervision, or in the collaborative writing, the reader is built into the process. One does not have to go begging for a reader. Well, it's built in, in theory. I hate it when I have worked really hard on a draft of one of our papers and I send it off into the ether only to be met with total silence. Everyone is too busy, too pressured with other things etc etc to reply. Forgive me for individualising, but you never did that – were never too busy to reply to my draft or anyone else's. The rapidity with which you reply to these letters is part of the energy and pleasure of it for me. Only one part of course, but (here I go individualising again) I never have been very good at dealing with silence, and so to have a responsive writing partner is a real buzz.

So . . . the workshops for me have rarely been the problem, though some participants have said I am blissfully unaware of how anxious some participants get about whether their stories are 'good enough' or whether they understand the collective biography process well enough. Or whether they have got all the clichés and explanations out of their stories. Or whether they have enough to offer to be a valued member. I just proceed as if it is perfectly obvious that everyone is valued since everyone has something interesting to contribute – as they always do. We get through the workshops without any visible grief. We almost never get through the collaborative writing without grief – from at least one of us.

The question is, perhaps, why we see it as grief. Why isn't it just the interesting thing that Deleuze describes when he says: 'I'm interested in the way a page of writing flies off in all directions and at the same time closes right up on itself like an egg. And in the reticences, the resonances, the lurches, and all the larvae you can find in a book. Then we really started writing together, it wasn't any problem. We took turns at rewriting things' (Deleuze, in Deleuze and Guattari, 1995: 14). Why do we define our own reticences and our lurches as so unspeakable and so dreadful? After all, we do 'really start writing' despite, or perhaps because of what Cixous calls 'that lava, that flesh, that blood, those tears' (Cixous, in Cixous and Calle-Gruber, 1997: 12). Is it that we tend in our writing, each of us, to close the writing in on itself like an egg, sealing it up, not wanting to know or daring to know what it might come to life as? Or, perhaps, anticipating something like the birth of a nice puppy, when what hatches is a dragon that eats puppies? Or the precious golden egg is ignored or misplaced and someone goes and hatches a cuckoo, so that lines of thought are flying off in all directions? Those unexpected lines that might provoke anxiety about not understanding? Am I dramatizing it too much? Is it not really that bad? On the positive side, when the egg, or a new line of thought, is ignored or misplaced it lets us know it was not visible enough, it gives us a reason to more clearly and vividly articulate its lines, its shape, its detail, its connectedness to the rest . . . Going back to what you say in your last letter, if the writing is a gesture of love, does the overwriting come to be experienced, sometimes, as a negation of that love? Or is it just that the lives we return to when we leave the workshops are so busy and fractured that we become less able to write and read with love? Or do we need to think more carefully about the metaphor of love and see what booby traps it has hanging off it?

I like what you wrote, following Cixous, how 'We are already, and continue to be, text'. During the collaborative writing we are already, and becoming a messy and unpredictable text – the writing is close to the bone, the nerve, the skin – it is the bone, the nerve, the skin, in a process of rapid transformation that we are only in part in control of. Monne wrote in an email at the end of the last paper:

> I think it would be real nice if somehow it would be possible to support the writing a little bit more and I feel that it was real hard to give all of the drafts a close up and profound prospect/chance, in the writing. Sometimes maybe, its just some specific words that need to be shifted or elaborated on, some headings, or grammatical changes, or to introduce a good metaphor, or finding the right quotations etc., well you know what I mean . . . and this time there was some major changes from one paper to the other . . . well I was doing my best to 'hang on to the swing' (Swedish saying) trying not to fall off . . . **BUT the outcome of it was extremely good. In this discourse, one of the best papers I read. Monne**

In other words, the collaborative writing was tough, but it has paid off.

I keep coming back, then, to what was tough. Can we say something insightful here about the trauma of the writing? What can Monne possibly mean by supporting the writing more? Who might do this and how? Can we delve into the specificity of the trauma in such a way that we can then resurface and say something that gives rise to the collective sigh – yes, that was it, that was it, precisely? When you and I experience that moment, I agree it would be good to send it to the others for feedback. But not before.

Hi Bronwyn,

I'll start with a vignette of the fragmented and fractured selves we are in our every day busy lives – it's 10.30 pm here on Thursday night, the week before Christmas, and this is the time I've scratched out to (begin to) respond to your message. I only have one more day at work before I drive into the distant west to 'go home' for a few days. So many obligations pile up on top of one another and all of them are urgent and immediate. You were so shocked that I hadn't read your latest contribution by this afternoon but I told you I was sav(our)ing it for later. You weren't convinced. Later it is now, but I'm tired and all that's happened between now and then is that a couple more deadlines have fallen onto me. I read the paper on the way out to the car and went over the new sections again at the traffic lights on the way to the plaza for a massage – shoulders, neck and arms – the parts that I need working to do this work and to drive for ten hours on Saturday. They're tingling as much now as they were before the massage after a few more hours at the computer tonight. Amongst the other things were proofs to check of two other papers – one of them our reflexivity chapter. Every day's like this for all of us – worse for those with partners and kids at home. The metaphor of love is certainly a romantic hook (perhaps I am too easily seduced by Cixous) and one of its most banal barbs might be that people make choices away from the workshop that they do not need to make during the workshop. We might choose to be hurried and inattentive to the paper because that has less personal cost and – away from all of us and that place and time – less emotional trauma than inattention to the people and other tasks close to home. We schedule in so many hours, a morning, one day of the weekend, so we can do all the other things we need to and when a task is finite like that perhaps it's easier to pass it on (or pass on it). I wonder what would have happened if we had had no deadlines – if we'd said sit on it, live with it, think your way inside it for as long as you need to take to feel that it is yours (and ours) and pass it on when you want to. A bizarre suggestion I know. It may not have taken longer than it often has. As far as individualising, remember that I am a responsive partner because there is no one else at home for me and I am too readily prepared to have an unhealthy life – eating over the keyboard again and writing into the night.

. . . Now I'm at work – writing into the fissures of another day. All of the preceding is irrelevant really, should be, but it isn't at all. As we found in our embodiment workshop, and you found in your other research (Davies and Petersen, 2005b), this is how we work and there is a toll on our bodies and in the quality of attention we can bring to bear on our thinking and writing. Remember Margaret's response after that workshop:

> It is not often I have an experience in my life that feels profoundly transforming, at the level of shifting the cells in my body. This has been one of them. Often for me these experiences have involved body/landscape but this time it was not the landscape although that played a part. It was the space shaped by the women and the interactions between them. The talking, cooking, eating, reading, thinking, body work, care and attention that was enacted in the space of that house, that garden, that place. I always say to my students that you know when you are doing good research, research that is actually making new knowledge because it will surprise, shake your certainties, change the way you see things. It always involves moving beyond your comfort zone. This research has been all those things.

Just as you say, the living workshop was a wonder but the process of writing that paper (that became two papers) was incredibly difficult. It was hard, months later, to retain this moment but it was true for all of us at the time – and I note now that this comment was qualified as '*Overall response (as of this moment)*'. We can only ever comment from our particular situated positions however fleeting or momentary they may seem. The workshop space is an escape from our everydays – a sort of holiday into deep thought and reflection – whereas the writing process happens inside the grit of our everyday lives.

Yet, looking back at what I wrote last night, I see I have slipped too easily into characterising some processes as successful and others as not. The fact that we take up our turns 'differently' is interesting and unpredictable. Several times I have felt that I have made my most effective contributions when the person preceding me has herself been unable to work on the text of the paper (for diverse technological and personal reasons) but has given such a close and careful reading of the draft that I have used her suggestions as my starting point (or several of us have given very close feedback just before I take up my turn). That woman might have 'passed' on her turn (as in the self-abnegating messages I quoted earlier) but the reading has itself been a writing, or an enabler of the writing to continue as a collective process rather than an individual intervention. On these occasions I have felt like I am not 'overwriting' other people's work in some violent or traumatic manner but that I am better able to proceed with love and care in incorporating the responses of several of us into my turn at the 'text work'. I've not felt inadequate or uncertain but confident to proceed. These processes have been entwined and continued to be collective. I noticed that in one of your messages in the reflexivity paper you send your draft of the paper on with this comment:

> I've forgotten now who is next, hence sending it to all – which may irritate some – and for that I'm sorry

How curious this comment seems now. Perhaps you were acknowledging the busyness of everybody's lives but this part of the process may be the most essential thing for an ongoing sense of collective venture, for nurturing a sense of each draft as tentative and collegial rather than as a secret text to be passed in turn from one to the other along our conga line. Making space for careful (collective) reading is as important as making space for (collective) writing. I am saying the most obvious things again – and this is what has mostly happened every time anyway.

The changes authored from draft to draft are amazing and yes, sometimes shocking. I don't know how we could come up with any generic way of 'supporting the writing more', but perhaps one way would be to foreground the reading of a draft-in-process – naming that reading as a critical part of the writing – whoever's turn it is 'next' to write. This brings in another problematic – the need for a writer to navigate and attend to possibly contradictory advice. When it happens that we are able to integrate all the feedback and write from what feels like a collective place it is amazing and can feel like a great leap forward. Or it might feel like a violence has been done. Nothing is predictable. Everything is dangerous. I find this exchange about the paper as a 'phoenix' between two of us (actually between us two) in one of our strings:

> I get the feeling as I let go of it now, that I can glimpse a truly magnificent jewelled phoenix rising from the fire, but it is only a glimpse and I must now hand over . . .

By the way I've been reading about phoenixes – did you know this: 'when the phoenix was about to die, it returned to the Temple of the Sun in Heliopolis ("Sun City") Egypt . . . On the altar at Heliopolis the great bird proceeded to make itself a nest out of twigs of cassia and myrrh. It had brought with it a great ball of myrrh which it shaped like an egg, then hollowed out; it buried its "parent" inside it. The nest completed, the phoenix became hotter and hotter and redder and redder until it turned to ashes; a new phoenix then emerged from the egg of myrrh. The process took three days [perhaps that's the optimum turnaround for these papers]. The fabulous bird lived alone in the universe. Like the sun, there was none like it; it was monos, singularis, unicus. There was no way it could generate off-spring because it had no mate; it therefore had to renew itself out of itself.'

(Visser, 2000: 352)

In using this metaphor we imply that there is some organic perfect unity of form (thought) – 'monos, singularis, unicus' – that our task is to uncover, reveal, 'birth' in another of the metaphors that we use for this writing. That each collective has a perfect body of (textual) work – if only we can persist long enough, strain hard enough, suffer the flames and pain for the beauty to come to fruition. A phoenix 'egg' is not a separate object laid by a 'parent' but death of the 'sacred originary' (the fracturing of the collective?) is inherent in its re-birth into something other/more beautiful. I may have strayed too far into fantasy here, or, more likely, I may be inadvertently mobilising a Christian/Western discourse of suffering as necessary for birth, or a psychoanalytic discourse. So I will veer sharply away from here . . . but the suggestion of an optimum turnaround of three days implies that submersion and speed are beneficial to our process. They were for me when I was not working fulltime but a rapid turnaround was highly distressing for others (and would be for me now too).

Some traumas came from our feelings of inadequacy or different understandings of theory or concepts that we might have been meeting for the first time in these workshops. Coming to grips with theory was particularly difficult as (our roles in) the workshops were never, inevitably, completely equal. You were always the one with more experience than all the rest of us. You created these workshops – in part – as a teaching tool for your postgraduate students and as the workshops progressed over several years, one by one we graduated and acquired another sense of ourselves as competent and familiar – the 'old hands' of the process who took it upon ourselves to reassure 'newcomers' (shame-faced I catch myself out doing this everywhere I look in our strings of email messages). You were the senior researcher for the reasons you named early in this correspondence – and also because you have been a researcher and reviewer for longer than all the rest of us. Not that this made you necessarily more 'right' than others, or more able to shift a paper in a new direction, but it gave you a certain authority, an obligation, to speak when you thought a paper was 'losing it'. So in a partial response to your question about supporting the writing – 'who might do this and how?' – I could answer: 'You Bronwyn, as you have up to this point'. Whether this is fair or it could be rotated through participants whose particular topic/area is under investigation might be one logistical question we could ask. But it would enter that problematic space of our desires for a feminist practice of equity and collectivity, which brings me to my next point, the stories themselves.

I think that trauma was particularly evident when the stories were cut. Every time we moved from a story from everyone, to just those stories that made our argument, it was felt like an exclusionary move, like a sort of violence, like a hierarchy was enacted of stories that were 'worthy' and others that were not. Although each time we said we would try to retain one from each it often became necessary for the integrity of the paper/ argument to cut. I think that perhaps we have not worked ourselves apart from the humanist selves who are committed to these stories (to the selves that we create in these stories), towards text-workers theorising around discursive fragments (this time, in the form of memory stories we contributed to a collective pool – like Rushdie's fable/fabulous 'sea of stories' (1991) – rather than interview transcripts or whatever other sorts of data we might use). I still read these stories in the published papers with an acute consciousness that this is 'X's story' or this is 'Y's story' and that there is a vast sea of wonderful stories out of which we have only fished out a few for the particular dish that we might be baking this particular time.

So Bronwyn, I think I have answered none of your questions, I have flown off in all directions, muddied the waters, drawn out some red herrings. Rather than resurfacing with some bright shining truth about our collective writing process, I feel caught in an eddy, swirling deeper and deeper. Adding more and more bad metaphors and sentence fragments to this text. Drowning . . . Each collective and each experience is unique, each paper has its own traumas, sticking places and moments of breakthrough (which are read differently by each of us anyway). The collective 'sigh' is differently nuanced in every group – how can we hope to find the words to say 'yes, that was it, that was it precisely' in a way that will resonate with every one of these ventures?

(February)
Dear Sue,
After I received your letter reminding me of the fact that Christmas was coming and that life was (ab)normally hectic I figured it was time to seek the feedback that you suggested we should invite from all of the others who have participated in this writing: Anne Britt, Babette, Barb, Cath, Danielle, Eileen, Eva, Helen, Hillevi, Jenny, Lekkie, Margaret, Monne, Phoenix, Sharn and Suzi. There are eighteen of us altogether if we count our inception as the schoolgirls paper that we ran the workshop for in 2000. There is the earlier paper on silence, and the workshop I wrote up myself for *(In)scribing body/landscape relations* (2000a). But the schoolgirls paper is the first collectively written paper by members of this group meeting together on Magnetic Island. It has been totally fascinating reading the various responses to our correspondence that have come in over the last five weeks. I think the insights offered in those letters allow us to come to

a number of insights, the sigh, the aha, about the collaborative writing process and its difficulties.

The biggest aha comes from the recognition of my greater power and my difference from the rest of the group. When the 'we' that you wrote was interpreted as the 'not-Bronwyn' we, and questions raised about your ability to 'represent' that we, I began to see the conflicting constitutive discourses at play. When I had read your 'we' I consistently read it as including me, though I knew from many conversations that I was sometimes not included in the group's understanding of 'we'. Still I read it that way without any tension or struggle, even without noticing that I was doing so. As my different and more powerful positioning dawned on me, as I read all the emails, I began to reread aspects of what I had said and done. My expressed delight to you, for example, about your fast responses to my own and others' drafts could be re-read as abusive, especially when I read again the pressure you put yourself under to reply quickly. To make sense of this double reading, requires recognising the conflicting discourses through which we constituted what we were doing. There was an intertwining and tension between the collaborative feminist discourse and the pedagogical discourse through which we constituted the workshops and the writing.

As a result of reading the comments everyone has sent in I have gone back and revised some of what I wrote to you, in the previous letters. I have, for example, taken out a long and boring quote from the traumatised email I wrote when I was upset at my words being overwritten and I have also changed from using people's initials to their full names following Lekkie's observation that the use of her initial felt like it was obliterating her. The email comments have not only been about the collective struggles of writing our papers, but also about what you and I have written here, and how we have written it. Hillevi coments, for example, that it is problematic if we present these letters as if they are authentic. I didn't know what she meant at first, imagining a theoretical problem about the fictional nature of 'authentic selves'. Then it occurred to me that it might seem unlikely that we really had written this exchange as an email exchange, just as it appears. But in that sense it actually is authentic. Except for these changes I have made now, that will in turn require you to modify some small aspects of what you have written to me.

Some of the responses to what we have written are heart-warming, and some have been anxiety provoking as they touch on some of the difficult issues that are so hard to get out into the open safely. What I want to do in this letter is gather the threads together of what I think everyone has said. (As you know, I first cut and pasted all the responses into the document and sent the complete document to everyone so they could see the flow of responses easily and think about what else they might want to add. Although some did not reply to our initial correspondence and some replied quickly, promising more later, there have been more than 30 pages of responses – so far. Helen strongly argues that we not continue in the way we have begun with our two-way conversation:

> Given that the papers have all arisen from a group process, it is not clear why you're now writing to each other only (I know that we're being invited to respond, but it seems less integral). I'm not clear if the letters are being written as your (both) individual responses and thoughts on the process/difficulties or if you're employing them as a writing genre with which to express a collective response, trying to take up all of our thoughts. If either of these, it doesn't seem appropriate or satisfactory so far. In the first instance, why not include all of our thoughts in an equal way given that the group process has been essential so far? In the second, it seems important that we each be allowed to express our own responses rather than have you speak for us. I understand that there are practical reasons for not doing this, but I do believe that a more genuinely collective bio approach to developing the new 2 chapters would be more appropriate and allow us to more adequately examine the important, unexamined issues of silence, power and collectivity. Helen

I sympathize with what Helen is saying, but I don't think it is possible (or do I mean desirable?) for us to create an eighteen-author chapter. It is always an issue when a suggestion from one of us comes up like that. The others rarely (if ever) email in agreeing or disagreeing, and given the busyness of people's lives and the number of such issues that come up, discussion amongst all members and voting is unrealistic. So I am going to continue in the way we have begun, but attempt to synthesise and respond as best I can, to the emails that have been written in response to our conversation. The 'unexamined issues of silence, power and collectivity' that Helen raises will be central to what I try to cover in this letter.

But first, it was heart warming, wasn't it, when we received positive comments? Monne felt uncomfortable with the focus on the difficulties: 'I don't want to emphasise the struggle, anxiety, bumpy, tearful, hard doing etc, since I think it is a wonderful journey, an opening up for "seeing" possible and alternative views, which can only be talked about as an adventure.' Sharn wrote, of our conversation: 'What you are attempting and achieving in the content and structure of this chapter is courageous, compelling, inspiring, instructive'. And Hillevi wrote of 'this brave and in parts beautiful dialogue between Bronwyn and Sue'. Though Danielle remarked to me on the phone that she had noticed that the nicer the beginning to an email, the more likely something sharp and critical was to follow. Helen, whose critical comments I quoted above, for example, wrote:

> The letters you've sent to each other and then to us are very brave.

You have dared to open up for discussion the collective biography storying and writing process that we've all experienced. Many of us have alluded to so many facets of the process in the course of our emails and face-to-face discussions, but we have never followed through with a thorough examination of the process, to my knowledge, before. So, I'm glad that someone has begun this examination. I think you said, Sue, that the 'I' is exposed – as we all know, this can be very dangerous – rather than resting in the seductive (and to a large extent, imaginary) embrace of the 'we'. You have both dared to name and make visible your thoughts and feelings. Helen

Of course I read both of these comments from Helen as true. What we have done is brave and it does open up the space we haven't ventured into before. But there is, as Hillevi pointed out, a whole complex issue of power and shifting positionings in this collaborative work, that must be addressed. I realised from what Hillevi and Helen wrote that we had two major and partially conflicting discourses at play about what we were doing: the feminist discourse on collaboration and equality, and the pedagogical discourse that was the initial motivation for the workshops. Hillevi wrote:

> The other issue is of course the issue of power and shifting positionings. One of my readings of the dialogue is that Sue becomes a representative of the 'Other than Bronwyn', who is the initiator, the senior researcher, the supervisor of most of us etc. So, just as I did in the beginning of this e-mail, Sue starts off with talking about the writing-process as love etc., as a response to how she herself and to as she knows all of us feel about this process; adoring and loving the context of being, living and writing together as intellectual women, and all of us immensely grateful to Bronwyn who got us all there! So, what Bronwyn is asking for – writing about the difficulties – is a hard task for Sue to – alone – voice from the perspective of the 'Other than Bronwyn'. Bronwyn has to repeat her request to make Sue write it, and I can sense that Sue is aware that all of the rest of us are in a sense also to be voiced in one way or the other. Or is it actually possible for Sue to respond to this request individually? Perhaps this is what she has done, but I am not sure she can answer that question herself because, as Cixous says: 'a memory (is) composed of all sorts of signifying elements that have been kept or noted – or events that time has transformed into signifiers . . .'
>
> The point of this is that all of us know what it is to be 'other than Bronwyn', but we also know what it is to 'be Bronwyn'. . . . As teachers, supervisors etc. we know of the different kind of responsibility involved and power-production in being the initiator etc. of a collective learning-process, no matter how equal we try to make it.

We know about positioning ourselves as initiators and we know about positioning ourselves as students and learners. Hillevi

I was almost shocked when I first read Hillevi comparing the work-shops with teaching undergraduates. The feminist equality discourse had become so dominant in my thinking as to make my pedagogical power unmentionable and somehow suspect. But as some of the participants point out, in response to emails taking up the feminist idealistic position, they had never lost sight of pedagogy as the main game. Cath wrote, acknowledging up front the wish to have been included in this conversa-tion between us, and then explains that the pedagogical nature of what we were doing had always been in the forefront of what she thought we were doing:

> I have now read the chapter and wish I had been there! For me the data/writings were perhaps collaborative but there was always a sense for me of Bronwyn as guide – of getting it right in terms of wherever Bronwyn's thinking was taking me. I did/do not find this at all problematic and relished wherever her thinking took me. So as far as 'collective' writing of the papers whether Bronwyn thought it was 'good' always mattered/s. I guess in this sense I wonder about what we mean by 'collective' – much of the pain I believe I/me/others experienced was not so much in terms of the difficulty of the writing but in getting it to where I could feel that it captured the 'aha-ness' and 'yes-that's what I meant' of my guide. So, as always, it is fine for me for Bronwyn and Sue to take it wherever it goes next. Cath

For others, the feminist collaborative discourse was more dominant. Sharn wrote for example of its centrality and hints at its problems:

> Openness is difficult to achieve yet necessary to achieve authentic, collaborative or collective writing. My experience of participating in three MI workshops and having the privilege, due to geographic proximity, of conversations with participants in others (and with you B, I think in every instance), tells me that openness and collaboration have always been motivating concepts and good intentions at the heart of the work. It also reminds me of the old adage, 'easier said than done'. By the time we were confronted with it, we were aware that the prospect of collective writing poses both threat and promise. Sharn

Barb wrote about her disengagement arising from our failure to fully practice this ideal in the writing, though at the same time takes up the pedagogical discourse along with Cath as one which informed her understanding of what we were doing:

> Although there were unequal power relationships in the workshops

we had the opportunity to express, share, modify the stories and know that we were making a contribution. I found it very difficult after this. When we stuck to the theorists we had used in the workshops it was possible but when new material was introduced that other authors were currently working with it became a time consuming task to keep up and this was often at the expense of close & deep analysis. I sometimes let drafts pass by without the attention I should have given them and when I was not happy about the analysis. Another reason for this apparent disengagement was that unless the work was rewritten little notice was taken of suggestions. Basically I felt much the same as Cath. I was happy to go along with Bronwyn and only if something really jarred did I have much input. I was certainly not powerless but the major power resided in those who wrote more prolifically and who were currently engaged with similar materials (I could be wrong, very difficult to unpack). Barb

Aha! A clue here that seems important. I was consistently puzzled when there were complaints about me bringing in new references that we had not discussed during the week. Sometimes a suggestion was made at the workshop that we not go outside the readings we had used to inform the workshop. I rejected this suggestion out of hand, since when I am stuck with writing and can't solve the problem to be solved I start reading. I look for conceptual material to get me beyond a dull and sticky point in the writing. This sideways move is the main strategy I have for getting unstuck, for solving problems. I have not, as an all-knowing leader might, provided all the necessary material before the workshop, since the work-shop and the writing of the paper are an attempt to achieve a clarity about a concept or topic that I do not already have. What appeared to Barb a wilful importing of new material from my other work was, rather, a hard earned struggle to solve a problem in the paper. I don't remember if I ever explained that. Probably not as it seemed to me terribly obvious.

Hillevi's recommendations for how we overcome what she experienced in the difficulty of writing require me to acknowledge and keep sight of my pedagogical role. She says:

Bronwyn's initial letter to Sue starts off with polarizing 'planning' as opposed to the impossibility of planning a collective writing, without at all describing the preconditions of the process. I think this question of 'planning' is relevant and should definitely be discussed in relation to the preconditions, rather than made into a simplified polarization. What does it mean to plan? In the quote by Deleuze on his writing-process with Guattari, it is evident that they went through a process of 'planning'; i.e. a process of a collective meaning-making, which must entail differences in how they understood concepts and relations of meaning (sometimes discursively conflicting meaning-making that needed time). A plan/organisation for a process of collective writing could, for instance, be to take turns in writing freely around significant concepts to be used in relation to the initially chosen stories, and work them through via e-mail before starting the process of picking out the bits and pieces of that writing and transforming it into a paper. What does it, for instance, mean to at all do multiple readings? What does it mean to read (or write) from a psychoanalytical discourse as opposed to a poststructural? (just to refer to the issues raised in the dialogue between B and S.)

To get back to the point: In trying to take an equal as possible responsibility in a collective process of writing, I – personally – find it important to have an ongoing dialogue in relation to such (theoretical/discursive) issues, and collectively figure out what discourse it is that we are writing from/within, not the least, to be able to transgress it! In a situation where I write with Ulla Lind, whom I have worked with for 10 years now, we can figure these things out within the actual writing-process. However, to meet up with persons you don't know for a week under extraordinary – wonderful! – circumstances, and then simply start this process IS definitely a much more complicated task than the collective writing of Deleuze and Guattari. And it is certainly an extraordinary challenge that Bronwyn has made possible for all of us!!!! (as well as a challenge for the academic community – it is thereby utterly important!!!!!!) My personal and 'Scandinavian' critique referred to the lack of such a negotiated understanding in relation to key concepts and feminist poststructural discourse as such. Hillevi

And now I must ask myself, have I simply been self indulgent all these years, revelling in the collective pleasure of working as equals at the workshops and then coming undone in the writing, knowing full well I have to position myself with final responsibility for making the paper publishable, a positioning which does not sit easily with the balm of the way we worked together at the workshops (or the way I thought we were working together)? I need to remember here though that Hillevi participated in the first workshop and that since then we have become much more organised, selecting relevant readings, sending them out and discussing them at the workshop. We have also changed the original practice of not sending each draft to everyone. In more recent workshops we have sent each draft to all participants and invited comments from everyone. The process has evolved as problems became evident along the way.

But one way or another the issue of power and shifting positionings is clearly of vital importance in unpacking the dis-ease that often surfaced in the writing process. We were a mix of current PhD students studying with me, ex-students of mine who now had their PhDs and wished to continue their involvement, others' PhD students who had asked to participate, invited international guests who were usually also PhD students, co-opted members like Barb who had studied with someone else, and one undergraduate honours student. It is quite shocking to read about how anxious some members of the group felt about the writing. Phoenix writes for example of how warm and welcoming the workshop was and how difficult the writing space was in contrast because of the separating out of the I and the attendant sense of vulnerability:

> I will always delight in the memory of the delicious tropical feast of a breakfast Bronwyn so carefully prepared for us on the first morning, and telling us that this was the one and only time she would prepare food for us. Having food prepared for me is a rare pleasure and this gesture was very welcoming. It clearly showed Bronwyn's sense of responsibility to begin, and asked that we all assume the responsibility for making it wonderful. Love and openness were indeed offered to me by Bronwyn and Sue, as possibilities and pathways into the collective.
>
> The email space and the writing process were altogether quite a different experience from the actual week on the island, from my perspective, not that love and openness weren't apparent.
>
> On Magi Is, the opportunity to get to know the other women and find a position that could be negotiated and massaged through talk was possible. However on email, one has to blah out a position without much opportunity to feel a way through, and into, differences. Even when the blah is carefully constructed and well thought out, (or more so when it isn't), it sometimes felt like 'over exposure' entering the email discussion about the writing.
>
> I sensed that other participants avoided that over exposure on occasion, by direct contact with particular members of the collective rather than blah into the collective email space. Which is bringing me to my point. As Sue writes in the chapter, that she becomes an individual (/other than Bronwyn) in responding to Bronwyn, it is like that responding to the group – my responses expose my individual self (in all my rawness and inadequacies, less experienced/ less knowing etc, that is, in all my fear) and I feel as tho I leave the collective space when I offer my thoughts (for a time that becomes concrete in the electronic word). In email and in electronic passing of the edits of the paper I can't/couldn't tentatively look for signals and weave a response that is generated by the conversation-in-motion, cooperatively or collectively. Hillevi's point that power, responsibility and positioning are complex and shifting is more obvious when the work moves from actual physical space to virtual space.

I have noticed similarly in other email groups that responses I would not hesitate to make in person can feel like over exposure on email. I sensed in Lekkie's reply a trace of the risk taking, and the kind of trusting that I would be heard and understood that this relative 'over exposure' produced in me on email and edits.

Eileen's message asks about the difference between the virtual and the actual space, and this 'difficulty' of mine is really one of electronic communication rather than specifically collective writing, but distance and time necessitate electronic conversations and such difficulties that could be more deftly handled in actual face to face conversation, become more obvious.

I followed the movement of the paper I was involved in and I participated and I know it exists with me in its bones too. The difficulty (if it must be described that way), for me, was the power/responsibility nexus required greater risk-taking on my part when the writing space was electronic. I needed more courage to take my own steps to prevent collapsing into the possible self–other binary divide electronically. It was easier personally in the warm humid and loving environment of Salty.

In other words, the 'we' as Sue puts it in the chapter, wavers for me, more dangerously in the electronic space where the negotiation of power/responsibility and positioning becomes somehow more unidimensional rather than an embodied response I can negotiate.
Phoenix

Danielle, as our only undergraduate participant expresses an even more raw sense of vulnerability:

When I was invited along to the Magnetic Island workshop, two years ago, I felt like a little kid with a C+ average, who had been invited to a 'Writers Camp' by accident. The kind that my 'gifted' best friend went on when we were in grade six. After all, I was a university student that was hoping to write an honours thesis as part of the fourth year education program. I am by no means trying to suggest that I was brain dead. Rather, I am trying to make the point that I had been dragged reluctantly from a university environment where my peers were coming to me for help, into a scary situation, where instead of seeing my lecturers out the front of the room (from a distance), I would be staring at them at eye level and asking them if they could pass the cornflakes over breakfast. I was not looking forward to the trip! If I could have thought of an excuse that I thought was good enough for a university Professor to believe, I would have used it to get out of the whole thing.

I had been sent some required reading which only served to make me feel even more insecure. After filtering my way through these readings I had become acutely aware of the fact that I had bullshitted my way through university thus far . . . and no amount of bullshitting was going to help me on this trip.

Staying at the house for the week together was a great distraction. Seeing all of these extremely intelligent women doing day-to-day things and talking about tragic relationships and other topics that I could relate to served to close the divide that I was feeling between them and me. But when talk around the topic surfaced I felt like I was out of my depth. The Magnetic Island trip had exposed a person that was incapable and unsure, as opposed to the capable, pushy, group leader that I had come to know and feel extremely comfortable with during my uni life.

Writing stories was also a time when I felt like I had forgotten to wear my knickers to school. I felt like this because of the time constraints and my lack of knowledge surrounding the topic. I had been used to feeling confident about sharing my ideas and now I felt embarrassed that I was reading out something I had written and I wasn't even sure if it made sense.

The week was also filled with lots of enjoyable things. I enjoyed listening and learning. If I had not ventured outside of my comfort zone I would never have met the friendly and nurturing group of women that I encountered on the trip. I enjoyed great food, conversation and met some really diverse and interesting people. I spent a lot of time reading body language and felt a great sense of relief when I noticed that other people were also feeling a little uneasy at times. The 'immediacy' I experienced on the trip was something I really enjoyed.

I enjoyed the way the women I was with trod carefully at times over stories we shared. These women were very intuitive and understanding and made me feel welcomed and valued. When something was shared that could have been taken to mean something completely different (perhaps offensive), a space was provided for clarification and teasing out, that I think is not as readily available by email.

Finally, I believe that it is this lack of immediacy that prevented me from feeling comfortable to contribute by email to date. I can't see your faces when you are reading this and it terrifies me in many ways. Is what I have written completely irrelevant? Have I offended anybody? Will anyone tell me if they did feel offended? Can anyone relate to my story? How many spelling mistakes have I made? Must go, I hope my simple recount is of some use. Danielle

On the other side of this vulnerability and struggle are the wonderful stories that Hillevi and Helen have told of the ways in which the work we have done together has spilled over into their teaching and research. The process, with all its flaws and all its struggles, seems to matter. It seems to impact on us as academics, as teachers, as researchers. Babette's response brings these threads together and back to the practices of writing in the social sciences. She says:

> Reading Sue's and Bronwyn's exchange of words and stories (of ourselves), it is as if I am propelled back into that space. I have not forgotten how this collective working and writing was then – tedious, passionate, risky, fun – yet writing my thesis now I am a solitary writer once more. In this sense, classic social science, although the 'social' sounds rather like a paradox, is quite asocial when it engages in this traditional kind of writing. When I teach 'research and writing' to my students nowadays, I witness their shock that 'something like this', that is collective writing, is possible as well as 'scientific'. I suppose that a lot of them do think of shared work and thus only half the suffering. I do not tell them that it is both: multiplied suffering but also multiplied pleasure.
>
> Are we supposed to offer another memory? Then here it is: I remember to have been most surprised that this method of collective biography originated from Germany. Germany of all countries did not seem to me as being a sphere of collectivist action and thinking, or at least not in the positive supporting, warm – feminist romantic – sense that Magnetic Island then proved to be. Reading you two and us again – in this multi-logue – I am propelled to try to reach other islands again. Babette.

Not long after I finished this letter to you, Sue, the letter below arrived from Eileen. I think we could close this chapter with that letter, ensuring that what we have here is beautifully rhizo-vocal text.
Bronwyn

Hello All,
A very belated response to the collaborative writing from Sue and Bronwyn and the responses to that writing from others. I have a brief window in my day and hope to be able to complete this thinking/writing in that time. But it is a narrow window!

My position
Who is the 'I' responding at the moment, and how is that 'I' different from the one who engaged in various collaborative writing exercises?

I've known Bronwyn for years, longer probably than anyone else in this group so that is a big part of this 'I'.

Here's a bit from my thesis that may have something to do with writing, myself, and Bronwyn.

One of the methods I have used to attempt to make my embodied self visible in the constituting process of the discourses that I write about, and write in, is through the use of memories that I have constructed as poems or stories. I sheer away from the term *poem*, as I am still bound to the discourses about poetry that I learned at school. My stories are lyrical in a poetic kind of way, but mostly, they are intensely personal, as they try to capture the images, senses and sounds of a particular moment that I call on to help me describe the way I felt/am feeling as I am constituted as a subject of and in a discourse. As I contemplate how to locate myself as a writer, this story appears on the screen before me:

I wrote a poem when I was about thirteen.
I remember the writing of it
Sitting hunched over the fireplace in our lounge room,
Watching the desolate day raining outside the French windows
A notepad on my knee.
But mostly I remember the A+ + +,
Scrawled in red at the top of the page when it was returned to me
The joy and excitement that rushed through me
As I basked in the glow of praise from a teacher

Almost thirty years later I experienced the same joy and excitement when I read Bronwyn's comments, her authorial interruption, on a story I had written for a collective biography exercise. I had moved her, my writing had inspired her to be amazed, impressed and appalled (Davies, 2000a: 56–57). These memories of writing, and more importantly of the validation of my writing, have contributed to the way in which I set out to write this thesis. I wanted to include stories that expressed my gut reaction. I wanted to include stories that would amaze, impress and appall (Honan, 2001).

To me this collaborative writing process was always bound up with my need to 'amaze, impress, and appall,' Bronwyn!! So this takes me to my next subheading.

Power relations

The whole writing process, each person's reactions to it, and most interestingly I think, each person's reactions to this writing of Sue's and Bronwyn's is a fascinating representation of power relations. I think everyone who has responded has mentioned these relations in some way. To me the most important of these are, the relations represented in the positions adopted by Sue and Bronwyn as the authors of this chapter, and the relations between each of the members of the workshop groups and Bronwyn herself. I cannot move beyond these relations as I begin to try to make sense of the difficulties, frustrations, joys etc involved in writing collaboratively. Although I am now a 'doctor', an 'academic', a 'published writer', Bronwyn, as well as being my dear friend who I love, will always be my mentor, my guide, my supervisor, my teacher. This has to have something to do with the writing process: my desire to please Bronwyn, my desire to appear to be a good writer in her eyes, my desire to appear to be a competent professional, all affected how I responded to various drafts of the writing.

It also affects how I read her collaboration with Sue, and helps to explain my resentment, envy even, of the close relationship evidenced in the writing.

It also helps explain how I dealt with drafts that Bronwyn had radically reworked during the collective writing process. Usually I thought the reworking made the draft better, sometimes I was frustrated because she brought in other texts that I had to then try to read. And I really can't imagine how I would have dealt with the question of two different drafts to choose from, one by Bronwyn and one by someone else. I'm glad I wasn't in that group☺.

But bottom line I guess, and I know that writing this may upset you Bronwyn but here goes anyway: I always knew that you were in control. There was no way that you would allow a piece of writing to go to a journal with your name on it that you weren't happy with. I always felt that I could contribute, and I was wildly happy when some of my writing was included in the final draft (if I could recognise it, another interesting point made already!), but I always knew that Bronwyn had the final say, so I wasn't upset when my writing was excised. And that goes for the stories as well as the draft writing. I don't know if it was Cath who told Bronwyn to 'get over it', but Cath I can hear you saying that, and I'd always hear you saying that to me if I started to get precious about part of my writing that had gone.

Now that all may be contradictory to the 'collective' of a collective writing exercise, but I've never really engaged with the liberal/radical feminist notions of a collective. All that passive equality crap! I've been thrown out of feminist collectives for not being lesbian enough, for not agreeing to stop shaving my legs, for having a boyfriend. My sister was thrown out of one because she had male children!! So I'm a bit wary of the peace and love, women together discourse that's in a fair bit of what Sue has written. Sorry Sue, but while I had a fantastic time on Maggie, and each time I was there was terrific, I do remember pretty vividly some times when we were not all madly in love with each other.

Time

The day-to-day business of being home has also been commented on by others. I had the luxury of a year off work to write my thesis, and I remember joking to someone that I was always first to respond to emails as part of my work-avoidance techniques. The two workshops I was involved in, reflexivity, and embodiment, are taken respectively from 'my thesis writing time' and 'my new academic working full time at a university time'. I can certainly see a difference in the way I worked on these two papers.

I was interested in someone's comment about what would have happened if we hadn't structured deadlines into the process.

The writing process

I think the time issue has a big impact on the writing, but also the commitment. I think there is always a different level of commitment to the writing, expressed as ambivalence, or silence. I know sometimes after 8 or so drafts, I couldn't care less any more (and usually said so!!). So why didn't it become part of the process that you could 'drop out' but still have your name on the final draft? I know Bronwyn has written about her reading of silence, but usually my silence was because I had nothing to say!

Ok I could probably go on and on, but my window has closed and I've got to move on to more pragmatic writing (Unit guides yippee!).

I hope I haven't offended anyone here but what I find especially joyous about ps theory is that it allows me to analyse what people say/write so they don't take personal offence, and I'm writing this to other poststructuralists aren't I?

Ok love to everyone (even if it's not lovey dovey love☺).
eileen

In the next two chapters we directly tackle two knotty concepts: power and the subject. The chapters thus far have already made use of these as conceptual tools for thinking through specific contexts and the processes of our collaborative work. In the remaining chapters we turn our attention more minutely to their theoretical import.

8

An archaeology of power and knowledge[14]

Our question in this chapter is twofold: how might we use Foucault to read our embodied memories of power and knowledge; and how might we use the analysis of those stories to enable us better to see the implications of Foucault's writing for the analysis of subjects' enmeshment in power/knowledge relations? We use our own embodied memories of achieving ourselves as appropriate(d) subjects (as girls and women, in relation to men – fathers, lovers and husbands) generated through the strategy of collective biography. We set out as archaeologists of our own lives, searching for moments in which power and knowledge might be said, in a Foucauldian sense, to intersect, shape each other and act as lines of force in relation to each other. We thus use our embodied selves as vehicles for observing the plays of power and knowledge in relation to the processes of (gendered) subjectification. In doing so, we do not assume 'real' or essential selves or that we have found the 'true' story in these tellings. In telling and writing our stories, and in using them for our analyses, our purpose was not to find or reveal a true interiority, or forms of thought that reveal that interiority. Rather we have sought to map the rationalities that are available to anyone. They are the material out of which social action is shaped, and the material out of which interiorities are themselves produced.

We organized our work of remembering around topics that had emerged from our reading of Foucault. We asked ourselves what our first memories were of:

- power as multiple lines of force, adding one's own line of force to one's own submission to another
- conducting the self as appropriately submissive, desiring to submit to another
- becoming a line of force, desiring not to submit, refusing submission
- working to change thought and to change relations of power.

At the outset we decided to restrict the stories we would tell to male–

female relations. We could equally have chosen, for example, mother–daughter relations or teacher–student relations. The choice to focus on gender relations was in one sense arbitrary, and in another sense, a quite predictable choice for a group of women thinking about relations of power. In each of the sessions we told, and then wrote and rewrote multiple stories from early childhood, from adolescence and from our earlier and later adult lives.

The explanations that, as usual, we sought to remove from our stories might be compared to those explicit bodies of knowledge (*connaissances*) and to the broader rationalizations that Foucault recommends we avoid. These, by their very nature, rely on and invoke bodies of knowledge *external* to the remembered event. The purpose of rationalizations is to articulate and repeat the dominant device of cause and effect in such a way that the actual detail of the event is obviated by the imported, value-laden discourse. We thus sought not to try to justify or make sense of ourselves in our stories, but to make them, rather, imaginably able to be lived by any reader/listener.

In addition to developing this particular mode of writing, relevant to the method of collective biography, we sought to elaborate the *specific rationalities* at play within each of our stories. Foucault suggests that we 'analyse specific rationalities rather than . . . invoking the progress of rationalisation in general' (2000b: 329). Specific rationalities are those aspects of knowledge without which the events could not, in any meaningful sense, have taken place. Rationalities are the forms of knowledge that are presupposed and actualized in the relations of power that unfold in each specific scene:

> [I]n a society, different bodies of learning, philosophical ideas, everyday opinions, but also institutions, commercial practices and police activities, morés – all refer to a certain implicit knowledge [*savoir*] special to this society. This knowledge is profoundly different from the bodies of learning [*des connaissances*] that one can find in scientific books, philosophical theories and religious justifications, but it is what makes possible at a given moment the appearance of a theory, an opinion, a practice. . . . It's this knowledge that I want to investigate, as the condition of possibility of knowledge [*connaissance*], of institutions, of practices.
>
> (Foucault, 1998b: 261–262)

After the workshop was over, and we were once again scattered geographically, we typed up and revised our own stories and began to trace the rationalities that seemed to give them sense. We each further developed the analyses of our own stories that had been collectively undertaken during the workshop. We noted any further details that unexpectedly arose from the fractured bedrock of our memory. When this individual work was completed, each document was sent to each member of the group. Then we began a collaborative process of writing and rewriting this chapter based on these collective and individual lines of thought. This done, Bronwyn wrote the first draft and then passed it on to the next writer. Our task in writing was to find a language that enabled us to see the stories against the grain of old sedimented discourses, and through which women are usually constituted as powerless and men as powerful. In elaborating the relations of power between men and women, and looking for the rationalities that make those relations seem reasonable, even inevitable, we do not, therefore, set out to tell a depressing story of the inevitability of current patterns of domination. We are more interested in disturbing and destabilizing sedimented thinking: our aim is 'to identify some of the weak points and lines of fracture in our present where thought might insert itself' differently (Rose, 1999: 276–277). To that end, we focus on the ways in which our subjectivities are shaped in terms of rationalities of power – on the ways we become governable and actively engage in the conduct of our own and others' conduct. With such knowledge, we have found, lines of fracture may well open up, which hold the possibility of different lines of action. We are interested in the ways in which power, and the related forms of knowledge, act – in specific instances – on the subject to make the subject possible and in the ways the subject takes up and reiterates those conditions as an active subject (Butler, 1997a: 14).

By insisting that we make sense of Foucault's writing about power through our own experiences of being in the world, we find ourselves interrogating the deeply subjective, deeply sedimented, deeply emotional arena of subjectification. We engage in an analysis of power 'at its extremities, in its ultimate destinations . . . where it becomes capillary, that is, in its most regional and local forms and institutions' (Foucault, quoted in Richer, 1992: 114). We work at the level of the body, which is 'the only irreducible in Foucault's theorising' (Bell, 1994: 12). We analyse 'the forms and means of power focused on individuals and the details of their behaviour and conduct' (Gordon, 2000: xxiv). We see our responsibility as researchers of power/knowledge not to lie in representing things in themselves, but to lie in representing the web of 'structure, sign and play' of social relations (Derrida, 1978: 287), in 'seeing what frames our seeing' (Lather, 1993: 675).

Power/knowledge

Our interest in the concepts of power and knowledge and how they play out within gendered social relations is necessarily informed by our feminist sensibilities. Feminist social analyses of the gendered politics of everyday life have been prolific in the past decades but many of these analyses, particularly in the early days of feminist research, have been grounded in liberal humanist thinking. In writing this chapter we found ourselves, time and again, caught up in these usual ways of seeing. Old assumptions about power being held and wielded by those in positions of power often lurk at the edges of feminist analyses of lived social relations between men and women. This is inevitable, as even in a post-humanist world – humanism is 'our mother tongue' (St Pierre, 1997: 406). Our struggle in writing this chapter was to find a way to make meaningful the fluidity of power and the intersecting lines of power, knowledge and subjectivity, and to move beyond, in successive drafts, the more usual ways of lodging power *in* boys/men and vulnerability *in* girls/women.

In order to highlight what is new in the approach that we take up here, we will begin by summarizing humanist perspectives on power/knowledge and then detailing some of the shifts away from these that Foucault's work entails. What follows is an elaboration of the particular Foucauldian shifts in thinking about power and knowledge that we have found productive, and provocative, in work with our memories of power/knowledge.

Humanism, as Foucault stresses, is not monolithic, it is a 'theme or, rather a set of themes that have reappeared on several occasions, over time, in European societies' (1997c: 313). Despite the supple, diverse and inconsistent nature of 'the humanistic thematic' (Foucault, 1997c: 314), broad characteristics can be identified that are disrupted by Foucault's work. In humanist thinking, power is perceived as unidirectional, hierarchical and negative. It manifests in the effects of some subjects upon other (less powerful) subjects. Power is oppressive, a force that 'challenges both the natural and political liberty of the individual' (St Pierre, 2000: 489). Power is a quality that is (differentially) possessed and deployed and is the product of an individual's agency (St Pierre, 2000: 488). With increased agency comes increased power (and increased opportunity to abuse that power). Within humanist social justice frameworks, power is sometimes perceived as 'inherently evil', as something that might be given away to 'avoid domination . . . to "empower" those less fortunate' (St Pierre, 2000: 488–489). It is a 'humanist tradition,' Foucault suggests, 'that once someone gains power he ceases to know . . . [O]nly those who keep their distance from power . . . can discover the truth' (1980b: 51). Thus there are zones implied, in humanist thinking, that are power-free, neutral, uncorrupted, where knowledge is untainted and truth is possible.

Knowledge, within the Cartesian traditions of humanist thought, is rational, progressive, objective and productive of truth. It is something that has existence outside the humanist individual but it can be acquired, internalized and utilized in diverse ways. Individuals have varying degrees of access to knowledge and there are various domains and hierarchies of valued knowledge. Acquisition of highly valued knowledges can be 'empowering' in certain ways to the humanist individual. Thus knowledge pre-exists and is something separate to power. Within humanist thinking, power and knowledge are instrumentally related. In contrast, through a series of complex conceptual shifts away from the tenets of humanism, Foucault develops a version of the power/knowledge nexus wherein they are intimately and integrally related to one another. They are not only interdependent but they are productive of one another.

The first shift in Foucault's theorizing of power that we found important in our work is that power must be understood as in motion, never in any fixed relation to knowledge or to subjectivity:

> Foucault talked of lines of sedimentation but also of lines of 'breakage' and of 'fracture'. Untangling these lines within a social apparatus is, in each case, like drawing up a map, doing cartography, surveying unknown landscapes, and this is what he calls 'working on the ground'.
>
> (Deleuze, 1992: 159)

As Deleuze points out, Foucault's analysis of social apparatuses [*dispositifs*] is that they are not only in motion, and tangled, but that the multiple lines continually change their relation to each other, change direction, bifurcate, fork and drift. That which we can formulate, or seem to fix, is best understood in terms of 'vectors and tensors' (Deleuze, 1992: 159).

We use collective biography (rather than cartography) as a way of positioning ourselves, as researchers and as subjects, 'on the ground', in order to see the lines of descent, the tangles, the sedimentations, and the fractures and breaks. We pull our memories up out of the tangle of lines of force to examine them more closely, while recognizing at the same time that they are always in motion. And we descend into the watery tangle to find the intersections with other lines.

The second shift that we found critical in our work is Foucault's insistence that power can be a *positive* force. This thought disrupts the humanist assumptions made about power in Marxist and critical theories and various feminist theories, and which underpin common-sense understandings of power. He rejects the conception of power as a solely negative term. Power does not 'only weigh upon us as a force that says no but traverses and produces things, it induces pleasure, forms knowledge, produces discourse' (Foucault, 1980c: 119).

The third shift, closely related to these first two, is the Foucauldian rejection of the idea of power as a possession: 'power is not the property of the dominant class but the strategy of that class in action' (Deleuze, 1988: 30). Power itself 'has no essence; it is simply operational. It is not an attribute but a relation . . . a set of possible relations between forces which passes through the dominated forces no less than the dominating' (Deleuze,

1988: 27). Struggles against power are not themselves without power. The 'dominated' are not in a binary relation to those who exercise power, but are themselves integral to and operating through the relevant lines of force. Thus power moves through multiple lines of force. Using metaphors like chains and nets, Foucault envisages each person as simultaneously undergoing and exercising power. We are not only the 'inert or consenting target' of power, but also involved in its articulation. The lines of force are not separate from us, acting on us, rather, we circulate between their 'threads'. Thus individuals become 'the vehicles of power, not its points of application' (Foucault, 1980a: 98).

The fourth shift that was essential – and problematic – in our analyses is Foucault's distinction between violence and relations of power. Violence acts directly upon the other in that 'it forces, bends, breaks, destroys, or closes off all possibilities' (Foucault, 2000b: 340). In contrast, a power relationship necessitates that the one over whom power is exercised is recognized and maintained as a person who acts, who has a degree of freedom (Foucault, 1982: 221). The exercise of power is therefore always a way of acting upon an acting subject by virtue of their acting or being capable of action. Power relations do not exclude the obtaining of consent or the use of violence, but the important point, according to Foucault, is that *neither consent nor violence constitutes the basic nature of power*. The exercise of power is 'a set of actions on possible actions; it incites, it induces, it seduces, it makes easier or more difficult; it releases or contrives, makes more probable or less; in the extreme it constrains or forbids absolutely' (Foucault, 2000b: 341), but it always acts upon acting subjects. While violence is the brute, destructive force of one person upon another, the play of power includes, by definition, the possibility of refusal or the counterforce of revolt: 'If an individual can remain free, however little his freedom may be, power can subject him to government. There is no power without potential refusal or revolt' (Foucault, 1981: 253).

The fifth shift moves us from the view that knowledge in itself can be pure and outside of power. Foucault asks how do the fluid tangled lines of force or vehicles of power relate to knowledge? He talks about the fundamental difference in kind between knowledge and power, characterizing knowledge as more like formed matter. The relation between knowledge and power is that relations of power both (and at the same time and through the same processes) presuppose and actualize knowledge. The lines of force of power relations make us see and speak in certain ways, though they do not themselves see and speak. Power 'comes from below', operating like a blind and silent 'mole that only knows its way around its network of tunnels, its multiple hole' (Deleuze, 1988: 82). Relations of knowledge, manifested through seeing and speaking, 'are always already completely caught up within power relations which they presuppose and actualize' (Deleuze, 1988: 82). While 'power relations imply relations of knowledge, the latter also presuppose the former' (Deleuze, 1988: 83).

Foucault suggests, in *a sixth shift*, that to understand how relations of power are put and held in place we examine not violence, but the specific forms of knowledge, or 'rationalities', that make any particular form of power seem reasonable or inevitable. Research into lived experience, the archaeology of the everyday, necessitates the excavation of the rationalities that underpin these events. Rationalities are closely linked to the forms of knowledge that Foucault calls *savoir*, implicit knowledge. Foucault closely links implicit knowledge and rationalities to the concept of governmentality – or the conduct of conduct – which he describes as 'the encounter between technologies of domination and technologies of the self' (1997a: 225). In our analyses of the memory stories, we consider how the specific rationalities that give sense to an event are taken up by us within our repertoires of technologies of the self: they assist us to perform the necessary 'operations on [our] own bodies and souls, thoughts, conduct, and way of being, so as to transform [our]selves' into appropriate(d) subjects within the networks of relations of power of each moment (Foucault, 1997a: 225). As feminists choosing to examine gendered social relations in our memories, we do not intend to rail against the powers of patriarchal oppression, but rather to look (below) at the forms of rationality through which the particular relations of power manifest in our memories are constituted and maintained.

The stories

The first of the stories we've chosen is of a father–daughter relationship when the girl was six years old:

> *The long drive to the beach over the mountains took them over winding dusty mountain roads, through rivers with no bridges and through numerous shut gates. Four kids in the back. Two adults in the front. The kids took it in turns to open the gates. The older kids. The father was irritated by their slowness and incompetence. The tension in his back and the smell of dust and cigarettes always made her feel sick. Now, at six, she was old enough to take her turn at opening the gates. She feels sick in anticipation. She'd rehearsed the detail in her imagination. She'd watched where the others had got it wrong, swinging the gate the wrong way or letting it swing open and then get stuck on a rut in the road, not wide enough open for the car to get through. Or they fumbled with the gate lock, or dawdled back to the car. She knew they were not good enough because she could feel the rising tide of her father's irritation. Now it was her turn. She opened the car door, jumped out of the car door and closed*

the car door all in one smooth movement. She ran to the gate, looking to see which way it swung open. Tiptoe, lift the metal ring up over the post, smoothly, evenly, so it doesn't get stuck, pass it through the small hole in the gate. Turn it the right way so it will fit through. Lift the gate so it doesn't get stuck on the ruts, run out with it all the way so it's fully open. Lift it again the moment the car passes through, swing it back, hold it steady with your foot while small hands thread the metal ring through the gate, pulling it tight. Panic. It won't fit over the post. Adjust the gate, hold it, pull again, wriggle and twist, get it over the post. It goes over. Quick rush of air out of her lungs. All done in a few seconds. Run, jump back in the car. He's not irritated. Good. She got it right. No one says anything.

This story was initially told as an example of adding one's own line of force to one's own submission. When we subject it to analysis we find this common-sense understanding of the story dissolving.

No words are exchanged in this memory. There is no evident imposition of knowledge on the girl. Yet the girl works hard to embody the skills she sees as appropriate for her to have. The rationalities that give sense to the episode are, from the adult point of view, that as children get older they develop new competencies; not all children are equally competent; open comparisons between children should not be made; children must be given the opportunity to practise new skills. From the girl's point of view, there is pleasure in the acquisition of new competencies: power 'induces pleasure, forms knowledge, produces discourse' (Foucault, 1980c: 119). But the urgency of her performance suggests another rationality: that approval (identity?) comes to those who are visibly competent. In this she exemplifies Butler's observation that: 'Subjection exploits the desire for existence, where existence is always conferred from elsewhere; it marks a primary vulnerability to the Other in order to be' (Butler, 1997a: 20–21). The multilinear ensemble draws together, with pleasure and vulner-ability, power and knowledge, working together to produce the subject. The girl works to become an appropriately subjected being in order that she can have existence (a particular form of existence that she desires) conferred on her by her father. Even if his conferral is in silence. The power exercised by the father need not be read as an assault in this instance, since it is taken up by the girl, actively, as a force that she will bend to her own will – the will to become recognizably competent. As Foucault observes:

> Power would be a fragile thing if its only function were to repress, if it worked only through the mode of censorship, exclusion, blockage and repression. . . . If, on the contrary, power is strong this is because . . . it produces effects at the level of desire – and also at the level of knowledge. Far from preventing knowledge, power produces it.
>
> (Foucault, 1980d: 59)

The knowledge produced by the girl's exertion of power on her own body, is the bodily knowledge of how to open the gate, and also the knowledge that she can do it, perhaps better than her older, more laid-back siblings. She anticipates a particular kind of existence being conferred on her by Others. The line of force she reads from the father (and related to rationalities that suggest she should at this age develop these skills), are taken up by her as power that she exerts on her own body in acquiring new skills, and perhaps a new recognition of who she might be able to be.

Deleuze suggests we might distinguish between active and reactive effects. The girl's action upon her own body might be read as reactive, by definition – in that she reacts to what she reads on her father's body. It is also her observation that her older siblings are less concerned to react to their father's will. She is able, in a sense, to use their non-reaction to her own benefit, to carve out a small arena in which she might be recognized, comparatively, as having competence, and thus as recognizably existing. In this sense the active and reactive lines of force become one another, they merge in a movement in which she takes up as her own the line of action out of which and through which she is subjected and becomes an active agent. To reactively engage power is not, Deleuze points out, to be passive, but to be caught up in an 'irreducible encounter' between action and reaction:

> To incite, provoke and produce . . . constitute active affects, while to be incited or provoked, to be induced to produce, to have a 'useful' effect, constitutes reactive affects. The latter are not simply the 'repercussion' or 'passive side' of the former but are rather 'the irreducible encounter' between the two . . .
>
> (Deleuze, 1988: 71)

The girl's action can also be understood in terms of the 'conduct of conduct' as she carefully attends to her behaviours, actions and comportment (Dean, 1999: 10; Foucault, 1982: 220–221). She experiences herself as behaving autonomously, conducting her own conduct, while at the same time both parents sit watching her through the car window, an audience who might judge whether she gets it right or not. The metaphor of 'conduct' is compatible with her 'rehearsal' of the act in her mind. She conducts her own performance, and calculates how to get it right. She forms an idea in her mind of the perfect action and organizes her body to perform it. She judges whether it is good enough, not only against her imagined image, but through the audience reaction. Her father is not in a negative state, so she reads herself as having conducted her own conduct in a successful performance. She has not only not dis-pleased her parents, but she has conducted herself in a way that gives her a pleasurable sense of her own competence and agency.

Our second story is also of a father–daughter relationship. Now the girl is 14 years old, and in this story the line of force emanating from the father is more explicit. The multilinear ensemble of lines of force bifurcates and forks:

I was thirteen or fourteen years old and my best friend had a party at her house for some of our classmates. My father had told me to be home by 11 p.m. At 11 p.m. everybody was still at the party, and I was the only one who had to leave this early. I didn't want to be the first one to leave, because my classmates used to tease me about my parents being so strict and about me being so obedient. They had nicknamed me 'the angel'.

I delayed my departure until 11.30 p.m., hoping that my father had gone to bed by the time I got home. On my way home I walked very slowly, folded my hands and prayed to God that my father would be asleep and not notice that I was late. Coming closer to our house I could see that the lights were still on in the living room. I prayed that he wouldn't be angry. Carefully opening the door, I saw him sitting in a chair. He just looked at me in silence. Waiting. This awful, angry silence. I started explaining that we had so much fun that I forgot the time.

'Didn't we have an agreement?' (sharp tone of voice).

'Yes, I know, but nobody else had to go home this early and we had fun and I forgot . . .'

'I am very disappointed in you' (soft tone of voice). (Silence). 'You know that we worry about you when you don't come home when you're supposed to. I expected more from you.'

'Yes, I know, but . . .'

'You have really let me down' (sad tone of voice). (Silence). 'I thought we could trust you.'

The girl describes two external active lines of force running through her. She is not separate from those lines of force – cannot be indifferent to them or impervious to them. One line of force, taken up and spoken into existence by the father, both presupposes and actualizes the knowledge that girls are not safe – and in particular not safe unless they distinguish themselves from other girls. Her father establishes this difference through his insistence that she become the kind of person who makes and honours agreements with him. The other line of force, taken up and spoken into existence by her classmates is that there is a problem with setting yourself up as different and better. They tease her for being different, for being an 'angel'. The girl already has these knowledges as her own – she recognizes them when they are spoken, and she takes them up as serious proposals weighing on her actions and on her subjectivity. The girl walks in the space between these two lines of force and calls on a possible third external line of force – God, who might intervene on her behalf.

What we are not interested in here are the father's intentions. The point of any analysis, Foucault suggests, is not to ask after the intentions of powerful individuals – we cannot know those – nor to ask who is dominating and who dominated, but rather to ask how subjection works to create subjects:

> Let us ask, instead, how things work at the level of those continuous and uninterrupted processes which subject our bodies, govern our gestures, dictate our behaviours etc. In other words, rather than ask ourselves how the sovereign appears to us in his lofty isolation, we should try to discover how it is that subjects are gradually, progressively, really and materially constituted through a multiplicity of organisms, forces, energies, materials, desires, thoughts, etc. We should try to grasp subjection in its material instance as a constitution of subjects.
>
> (Foucault, 1980a: 97)

The girl is caught between two demands or lines of force that, from a common-sense point of view, emanate from external sources and are imposed on her, but in a post-structuralist analysis, run through her and are taken up by her as her own contradictory desires. The first power, or line of force, actualizes the knowledge that she must establish a humanist identity, that is, an identity that is consistent, unitary, rational and predictable, and whose moral principles dictate, in this instance, that she honour agreements made with her father, and that she be, above all, responsible. Responsibility for her own actions is seen as 'resting on a moral base and entailing personal commitment to the moral position implied in [her] choices', as a rational humanist individual she is expected to be in control of this process (Davies, 2000b: 56). This requirement to be responsible/rational is endlessly repeated in the take-up of the discourses of individual-based societies, a take-up in which both the girl and the father are inevitably engaged. They both know that being read as someone with a consistent, predictable, rational identity is a prerequisite for being recognized as some*one*, and in particular as someone of value. In this instance her father can confer such an identity on her: 'existence is always conferred from elsewhere: [marking] a primary vulnerability to the Other in order to be' (Butler, 1997a: 20). In this story the father anticipates the conferring of such an identity and is disappointed to have to withdraw his recognition. Such recognition is inevitably highly valued by the girl – to be recognized as of particular value is integral to the ambivalent project of subjectification (Davies et al., 2001). The second line of force, taken up by her classmates, confers upon her the subject status of one who is too good, an 'angel'. She does not read this as a desirable form of recognition and stays at the party in a bid for a different kind of recognition – a recognition as one who can break with that form of identity. In the space in between these forces, the girl similarly rebels. She appeals to God to help her to evade the choice between good girl and bad girl, between identity and transgression. Her desire is, reasonably enough, to be able to refuse the forced choice.

The rationality, mobilized by the father, is one of care – parents do what they do because they care about you, they know the dangers in this world because they are older and wiser and have more life experience. Children should appreciate parents' care, and allow themselves to be cared for, *and* should become worthy of that care. In this formulation, the line of force or power, which incites the girl to be a particular kind of person, actualizes the enactment of formal educative patterns of knowledge:

> There is no confusion, therefore, between the affective categories of power (of the 'incite' and 'provoke' variety) and the formal categories of knowledge (such as 'educate', 'look after', 'punish', and so on), the latter passing through seeing and speaking in order to actualize the former.
>
> (Deleuze, 1988: 77)

In this sense power both presupposes and actualizes knowledge.

The father also engages a rationality of humanist/Christian morality in the conduct of his own conduct and in this sense the lines of force, on himself and on his daughter, coincide or draw together. But he positions himself as one who lives this morality and positions her as one who has failed in its terms, and in her failure he represents her as having a major impact on him – on his emotions. Even so he continues to conduct himself as a moral being in not losing his temper, not yelling or hitting her – he remains rational and in control of his feelings. This further cements the moral authority he has to tell his daughter what to do, and positions her as lacking moral rightness or authority (Davies, 2000b: 59). Rose elaborates this complex relation between rationalities and morality thus:

> [Rationalities] have a distinctive *moral* form, in that they embody conceptions of the nature and the scope of legitimate authority, the distribution of authorities across different zones or spheres – political, military, pedagogic, familial and the ideals or principles that should guide the exercise of authority: freedom, justice, equality, responsibility, citizenship, autonomy and the like.
>
> (Rose, 1999: 26)

In our next story the girl is confronted by the knowledge of male–female relations that the father may have had in mind when he set the 11 p.m. curfew. The lines of force here change direction, and become dangerous, they impact forcefully on other lines. The girl, now 15, is out on a date with her girl friend and two older boys:

She was 15. She was on a date with her best friend Sally. Bill was Sally's.

Phil was hers. Phil and Bill were older, working. She and Sally were still at school. They were going to the farmhouse that a group of Bill and Phil's mates had rented. Their first time living away from home. She carefully brushed her hair so that it looked straight and natural. She put on the black eyeliner so that it looked right – not too dark but clearly there. Not a baby but not a slut. She put on the pale, frosted lipstick. The black shirt. The black pants. She took such care with the dressing but it had to look like she had taken no care. A free spirit. They picked her up at last. She got in the front as it was Phil's car and they drove out to the farmhouse. This was a first date so she made no physical contact. They all sat on the back verandah of the farmhouse. They talked. The sun set and the dim lights glowed a kind of dull yellow. Inside the farmhouse about eight other males watched television and drank. Their voices and laughter growing louder. There was a girl inside – the long-term girlfriend of Bob. They had been going out for over a year. All she could hear on the verandah were the voices of the boys/men. Then she heard a scream. Not a 'no' but a scream. The laughter of the men grew louder. She sat still. Sally sat still. She tightened her body and pulled her legs closer together. Tightened them around herself. She looked at Phil and he went inside. He came back out to the verandah after about 5 minutes. Phil told them that they had better go. There was a gang-bang going on and the boys were drunk. She clenched her stomach. Bob's girlfriend had slept with someone else and as she was a slut they all would have her. Her screams were regular. And loud. Phil told them it was time to go; it could get out of hand. She felt warmth in her body. She would be protected. She was not the kind of girl who would be the meat of a gang-bang. She got into the car. She flicked her hair as they drove off and gave Phil her deep-blue-eyed look. She rested her hand on his leg. She would not fuck someone else if she was going with someone. She was worth looking after.

Later, after writing the story and pondering the rationalities involved, the girl/woman writes:

I remembered that there were two women inside the house. The other was the girlfriend of my first 'love'. We had moved on but I had a passion for him that stays with me still – as a fantasy. He had a passion for the second girl and the shock was the memory that they were also going to rape her, as she wasn't anybody's – she didn't like my beloved. I remembered that the fact that they would also rape her shocked me. I don't know whether they did or not as I had left. What a strange thing memory is – I had forgotten that about my beloved. The bastard.

There are parallels here with the first two stories. The parallel with the first story is of a girl actively positioning herself as someone who can be recognized as the right kind of person. She does this in immediate contrast with those who have failed to do so. From the beginning she conducts herself as the 'just right' girl, bringing into play discourses and actions that signify her as a girl who is free, but not a slut. She knows already that she must conduct herself so that she cannot be read as the wrong kind of girl. In the rape scene and her removal from it, she finds herself positioned as a girl who is worth protecting (and by implication, a girl who is also vulnerable). In finding herself so positioned, she also finds herself desiring the boy/man who saved her. Power is strong, in the Foucauldian sense, because it produces effects at the level of desire, as well as at the level of knowledge.

The second parallel is with the father in the second story. The boys/men use their force to educate the girls, this time with the knowledge that they are simply not safe if they are not positioned as the faithful partner of a boy/man. That knowledge is presupposed and actualized or made real through the exertion of their physical force on the body of the girl who has apparently displayed herself as not being faithful. The raped girl resists, she screams. The boys/men rely on the girl as the literal ground on which they violently display their power/knowledge, and she becomes the victim of that power/knowledge. The act is an assertion of power, but at the same time also an act of violence. Rape is a mode of action that acts directly and immediately upon the girl's body. It forces and destroys, and 'closes the door on all possibilities'. In this respect it is a relationship of violence upon the raped girl's body. In that particular situation she does not, in our view, have 'a whole field of responses, reactions, results, and possible inventions' (Foucault 2000b: 340) available to her.

While the screams suggest resistance, it is improbable that she could have saved herself. No one comes to her aid. Phil thinks *it might get out of hand*. The implication here is that it is not yet out of hand, although there is a girl being gang raped inside the house. Perhaps he has in mind a rationality that legitimates the government of unruly girls/women. No counterforce on his part appears to be called for. The logic of the scene is that the raped girl does not deserve to be saved – she is positioned as and becomes an immoral being, in contrast to good girls. Just as the father in the second story, whose not-acting-out of potential violence constitutes him as virtuous, inculcated in his daughter a knowledge of the importance of becoming recognizably a responsible and moral being, so these boys/men inculcated in the girls the knowledge and the desire to be the right kind of girl – a girl who conducts her own conduct, who governs herself, who actualizes knowledge of what a good girl is. The 'good girls' are removed from the scene by the 'good' boys/men. The knowledge of the power of the boys/men over the girls is made all the stronger by this removal, as is the girl's desire to be the right kind of girl/woman. The rape of the other girls thus works as an action upon her future actions. It is a power relationship in so far as the girls are recognized as free subjects who can choose several ways of behaving. It is an act of government, of structuring the girls' possible fields of action in the future. In this respect it is about 'guiding the possibility of conduct and putting in order the possible outcome' (Foucault, 1982: 221). There is however an important question that needs to be asked: to what degree is it possible for these girls to practice their freedom, given the way our societies presently structure gender relations? (We will return to this question in the final story.)

The girls who were raped transgressed the patriarchal order that dictates the particular form of female subjectification acceptable to men. The first raped girl was unfaithful to her officially designated lover. The second girl, the girl left behind at the house, remembered after the 'lie down' necessitated by writing up this story, became logically 'rape-able' because she 'wasn't anybody's', she had no status in the economy of sexual relations between men and women that would have engendered protection and respect for her as 'somebody's'. Even worse, she had rejected a desirable member of that group of young men, one who would have been willing to bestow his protection (based on exclusive possession) of her body.

In our fourth story the girl has grown up and become a woman, studying for a PhD. Her lover attempts to insert himself into the spaces of her study, wanting to direct and control them/her. She reacts, forcefully, changing the direction of the lines of force at play:

> *Her new lover called her mid-sentence when she was in a completely other head-space, trying to write something urgently. It was evening but she had been at the computer all day and all the day before – in the same sarong, the same books piled all around her, struggling with the same set of difficult concepts, starting to panic. He started waffling on and on about nothing while she 'mmm'ed and answered in an abstracted sort of way. When she said that she was sitting at the computer working, he shifted topic and began to talk about her fragile PhD proposal. He started to tell her how she needed to approach her project. She felt herself getting angry. She'd told him before to let it alone, this was her stuff, she didn't want to talk to him about it. She'd even called it 'secret women's business'. At this stage it was still too vague and she felt inarticulate when people tried to get her to talk about it. It was too difficult to find the right words to talk about it – with anyone.*
>
> *So when he started to tell her what she should do, that all she needed was the 'right research question' and implied that he could help her work that out, she felt a hot red rush of fury explode in her head and begin to form into words. Now you listen to me, she thought, and she began speaking very slowly:*
>
> *'How come you can tell me every little thing that you're doing but not ask me once what I might be doing, if I'm busy or not. I don't just sit here waiting for you to call me.'*

Her voice got harder and more sarcastic. The words just flowed out of her mouth:

'And . . . I don't need you to be my academic mentor. I have a mentor. She works at the university. She's called my supervisor. I have other mentors – the women I met at university, the women on my email list.'

She paused, and then spoke into the silence: 'What I want you *for is . . . sex.'*

She was actually thinking about what fun it had been when he'd sung to her and danced her around his kitchen. She was remembering lying on the beach with him on New Year's Eve watching the moon and how good it was to feel skin against hers again. But what came out of her mouth was the crude line: 'What I want you for is sex!' He hung up on her immediately and she flung herself onto her bed crying in fury at herself for sabotaging everything.

(She rang to apologise, she wrote him a letter, she even gave him some of her poems but it seemed she could not speak her way out of that shocking moment.)

The woman's words 'What I want *you* for is sex' made us laugh when we heard them. We could imagine any number of powerful outspoken feminist comedians uttering such an outrageous line, and getting away with it. But here there was no audience to laugh – only the man who could not tolerate her words and who withdrew into silence. Her words create a fracture or break in the line of force he is taking up, sending them in different directions. Men are no longer supposed to speak such words, he knows, so why should a woman speak them and get away with it? He breaks the relationship with silence, joining the father in the second story and the boys/men in the third story in the task of educating girls/women with the knowledge of how to be appropriate feminine subjects. His silence is very powerful. He may have temporarily lost the position of confident, dominating male, while she spoke her angry words, but he is nonetheless supported by 'the overall effect of [the] strategic positions' of men as a dominating class (Deleuze, 1988: 25). She panics. She reads his silence as a line of force on her actions and repeatedly tries to undo her words. She is no longer positioned as a good or worthy woman. Maybe she is also the slut the father worried about and whom the boys raped. These knowledges are inescapable. She cannot find the form of knowledge/power that will enable her to reposition herself as the right kind of woman. She seems caught, again, between two positions, but this time both are undesirable.

Her words seem to have been too much. Yet how could she not speak them? She knows (has access to explicit knowledges that tell her) that both men and women, nowadays, have the right to set boundaries. She also knows that men may not 'hear' or respect boundaries set by women. If men make mistakes these will be overlooked, or at least tolerated, by good women. On the other hand, women who speak directly risk rejection from men – desirable women are submissive, speak gently and are always available. Generally, she knows, women do not set agendas in relationships. Women who make mistakes may not get a second chance. She knows all of this. It is common-sense knowledge. But she is also a feminist and bent upon making life into its own *telos*. It seems that the two moralities that we discussed in Chapter 3 are also at work here:

> In the first form . . . morality is obedience to a heteronomous code which we must accept, and to which we are bound by fear and guilt. In the second, morality is an exercise in ascetics, whereby through experimentation, exercise and permanent work on oneself one can make life into its own *telos*.
>
> (Rose, 1999: 97)

But the man's withdrawal into silence makes the positioning of herself in the second morality a difficult one to maintain. Instead, she gets caught up in a morality of obedience to a heteronomous code motivated by fear or guilt – she repeatedly attempts to undo her words with gifts, but only finds herself reiterating the wrongness of what she said caught in the impossible, irreversible, fatal trap of speech where '[w]hat has been said cannot be unsaid, *except by adding to it*,' caught in what Barthes calls 'stammering . . . a message spoiled twice over . . . a *misfire*' (Barthes, 1989: 76).

The woman is caught, like the 14-year-old girl coming home late, in the guilty situation of having been found to be the wrong kind of woman. As one who conducts her own conduct, she finds her conduct faulty. She stammers, she stutters, her words are like a machine that signals it is not working. Her creative moment of freedom, in which she experienced herself as powerful, is not working. Her words were powerfully active, but so too is her lover's reaction – his withdrawal into silent disapproval. As Rose observes, 'creativity arises out of the situation of human beings engaged in particular relations of force and meaning' and out of the possibilities of any particular location. Our attempts at creativity or freedom, he says, are generally 'cautious, modest, pragmatic, experimental, stuttering, tentative' and they emerge 'in "cramped spaces" – within a set of relations that are intolerable, where movement is impossible, where change is blocked and voice is strangulated' (Rose, 1999: 279–280). They are opportunistic and prone to backfire.

In this story we see that the position of the dominator is not necessarily an unambiguous one. She takes control, he becomes silent, she is overwhelmed by grief. She wants to undo her own moment of ascendancy: 'the power-relation is the set of possible relations between forces which pass through the dominated forces no less than through the dominating' (Deleuze, 1988: 27). Power is not *held* by the woman, rather relations of power both presuppose and actualize knowledge: 'No doubt power, if we consider it in the abstract, neither sees nor speaks . . . precisely because it does not itself speak and see, it makes us see and speak' (Deleuze, 1988: 82).

In this sense, to return to the gang rapists, they are not the ones who produce and control the discourse that is actualized in their act of domination and control. They can nevertheless (and this is an important distinction) be held responsible and accountable inside moral and legal discourses. To the extent that they take the discourse up and make it their own as they carry out the act of rape, and to the extent that they do not seek alternative discourses, then they can be said to be agents driving forward the blind mole of power as they violently deprive others of their power. They may well be ambivalent about their own act, but they do not allow their ambivalence to surface. Phil, in contrast, can recognize the ambivalence and retreat: he has immediate access to another rationality, that of protecting his girl who is innocent.

In our final story the woman is now a wife. She is travelling with her husband and children in Yugoslavia in 1980. Here the bid for freedom from the control of others comes not as her own, but as a plan between her husband and a young man they meet on the train:

They are travelling second class through Jugoslavia. She already has an edgy feeling. Long bread queues and lack of even basic consumer goods in the shops unsettle her. Her children are inspired by the aura of revolution and the tall, strong, attractive people. She feels uneasy. They are being watched. Sullen, hard looks are directed at them by their fellow passengers. One of them leaves the carriage and comes back with two soldiers. Her husband's medical book is grabbed and taken outside the carriage. The other soldier produces a gun and stands guard over them until the book is returned. The pictures of naked bodies have been removed. This experience heightens her sense of apprehension and oppression.

They strike up a conversation with a young architect. He's trying to leave the country and he has to get his money past the guards. They share wine, food, laughter and stories. Her dark mood lifts. Maybe she is just imagining the threat. The wine is doing its work. She's lulled into a sense of security and drifts into a semi-drugged sleep. The voices drone on and on.

'Could I have your bag darling?'

Her bag is opened and money stuffed inside. He can't expect her to do this. She objects but he insists. She's angry but compliant. It's too dangerous to cause a fuss, there's a soldier stationed outside the carriage door. She spends the rest of the night fitfully on the edge of dreams. She feels overwhelmed by the image of being caught, and her terror is periodically exacerbated by torchlight sweeping across the carriage. The soldier is maintaining his vigil. She can't give the money back to him, someone might see, he might make a fuss, her husband would look a fool. If they're caught she supposes she'll go to prison. She will say it was her idea – at least her husband and children will be safe. Images flit before her of torture and deprivation, of isolation in a strange land. Years without seeing her family.

The train is slowing down. They've crossed the border into Austria.

'Wake up darling, give me the bag'. He slips the money into the hand of their friend. He leaves the train. They wave to him as he stands with the other illegal immigrants on the station platform.

The woman finds herself positioned as an attachment, but also a useful vehicle, for the men's grand adventure. She is silenced by the twinned forces of state and marriage. She reads the state she is travelling through as oppressive and dangerous, and her marriage as neither of these, yet it is the combination of both that works here to keep her silent. Her situation can be compared to what Foucault calls a state of domination:

> in which the power relations, instead of being mobile, allowing the various participants to adopt strategies modifying them, remain blocked, frozen. When an individual or social group succeeds in blocking a field of power relations, immobilizing them and preventing any reversibility of movement by economic, political, or military means, one is faced with what may be called a state of domination. In such a state, it is certain that practices of freedom do not exist or exist only unilaterally or are extremely constrained and limited.
>
> (Foucault, 1997d: 283)

The men can be seen in this story to be caught up in a grand narrative, involving state oppression and revolution, in which the stakes are high. They plan to overturn the state of domination in which the young man finds himself. They guess, perhaps, that the woman will be seen as an appendage only, and that the gun-wielding guards will not be able to imagine her as complicit in their adventure. Perhaps the husband judges that the risk to his wife's safety is not too great, as he joins in this line of action against the controlling state. In engaging that knowledge (rationality) of women's marginality in Yugoslavia at that time, he acts out and makes real that same knowledge, in a relation of power where his wife is completely silenced, and made vulnerable. Not through a state of domination based on 'economic, political, or military means' but on the sedimentation of husband–wife practices and knowledges. She will be silent to protect him, she will do as he wants, she will support his adventure, she will accept his moral stand, and she will, ultimately, if necessary, protect his life and the children's because that is what a good wife and mother would do. A story fit for an opera, where men and state engage in struggle, and good women love them and die for them, and where the men may die also, having claimed their fame through standing for something that mattered. In agreeing to be positioned as the woman and the wife who belongs in this way in this kind of drama, she might be said to be complicit in her own domination, to be presupposing and actualizing particular forms of knowledge and of power-relations between men and women. The husband's dominance in this reading is not an act of violence, because the wife has access to several ways of behaving. But that ignores the force of the state on her actions.

If we look at the husband–wife relation, putting to one side, for the moment, the role of the state, we can see the husband's dominance as a way of governing the wife's actions – as structuring her possible field of actions. Foucault points out, in examining the ways men and women relate to each other in the position of 'husbands' and 'wives', that 'one should not assume a massive and primal condition of domination, a binary structure with "dominators" on one side and "dominated" on the other, but rather a multiform production of relations of domination' (1980e: 142). The primary dominating line of force in this story, however, is the state. The state looms large in the wife's consciousness as a frightening and intractable force. At the same time that line of force is, in practice, linked to her subjection as woman. All the questions she asks herself about how to reverse the situation both presuppose and actualize the knowledges she has that bind her into her position as woman, as the one who does not have the right to protect herself. In the normal course of events, Foucault observes, those who are dominated by others in positions of power 'are not only its inert or consenting target; they are always also the elements of its articulation . . . individuals are the vehicles of power, not its points of application' (Foucault, 1980a: 98). The woman articulates herself as woman and is also positioned as woman, inside a context in which dissent from her womanly submission would bring very real danger to all of them.

This raises further questions: when do practices of freedom 'not exist' and when are they 'extremely constrained and limited'? What degrees of freedom are needed for power relations to be fluid? And when is 'liberation' necessary first? In elaborating the relations between power and freedom, Foucault invokes the image of a man 'chained up and beaten'. Foucault says this man is subject to force, not to power:

> if he can be induced to speak, when his ultimate recourse could have been to hold his tongue preferring death, then he has been caused to behave in a certain way. His freedom has been subjected to power. He has been submitted to government. There is no power without potential refusal or revolt.
>
> (Foucault, 1981: 253)

The wife's situation could be said to be close to that of the man in chains who speaks when he would choose not to. This wife is *caught* in relations of power to the extent that her identity is ensnared by those relations of power:

Power is not exercised simply as an obligation or a prohibition on those who 'do not have it'; it invests them, is transmitted by them and through them; it exerts pressure upon them, just as they themselves in their struggle against it, resist the grip it has on them.

(Foucault, 1979: 27)

Not only do they resist, as Foucault points out, but through the same process they become invested in the power that is held over them. The wife is also, at the same time, in a context in which several lives are at risk if she speaks. Her state of domination (in which the freedom to speak can be said not to exist) is achieved through the combination of three complex tangled lines of force: her embeddedness in relations of power in her family; the husband's location in an adventure that sets out to disrupt the state of domination experienced in a foreign state; and her location inside a moral discourse that makes it unthinkable to place her own safety before that of her husband and children.

And so . . .

In undertaking this engagement between our own embodied memories and Foucauldian theory, we have followed a path described by Deleuze (1995: 86):

When people follow Foucault, when they're fascinated by him, it's because they're doing something with him, in their own work, in their own independent lives. It's not just a question of intellectual understanding or agreement, but of intensity, of resonance, musical harmony.

The analytic strategies that suggest themselves from a post-structuralist point of view, and that we have taken up here, are ones that look for and work with the lines of fault, the forking and rupture of knowledges that are already in play. At the same time they require us to 'work on the ground' of our lived experience, to engage in a reflexive examination of our own discursive practices and to extend our knowledge of how speaking- and writing-as-usual create and sustain cultures of practice that we wish to move beyond. At the same time, knowledge cannot be changed without also addressing the relations of power presupposed in those knowledges. In undertaking this analysis we have dismantled everyday readings of relations of power between men and women. We have engaged in what Foucault calls a radical criticism that is indispensable to social transformation:

Criticism consists in uncovering that thought and trying to change it; showing that things are not as obvious as people believe, making it so that what is taken for granted is no longer taken for granted. To do criticism is to make harder those acts which are now too easy.

Understood in these terms, criticism (and radical criticism) is utterly indispensable for any transformation ... as soon as people begin to have trouble thinking things the way they have been thought, transformation becomes at the same time very urgent, very difficult, and entirely possible.

(Foucault 2000a: 456–457)

Our trajectory in this chapter has been double. First, it has been towards uncovering the ways in which girls and women might be said to be powerful, even when they are complicit in their own subjection. Second, it has been to show that when Foucault defines all acts of power to involve the possibility of resistance and freedom, and he takes the opposite, a state of domination, to arise from 'economic, political, or military means', he has not fully taken on board the extent to which the repeated, minute accretions of everyday practices can generate sedimentations of lines of force that may also be understood as a state of domination.

In the final substantive chapter we describe a collective biography that we convened in order to revisit the site of the radical theoretical break with the liberal humanist individual marked by the post-structuralist work of Henriques et al. ([1984] 1998) and the feminist post-structuralist work of Weedon ([1987] 1997). These writers suggest that the new subject of post-structuralist theory will be more open to the changes desired by feminist and social justice movements. They describe the break with the liberal humanist subject as a break that heralds new possibilities of personal and cultural transformation. In this chapter, using the medium of collective biography stories, we revisit the relation between the liberal humanist individual and the transformative possibilities post-structuralist writers envisaged for the new subject of post-structuralism. We situate the discussion in the context of our transformation into neo-liberal subjects over the last three decades. This last workshop of this series was conducted after Sue and Bronwyn had both left North Queensland and Magnetic Island and moved to the city of Sydney. It is conducted in Bronwyn's inner-city apartment but also on the nearby hotel rooftop looking out over the harbour. It took place in a much more pressured environment over three days, in the middle of which Bronwyn flew to Brisbane to speak at the memorial ceremony of her dearest friend Carolyn Baker who had died the week before. None of that grief shows up in the chapter, but here you will find little of the luxurious bodily presence of some of the earlier chapters.

9

Constituting 'the feminist subject' in post-structuralist discourse[15]

Thirty years on from the post-structural revolution and the radical revisions of what it meant to be a transformable subject in the context of psychological and feminist practice (Weedon, [1987] 1997), it is timely to revisit the questions first raised by post-structuralist thinkers, such as Foucault and Barthes, and taken up by feminists such as Weedon, psychologists such as Henriques et al. ([1984] 1998), and philosophers such as Butler (1993). The new feminist post-structuralist subject has been theorized as more open to the cultural and personal changes envisaged by feminism (Henriques et al., [1984] 1998; Weedon, [1987] 1997). That new subject has been theorized as fluid, fragmented, with more open boundaries (Davies, 2000a), as coexisting with the texts in which it is constituted, texts in which contradictions can be embraced (Cixous and Derrida, 2001) and played with, and, through that play, generate new possibilities of being (Barthes, 1977b). Barthes uses his own autobiography to explore what coexisting with text, and play with that text, might mean:

> Do I not know that, *in the field of the subject, there is no referent*? The fact, (whether biological or textual) is abolished in the signifier, because it immediately *coincides* with it. . . . I myself am my own symbol, I am the story which happens to me: freewheeling in language.
>
> (Barthes, 1977b: 56, original emphases)

This is not a freewheeling that is directed by the rational subject of liberal humanism who exists separate from the text, producing and directing its own trajectory. It is a subject inscribed and reinscribed with discourses that the subject did not produce and which always remain, at least in part, opaque.

Whereas liberal feminism had constituted feminist change primarily in terms of individual women's rights, and radical feminism rejected the male symbolic order in favour of a celebration of the feminine, post-structuralist feminism envisaged a radical deconstruction of the male/female binary and of essentializing practices that locked individuals into particular subject positions or categorizations (Kristeva, 1981). The categories themselves were to be deconstructed and along with them the modes of being that those categorizations had made real. This was envisaged as a move away from the liberal humanist subject. At the same time as feminist post-structuralist writers were exploring just what these transformations might make possible (for example, Davies [1989] 2003; [1993] 2003) another global, socio-political movement was under way. Neo-liberalism, driven forward by conservative political leaders such as Thatcher and Reagan, and now perpetuated and furthered by leaders of all political persuasions, envisaged a new hybrid subject – a subject with the flexibility of the post-structuralist/postmodern subject, but built on a radical reconception of an individualized, competitive, free and responsibilized subject, a subject that understands itself, in liberal humanist terms, as free and in control of itself and responsible for its own fate. This neo-liberal subject is primarily inscribed with economic discourses of survival/success, and has, as such, a commitment to the national economic project of competition and survival (Davies and Bansel, 2005; Davies and Petersen, 2005a, 2005b). The vulnerability of the subject to this inscription of itself as the neo-liberal subject is tied to the intensified dangers in late capitalism of non-survival. The will to become the new subject is necessarily a personal project taken up in the interests of individual survival:

> security is seen as emanating from people's capacity to adapt. Either they are flexible and adaptable, open to change, capable of finding new projects, and live in relative personal security, or they are not and will be put aside when the current project finishes.
>
> (Chiapello and Fairclough, 2002: 30)

Many feminists (including those in the public service who came to be known in Australia, often derisively, as the femocrats) were drawn to the neo-liberal forms of governmentality. Its seductive rhetoric included the promise to deliver gender equity and other forms of social justice. While neo-liberalism has undoubtedly delivered accelerated careers for some individual women, perhaps especially those who actively take up neo-liberal discourses as a form of management of self and others, its philosophy is one that is anti-critique, and in particular anti-critique of government (Sklar, 1980). Earlier in this book, in Chapters 4 and 5, we mounted a critique of neo-liberalism in our academic workplaces but our analyses demonstrated how we actively incorporated – despite critique and despite moments of resistance – these discourses within our embodied everyday practices, our modes of being and our desires.

In the writing of Henriques et al. and of Weedon we find a (relatively unexamined) claim that the post-structuralist analysis of the processes of subjectification opened the way for a new kind of subject who was more open to change. We can assume that it was not the flexible, changing, individualized, neo-liberal subject, exploited by late capitalism, that they had in mind. The changes they envisaged were linked, rather, to Foucault's later work in which he had turned his analytic gaze on how discourse and related systems of power work in the constitution of individual subjects to subjugate and govern them, and how that power might also be turned towards critique and transformation. He suggested that critique could make old forms of being no longer thinkable, no longer able to dominate and control: 'as soon as people begin to have trouble thinking things the way they have been thought, transformation becomes at the same time very urgent, very difficult, and entirely possible' (Foucault, 2000a: 457).

In Weedon's writing, the post-structuralist critique does double work. It shows, first, that the humanist individual is not what it thought it was. It is caught in fictions of itself as unitary, rational and centred, in control of its own subjectivity. And second, if that individual would look, she argues, with a 'post-structural' lens, it would see its own fictionality, its precarious, contradictory, constantly-in-process subjecthood. In the very act of taking up this new way of looking it would become someone else: a post-structuralist subject more able to turn a reflexive gaze on discourse and able to work on discourse itself in order to reconstitute the world in less oppressive ways. But what is the nature of this shift, this slide, this flight, into a new kind of subjecthood that can bring about change? What kinds of transformative possibilities are opened up in post-structuralist critique? What makes for a feminist or social justice transformation, as opposed to a neo-liberal transformation, in which subjugation to the interests of capital is taken on both willingly and (and perhaps a little) blindly?

Fundamental to the shift in Foucault's analysis of transformation is making the 'silent habits' of thought visible and thus more difficult to continue with. The shift takes place through the insertion of new ways of thinking and being into the disciplines and professions through which we are monitored and through which and in relation to which we go on becoming subjects. Such an awareness means we are, in one sense, no longer the naive liberal humanist subject – the essentialized, unique, universal and unhistorical subject who believes itself to be creating itself and is blind to the constitutive effects of discourses and systems of thought. This naive subject, one who has become an object to be observed and analysed by psychologists and by itself, occasionally reappears in our speaking and writing. Yet she has also become the one who we can no longer imaginably be (Butler, 1993: 188). This is so even though, paradoxically, our emotional and autobiographical roots are deeply entangled in just that specific, apparently unique, subject (St Pierre, 2000).

How might we make sense of this paradox? All subjects are produced not only through dominant discourses and regulatory practices but also through the opening up of new possibilities in language (Davies, 2000a). All subjects – including the transformed (or more correctly, the transforming) post-structuralist subject, who is capable of critically analysing the constitutive force of discourse – are always inside language. To change discourse is also, at least in part, at least for the moment, to change oneself. But while critique of discourse may work to make it, as Foucault says, *unthinkable*, the deconstructive process is always partial, messy and incomplete. The transforming post-structuralist subject is not the rational, unified subject, newly liberated from liberal humanism. The newly transforming subject is aware of its own messiness, its own vulnerability to the processes through which it is subjugated and governed, aware that reason 'is produced within discourses in which certain statements are privileged and others are silenced or excluded' and that 'reason is always situated, local and specific, formed by values and passions and desires' (St Pierre, 2000: 487). As Barthes points out, post-structuralist theorists do not have a place to go to outside of language that would enable them to look in on it and destroy it. When they make a critique of any discourse, or attempt to dismantle it, they are also inside it:

> In order to destroy, in short, we must be able to *overleap*. But overleap where? Into what language? Into which site of good conscience and bad faith? Whereas by decomposing, I agree to accompany such decomposition, to decompose myself as well in the process: I scrape, catch and drag.
>
> (Barthes, 1977b: 63, original emphasis)

Discursively constituted as we are, the constitutive effect resides not just in language, but in the affect of the material body. Decomposition is not just a play with words, but work on that material body.

The process of transformation, then, is not so much the result of a rational choice to be someone or something else in particular, but a movement, a 'decomposition', an engagement in a messy process in which one 'scrapes and catches and drags' in a complex process of reinscription, of rubbing out the unthinkable; a decomposition, and a fractured, messy recomposition – of thought and of body. In that work of re-imagining the possibilities we are always, also the inevitable *effect* of discourse, through the 'reiterative and citational *practice* by which discourse effects what it names ... [and] the reiterative power of discourse to produce the phenomena that it regulates and constrains' (Butler, 1993: 2, emphases added). The challenge of the post-structuralist transformative project is twofold:

- to see what the new questions posed by Foucault and other post-structuralist writers, along with their conceptual repertoire, enable us to see about *what we are now*
- and in making visible what we are now, to develop strategies (conceptual and practical) for making a radical break with current forms of domination, for imagining a new kind of subject.

What Henriques et al. ([1984] 1998) analysed in their book *Changing the Subject* were the processes of individualizing and totalizing that Foucault suggested we might refuse. They provide one of the best analyses of the ways in which individualizing practices are tied to governmentality and, in particular, to the ways in which psychology, as a discipline and as a set of practices, is implicated in the governing of individuals. In terms of what we are now, Venn ([1984] 1998) argues, the modern humanist individual can be seen to be historically specific, but its current forms have been interiorized and naturalized. In taking itself up as rational, and as wilful, the individual understands itself to be choosing what it will be, when it is actually being given little choice about those categorizations. It can conform to the categories inside of which it has been placed, within its own specific cultural and historical location, or it can resist and so encounter all the social, discursive, legal and disciplinary forces that will attempt to bring it into line. But it cannot undo, or avoid being positioned in relation to, the category itself.

In terms of developing strategies for change, Henriques et al. were optimistic that their deconstructive work could give rise to change. The deconstruction of common-sense knowledge about human beings and our lived experience, they say:

> involves prising apart the meanings and assumptions fused together in the ways we understand ourselves in order to see them as historically specific products, rather than as timeless and incontrovertible given facts. Such an analysis of the construction of the modern form of individuality is a prerequisite for understanding and bringing about change.
>
> (Henriques et al., [1984] 1998: 2)

Like Foucault, they see those changes as a continuation of earlier struggles, such as the feminist work towards consciousness change – the crucial shift being 'the necessity of understanding consciousness as something produced rather than as the source' (ibid.: 8). Protest movements and social transformations, they argue (ibid.: 3–5), become more possible if we imagine the self as not fixed, but as potentially entering into a kaleidoscope of possibilities.

In understanding this potential we are faced with another interesting paradox. If we understand ourselves in post-structuralist terms as constituted through discourse and as subjects in process, then the programmatic changes of social movements that we initially committed to may look different in light of new dominant discourses such as neo-liberalism. Or, through viewing feminist discourses, such as liberal feminism or radical feminism through the newly opened position of post-structuralist feminist subjectivity, the original commitments may (and one might even argue should) change. This is not to argue that post-structuralists are 'mindless relativists' who are incapable of being committed to and desiring specific changes (Davies, 1998), but the transforming subject we might become is not one that can necessarily be pre-programmed, or made immune to new and dominant discourses.

Collective biography as post-structuralist writing practice

In what follows we will explore the transformative potential of post-structuralist critique through collective biography. We will draw on Barthes's concept of decomposition and our own concept of mo(ve)ment. We will unravel – through focused collective work – the rational choosing subjects of our individual biographies, necessitating a shift from the rational possibilities of deconstruction to the embodied subject decomposing itself. We focus on the specific remembered moments and on the movement that becomes visible in the particular mode of memory-writing.

In this collective biography, we focused on the subject and how she might be read through humanist and post-structuralist discourses. As we have in other projects described in this book, we took up a dual strategy of retrieving memories and using those memories as data that can be analysed to produce insights into the processes of subjectification, that is the dual processes through which we become specific individuals actively taking up as our own the terms of our subjection, and through which we are categorized, totalized and governed. In our workshop we told and wrote stories from early memories: of 'being someone'; of 'being hailed as someone in a way that felt good'; and of 'being mis-recognized'. We chose these topics as triggers for memories that would take us into the earliest memories we had of being a subject, of taking pleasure in being a subject, and of defending our right to be a particular subject, in order to examine more closely these questions about being caught up in humanist forms of subjection and about the transformative mo(ve)ments entailed in reconstituting ourselves post-structurally.

Our memories tapped into our deeply felt and specifically liberal–humanist desires to be taken up (by others and ourselves) as unique and individual. The form of writing that we have developed in collective biography peels away those clichés, generalities and explanations that are the specific technologies of self used by the rational individual of liberal humanism, and attempts to lay bare the bones and flesh of ourselves as embodied subjects-in-process as we remember ourselves in one particular moment in time. We abandon the constructions of ourselves as who and what we should be, of the self that takes itself up within the readily available categories of everyday discourses, and that moves too rapidly from the specific moment to general observations. We work to recover the embodied detail of specific moments, details that might otherwise be lost in the rendition of oneself as a unique and rational subject who remains essentially the same over time and varying contexts. In doing so we constitute, through the mode of telling, another subject cut adrift from its liberal humanist moorings, and able to be seen in one particular moment, being constituted through multiple discourses, a subject who is in process, a verb rather than a noun, a subject with boundaries permeated by others, by discourse, a subject identical with the text through which it is being constituted.

We began this collective biography by gathering together relevant readings in order to begin thinking through the paradox of the subject and to generate the prompts we would use to shape our workshop sessions. Then we gathered together for three days in the heart of Sydney, far away from our usual meeting place on Magnetic Island. During each session, we took turns to tell stories relating to the topic of being a subject, of being subjected. We sought to tell the detail of the remembered moments, not as a story through which individualized, naturalized humanist identity is accomplished, but as a moment lived and remembered bodily. The rational moorings of the individualized subject are untied (for the moment) in this process.

When we wrote and then read our stories to each other, we asked questions of the writer until that precise detailed moment became imaginable in a lived bodily sense. How did it smell, how did it feel on your skin, your face, your stomach, your back? These are the kinds of questions that we asked. In this process of listening to and asking questions about each other's memories we found more of our own detail, sometimes in similarity, sometimes in contrast, and in the process, saw more of our own specificity. In that very specific detail we also found that our individuality is not as unique as we had supposed. The memories, in this sense become collective – collective because we have all imagined being there, in each moment, in intense bodily detail, and collective, too, because we have seen ourselves, in our memories of being constituted as specific individuals, as being constituted just like each other, through the same set of discourses and discursive practices – albeit each with her own specific history and her own bodily specificity. The commonalities became more readily visible, perhaps, than the specific differences as we began the work of decomposing the liberal humanist individual we had each (imagined we had) become. We looked at our memories as not just autobiographical, but also the means to make visible the discursive processes in which we are each collectively caught up. In this way the process of collective biography engages with the first challenge of post-structuralist work – to examine what we are now making visible, the constitutive power of discourse in constituting ourselves as subjects.

The subject re-membered

Our first memory is of the accomplishment of a complex task.

Buying the paper on Saturday morning
She looks carefully one way then the other then back again. There are lots of cars on Ogilvie Street on Saturday mornings. When the time is right she steps straight down onto the road and walks as quickly as she can, straight across, her hand in her pocket holding onto the coin that Dad has given her. She makes it to the other side, to the footpath in front of Dr Bennett's. She knows the way by heart. Down the side street, across the railway station car park and up the ramp, watching the sky with one arm bent back across her head to protect her scalp from the magpies that swoop down from the pines. Halfway over the railway bridge she pauses to look down onto the tracks. If she's lucky a train will come under while she waits. Then up the little passage between the shops, over Bair Street at the crossing and into the newsagent. She prac- tices the words in her mind before she says them: 'Can I have The Age newspaper please?' She surrenders the sweaty coin to the lady behind the counter and the lady gives her the paper and the change that Dad lets her keep for herself. She tucks the paper under her arm and walks down the busy street to her next stop. The Health Food shop has a whole wall made up of little wooden doors with glass windows that you can see through. She points up to one of them and walks out with a five-cent bag full of the jagged chunks of dark cooking chocolate that she loves best. Then she crosses the road again and enters the café. She uses both her hands to pull her body up onto a high stool at the counter and sits there, reading the list of flavours on the wall. But she has what she always has – Blue Heaven lemonade – in a heavy milk- shake glass with a stripy waxed paper straw. It's the clearest blue bubbly sparkly drink, like the sky in summer, or the colour of water in a swimming pool. The first sip is sweet and smooth on her tongue, and bubbly up her nose, the taste a little bit tingly like mint but different. She sips it slowly to make it last as long as she can. She slurps up the last traces from the bottom of the deep glass through her straw. She sits there quietly for a few moments longer. At last she slides off the stool and picks up Dad's paper and the chocolate. Her pockets are empty now but the sweet taste of heaven lingers in her mouth and her tongue is still as blue as a lizard's by the time she reaches home.

This memory can be reread in liberal humanist terms as the detailed telling of the successfully appropriate(d) individual. She is rational, autonomous and responsible. She has undoubtedly accomplished herself as a 'unitary, individual and rational subject' (Venn, [1984] 1998: 151). She knows how to take care of herself (the magpies), to take due care in dangerous settings (crossing the street), to act in a trustworthy way (spending the money as intended), to be articulate (asking for the paper), and to be literate and numerate (she reads the menu, she manages the money).

So how is a post-structuralist reading of the memory different from this and what does it make possible? How does post-structuralist writing and reading make visible the performative and relational nature of being a subject that is accomplished through specific discourses in specific times and places?

Through the specific embodied detail of the memory and also in the gaps and silences, we can see how the child is positioned by the father and by the townspeople at that time as one who can act autonomously. That available subject position of autonomous subject is one she can and does take up as her own. She rehearses the relevant lines and competences as she goes along, both rehearsing and competently performing them. The subject position she can be seen to be taking up is not only lodged within the discourses of individual competency and autonomy. It is also lodged within capitalism. She *has* identity because she *has* money to spend. Further, she is a 'girl' in this story, implicitly lodging herself and being lodged in a discourse of femininity, relationality and reliability. Although the memory is told without any other characters appearing in it, the relations within which she is made possible are everywhere evident in the story. As she judges when to step on to the street and cross it, we can imagine in the gaps the voice of the parent instructing her in this practice. She knows the way 'by heart', it is in her body, but the instructions are almost audible: it is Saturday morning, Ogilvie Street is busy, wait until there are no cars, walk straight across to the other side. We can hear the father pointing out the train, we can see the shop attendants listening to her and we can imagine her sticking out her blue lizard tongue when she gets home to show how blue it is.

At the same time as the girl constitutes herself in this memory as inhabiting the position of autonomous subject, we can say that her father has called her into that position by giving her the money and the responsibility. The townspeople, too, recognize her as legitimately occupying that position by not insisting that she go home, or treating her as if she is unsafe or untrustworthy. She is treated as a legitimate customer in each shop she visits and enters into transactions as if it is legitimate for her to do so. Such recognition, we might add, cannot be taken for granted – adult shopkeepers often fail to notice the child would-be customer. On this occasion they interpolate her into the subject position of responsible girl-child who is read as recognizably present, and having legitimate money to spend. The girl's quest for social recognition, for visibility, for association, for significance is achieved in this relational accomplishment on her part in interaction with others. In this way recognition forms the subject: 'the "I" neither precedes nor follows the process . . . but emerges only within and as a matrix of . . . relations themselves' (Butler, 1993: 7).

The ambivalence between the willed effect of the subject and the subject's dependence on discourse/the other is evident in the way the memory is told, with its emphasis on the solitary and heroic nature of her Saturday morning quest revealing the way that heroic narratives are woven into the accomplishment of herself as competent subject. She downplays the interactive nature of the encounter and constructs the tale of autonomy by papering over her dependence on the recognition of others and her subjection to the forms by which she has become recognizable as trustworthy and autonomous. This movement between the grand narrative and the small detail is one that post-structuralist writers are intrigued by. The heroic journey may be crossed out as the appropriate reading of what one is, but it nevertheless is there, in a partially rubbed-out palimpsest, criss-crossing the reading, informing its interpretation.

The memory might thus be said to 'reveal' the individual subject as she is constituted and constitutes herself through dominant discourses. The memory is vivid precisely because the fiction of herself as the autonomous subject is so skilfully achieved. The detail of the telling makes visible the constitutive work that is going on, and that has gone on, to make that (illusion of the) autonomous subject possible. In refraining from invoking the naturalized individual who can be described and explained as always having been this person, or this person in the making, the story opens another possibility: I see the way in which this kind of subjecthood is granted, and I therefore also see how, on other occasions, it might not be granted – to me, to anyone. I see my attachment to it, I see my dependence on it, and thus my vulnerability to it. The way opens in this visibility, in this shedding of the linear moorings to an explanation of 'who I am', an 'I am' that lies outside the text, to a recognition of the co-extension of oneself with the text, and thus as a text that can be rewritten, played with, opened up to something else. There is something deeply paradoxical about this moment. Having focused on what is embodied, on what may seem to have the ontological status of fact, we nevertheless encounter, as Barthes says, the sense that there is no fixed referent existing outside the text. We are the story happening to us, we are 'freewheeling in language' (Barthes, 1977b: 56).

The subject is always vulnerable to the possibility that the terms of its conferred existence might be disrupted by the withholding of recognition, or some kind of sudden break in the certainty of belonging (Davies et al., 2001, 2002). In our second memory, the child's confidence and competence is interrupted with a moment of loss:

Catching the train
Confidently, she walks towards the train, flanked by her father and mother, her small legs walking sturdily over the grubby platform. She has her favourite book tucked firmly under her arm – it's the one about Our Lady appearing to the three children at Fatima. It had beautiful pictures in bright, wonderful colours, especially the one of Our Lady balanced on a cloud over the small tree.

She sees the steam coming from the train; the hissing sound it makes is so loud and exciting. They are going on holidays and she is looking forward to reading her book again as they ride in the train. The pleasure of looking forward to a loved book AND a holiday makes a warm feeling spread from her stomach all through her body. And, she has a new blue overcoat, too, with black velvet collar and pocket flaps!

They are coming near the train – it looms big and black in front of her. There is a gap between the platform and their carriage, very big for her short legs. Her father puts out a hand to help her, excitement causes her to almost stumble and she drops her book. From the carriage, she peers back into the dark gap and sees the book's bright colours lying on the oily dirt of the railway tracks. She can't bear to lose it and puts out her hand as if to pick it up, but her father says it is too dangerous and she has to leave it. All during the train trip, she can only see her loved book, torn and crumpled under the harsh, uncaring, dangerous wheels of the train.

In this story we read a story of longing and belonging (Davies, 2000a). The child is constituted as one who longs for the book, to be the one who reads the book, who revels in its beautiful, saintly imagery. Her body glows with the idea of the book, her book. She *is* the book and its beautiful pictures, she sees them in her mind's eye. They are part of her. And now she is *also* the adventurer going on the train. The train looms huge and exciting. She imagines sitting safely within it, with her book, and rushing away on her holiday. Then there is a sudden break. A fracture. The book is lost and she is vulnerable. She reaches out to reconnect with the book, to save it, but it is not possible. Her father restrains her with rational argument – it is too dangerous to save the book. The book is torn and crumpled. The train is dangerous. It does not care for her. Its otherness, its dangerous uncaring force looms in her consciousness, separating her off from the landscape she inhabits. The child is constituted as transforming from the competent, confident child looking forward, into the vulnerable girl child, experiencing loss, no longer enjoying her adventure. The longing and belonging she tells of in the first part of the memory where she and the book and the train were one in an exciting adventure is transformed into an unfulfillable longing for the lost, damaged book with its beautiful images crushed under the wheels of the train. This memory gives us a glimpse of the clash of the father's rationality and the girl's desire. It opens up a moment to inspection of becoming the rational appropriate(d) subject whose sense of vulnerability and despair are made unspeakable since they lie outside the rational. The feeling is contained and focused in the image of the book crumpled and torn by the uncaring wheels of the train.

Our third memory is one of being mis-recognized. We have chosen this memory for its struggle with the constitutive work of the other.

(Not) smelling the roses
We were walking home from school, to my friend's house. Along the way we came to the most amazing garden full of roses. The bushes were laden with flowers – pale pink, deep pink, reds and yellows and whites. I was amazed at how beautiful they were, glowing in the late afternoon light. Let's smell them I said. My friend was hesitant. There was a neighbour who got mad at some kids from the public school who picked the roses. She knew those kids because she used to go to the public school. I looked at the neighbours' gardens and there was no-one in sight. She'll see that we're just smelling them, I said, it will be obvious we're not picking them. So we stood on the brick base of the fence, a wary eye out for peering next-door neighbours. We spread our arms out so our hands were visible on the top rail of the fence and leaned our faces towards the roses in sweet anticipation and with a faint sense of angelic virtue. Right then, from across the other side of the wide road, came a shouting voice: Stop picking the roses! You children! I know about you! I've seen you stealing the roses before!

She went on and on shouting. We stood down from the fence and out onto the footpath, our empty hands visible, but she kept on shouting. I was shocked. My head felt tight and my lips and throat went dry. How could she not see that we were not stealing the roses? How could she not see our uniforms? I was overwhelmed with embarrassment and hot with shame. I did not want to be this person who was being shouted at across this wide road, that I was a thief. I felt hot and angry. I wanted to tell her we were not picking the roses but my throat was dry and my voice could not have reached across that wide road even if I wanted it to. It would be rude to stand there shouting across the road. We will have to go over and tell her, I croaked, but my friend whispered, urgent and afraid, she won't believe us, we have to go. She was right. The woman was not normal shouting like that. We walked on up the road, the shouting voice biting into my back between my shoulder blades.

In reading the text as a post-structuralist performance we can see the text as presenting a girl who, through reiterations of 'recognition' of 'who she is', has come to believe in the predictability or reliability of those recognitions. Further she has invested herself in them – the private school uniform in particular signalling who she is and wants to be. Meadmore,

Hatcher and McWilliam write about the clad body being, in Foucault's terms, 'the inscribed surface of events': 'The school uniform is one such inscription on the body; it inscribes gender and class differences, and more subtle differences within, between and among students' bodies as well' (Meadmore et al., 2000: 467). The surface inscription of the girl's body through the private school uniform, as one who will behave in trustworthy and responsible ways, offers not merely the possibility of a performance of 'private school girl', but a form of understanding and a pattern of desire and a clear set of constraints. She does not read the inscription as constraint. It is, as far as she is concerned, who she is – she is one who does not contemplate stealing the roses. Her inscription thus prescribes what she can do, and her actions are predicated on others knowing that. She depends on that knowledge for the small risks and freedoms that are possible within that particular inscription. She can be read, with that knowledge, as not picking the roses and so she is free to smell them. She is shocked when her uniform does not guarantee the recognition such knowledge would give. She is bodily shocked at the (mis)recognition accorded to the one she takes herself to be.

In this way it is interesting to see the force of self-inscription – the stranger cannot read the inscription of herself as she does, and she is outraged at her failure to do so. She expects and desires her inscription to be read correctly – that is, as she reads it. She is subjected to a certain discourse about how her behaviour will be. She takes this up as a form of power. She reads it as granting her certain freedoms – the freedom in this case to engage in risky behaviour and be read as innocent where others have been found guilty. Her subjection to the category of private school girls is thus also empowering, but that power depends on the capacity of others to read the category she has been subjected to. The failure of the other to recognize her gives her a sense of vulnerability. The predictability and manageability of the world are undermined by the other's (mis)recognition. Unless, of course, the other can be read as faulty – as mad – as an other who is incapable of reading correctly. She produces a reading of the woman that deprives her of her power and *at the same time* she still experiences the vulnerability that the shouting produces.

This reading shows the girl as being subjected through the discourses of her middle-class school, taking them up as powerful signifiers of who she is as an individual, and able to be used by her to take certain freedoms that others might not dare to take. Subjection and mastery coexist here, and that coexistence is made starkly visible by the (un)expected interruption to the moment of mastery. As Butler says: 'A theory of the subject should take into account the full ambivalence of the conditions of its operation' (Butler, 1997a: 14–15).

What, then, of the second task Foucault has suggested, of developing strategies (conceptual and practical) for making a radical break with current forms of domination, for imagining a new kind of subject? We argue that radical breaks are difficult, that this new subject is elusive and appears in mo(ve)ments when habitual ways of thinking are dislodged, are pulled out from under. This work can be done collectively, through interrogation of the selves that we habitually tell ourselves (and others) that we are. We can trace those mo(ve)ments in our memories, and in our work in rewriting those memories into this collective discursive space. Deconstruction is the name we give to the critical analytic work through which relations of power and the constitutive force of discourse is made visible. Decomposition is the name we might give to subjective movement through which we unmoor our embodied selves from those discourses we have worked on deconstructively to make them unthinkable.

What this re-examination of the post-structuralist subject and its transformative possibilities has made visible is the extent to which we are always caught up in the specific reiterative practices through which intelligibility is made available to us and through which we make ourselves intelligible. Our vulnerability to those discourses and reiterative practices and their sheer reiterative nature means we cannot always analyse, critique and successfully deconstruct, as it appears, a new set of discourses and practices. A new dominant discourse, such as neo-liberalism, may take us over, reinscribe us, transform us, without us having realized that it was in urgent need of deconstruction and resistance. When new discourses colonize existing discourses we may easily miss what is problematic about them – their capacity to negate, for example, the power of feminist discourses by deeming them to be no longer relevant. The work of feminist post-structuralism is, by definition, work that it can never complete.

And so . . .

Post-structuralist theory provides a set of theoretical propositions that attempt to articulate the ongoing process of being subjected, of subjectivity, of the relations between the outer and the inner, of the constitutive force of discourse. The individual as an observable, describable object (and product) of the scientific gaze, which exists independent of any description of it, is put under erasure. This does not mean that that individual is eliminated, but that the work done to constitute it is made visible, its existence independent of discourse is called in question. In this mo(ve)ment we see the possibility of a different discursive constitution opened up, first through a critical post-structuralist deconstruction, and second through work on comprehending the processes of our own subjectification and decomposing those areas of fixity that are tied to discourses we are working to make unthinkable.

Post-structuralist writers engage in a private/public experimentation with discourse, with seeing, at one and the same time, the usual ways of seeing *as ways of seeing, and seeing against the grain of those usual ways*. The particular detail of specific subjects are interesting only in so far as they can be used to make visible the ways in which bodies/emotions/desires/memories become the inscribed (and reinscribed) public/private, inner/outer depth/surface to be read against the grain of dominant/humanist discourses and practices. In this process, who or what one is may become undecidable. The girls in our stories can be read as both rational, competent, humanist individuals and as subject-in-process who are working and worked on to appropriate themselves within a particular culture, in a particular moment and within particular relations of power. The post-structuralist subject-in-process in our collective biography writing is one who plays between a close and detailed observation of what she finds when she examines her memories, (un)hampered by the moorings of liberal humanist signifying practices, *and* one who recognizes the constitutive force of that same moment of speaking/writing such a description. In this sense the post-structuralist subject might be said to exist at the site of an almost intolerable contradiction, a contradiction that is necessary to comprehend subjectification. Butler says of this necessary ambivalence:

> the subject is itself a site of this ambivalence in which the subject emerges both as the *effect* of a prior power and as the *condition of possibility* for a radically conditioned form of agency. A theory of the subject should take into account the full ambivalence of the conditions of its operation.
>
> (Butler, 1997a: 14–15, original emphases)

In that ambivalence our subject-in process finds herself quite powerful, not so caught in definitions of herself as she might have been. She finds herself in mo(ve)ments, and as she *scrapes* her way through post-structuralist writing, *catches* herself in the act of being subjected and, sometimes, *drags* her individualized subjecthood behind her. She is above all, in process, vulnerable to inscriptions that may be opaque to her and yet developing the powers to make the discourses and their inscriptive powers both visible and revisable.

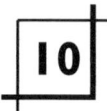

Collective biography as ethically reflexive practice[16]

Our responsibility, as educators and as social scientists, is to understand, to the extent that is possible, the complex conditions of our mutual formation. And we must seek to understand our own contribution to creating and withholding the conditions of possibility of particular lives. In order to achieve that understanding we must ask what it is that makes for a viable life and how we are each implicated in constituting the viability or non-viability of the lives of others. Dominant, normative discourses lend us a habituated sense that we know what is going on, and position us, sometimes, as those with authority to assert the correctness of our views. In contrast, through collective biography, we offer an ethical reflexivity that enables us not simply to reiterate habituated knowledges, but to see, feel, touch, and hear our own and others' ongoing vulnerability to those normative discourses and practices. In acknowledging our mutual vulnerability to those normative discourses we can begin to work towards an ethically responsible understanding of the part we play in granting or withholding recognition of the other.

Of such ethically responsible recognition, Butler says:

> Consider that the struggle for recognition in the Hegelian sense requires that each partner in the exchange recognize not only that the other needs and deserves recognition, but also that each, in a different way, is compelled by the same need, the same requirement. This means that we are not separate identities in the struggle for recognition but are already involved in reciprocal exchange, an exchange that dislocates us from our positions, our subject-positions, and allows us to see that community itself requires the recognition that we are all, in different ways, striving for recognition.
> (Butler, 2004: 43–44)

In the collective biography workshops we have worked to develop our capacities for paying attention to each moment of storytelling and listening in such a way that we are each fully present to the other, and at the same time vulnerable to the other, and vulnerable to our own incomplete knowledge of ourselves. This form of attention enables a recognition of the other, not as a fictionalized and completed subject who in her completeness is necessarily foreign, but a recognition that responds to our mutual vulnerability to normative discourses and to each other.

Ethical reflexivity can be an uncomfortable reflexivity that 'seeks to go beyond the confession/absolution tendencies of some forms of reflexivity, and, in acknowledging the impossibility of a thoroughly transparent and nameable knowledge of oneself, accepts "the uncomfortable task of leaving what is unfamiliar, unfamiliar"' (Ellwood, 2006: 5, citing Pillow, 2003: 177). The full knowledge of self that is implicated in humanist ideals of ethical practice, must, in this understanding, be put aside in favour of an awareness of the emergent process of mutual formation. The recognition of the unfamiliar in oneself opens up a new approach to the other, one that does not mark off such absolute boundaries between oneself and the other, between oneself as the known and the other as the unknown. In this model of reflexivity the recognition of the limits of self-knowledge and self-understanding opens up a different understanding of what it might mean to know the other and to act responsibly towards the other. As Butler says:

> I find that my very formation implicates the other in me, that my own foreignness to myself is, paradoxically, the source of my ethical connection with others. I am not fully known to myself, because part of what I am is the enigmatic traces of others. In this sense, I cannot know myself perfectly or know my 'difference' from others in an irreducible way. . . . I am wounded, and I find that the wound testifies to the fact that I am impressionable, given over to the Other in ways that I cannot fully predict or control. I cannot think the question of responsibility alone, in isolation from the Other; if I do, I have taken myself out of the relational bind that frames the problem of responsibility from the start.
>
> (Butler, 2004: 46)

This particular take on responsibility is almost opposite to the 'responsibilization' currently espoused in the neo-liberal forms of government that dominate the globalized world (Davies and Bansel, 2005; Rose, 1999). 'Responsibilization' in neo-liberal forms of government requires each individual to accept responsibility for self but to shed any responsibility for others – except to participate in acts of surveillance and control. Neo-liberalism heightens individuality and competitiveness, seeking to shape each of us as a flexible economic unit to be of use in a market economy. Neo-liberalism's (usually implicit) intentions have been to make democratic citizens both more governable and more able to service capital (Crozier, Huntington and Watanuki, 1975).

Neo-liberalism as a form of governmentality works by convincing students and workers that there is no choice at a systemic level. Instead, their power lies in their individual choices to become appropriate and successful within that (inevitable) system. Such a system is extraordinarily difficult to reflexively examine and may dismantle resistance to itself through discourses of inevitability (of globalism, of the dominance of information technology, of free markets) and of necessity (for individual and national survival). But as Saul (2005) points out, such discourses of inevitability and necessity signal a kind of fundamentalism that should be resisted.

The ethical reflexivity that informs the practices of collective biography is in profound contrast to the end-driven, market model of the individual. The social, psychic and intellectual work can better be described as an emergent practice (Somerville, 2005). Although collective biographies can be carried out with an end product in mind (a paper, a book), and can be carefully planned in advance, these organizational practices must operate in tandem with an openness to the unknown, and to the dynamic unfolding process through which a group of individuals work together to enable new insights to emerge from their collective work. Responsibility, in this model, lies inside social relations and inside a responsibility to and for oneself in relation to the other – not oneself as a known entity, but oneself in process, unfolding or folding up, being done or undone, in relation to the other, again and again.

In combining the collective biography workshops with my practices of supervision, I have run against the trends of neo-liberalism through which our supervisory practices are increasingly codified and audited and judged. It is important to ask, then, what alternative conditions of possibility have I created and maintained for myself, and for my students and colleagues in these workshops? In what ways do those conditions of possibility afford each of us, and others, a viable life?

In straightforward pragmatic terms, all the students who have participated in these workshops have completed their theses successfully. More importantly, they have written theses that open up new ways of thinking and practising. They have written theses that matter to them and that matter to others. The writing practices of the collective biography, both in the memory-writing and in the collaborative academic writing have made a significant contribution to the accomplishment of that completed work. Just as important as the acquired skills and pleasures of writing, has been the development of the group of participants as a collective, growing and changing with each workshop, but experiencing a commitment to the ongoing collective biography work and to the work of the individual members. That ongoing commitment was expressed through the wish of each participant to continue to attend the workshops and to participate in the email discussions long after their PhDs were completed. The ongoing discussions on our email list, which lasted for years, attended not just to the current collective biography paper, but to the struggles with thesis writing as well as the struggles with life and its multiple overlapping demands. The thoughtful listening and commenting that we cultivated in listening to each other's memories in the workshops was also evident in the ways each member listened and responded on the email list to the ongoing quandaries and epiphanies in each others' lives.

Another of the ways in which I ran against the normative forces of neo-liberal practice was that I failed to charge a fee for the students and colleagues who came from overseas to participate in our workshops. I regarded their participation as a gift; a gift of their presence, their insights, their memories and their friendship. When I have to, I can justify this failure to charge fees in neo liberal terms, as 'building international networks', but I feel dishonest and diminished when I do so. This was not our motive. We did not welcome their participation so that we could tick one of the boxes in someone else's agenda. To reduce their participation to this end-driven market cliché obscures, for me, the true gift of their presence.

There are many elements of intellectual work that cannot be grasped inside a neo-liberal mentality. Two such elements, that I want to focus on here, briefly, are the quality of listening and the art of being present in the moment of remembering. It is difficult to find a language to express this idea that does not immediately provoke an accusation of superficial New Age babble, or a neo-liberal cry that it is of no interest since it is unmeasurable. What I draw on for my understanding of listening and of 'being present', apart from practices of yoga and meditation, is the writing of such authors as Virginia Woolf, G.M. Hopkins and Basho. Each of these writers struggled to capture those intense moments of being when all the extraneous chatter died down and the present moment could be lived from within itself, not just mindfully, but bodily, through all the senses. Total attention comes not just with a focused consciousness, but also with the engagement of the bodily organs, including the skin, the heart, the gut and the bones. Some visual artists, too, re-evoke such moments of total attention, which are, perhaps, more common in childhood before so many governmental imperatives begin to weigh and wear consciousness down. Some paintings, just like some poems and some prose, take one instantly to a remembered sense of being aware of one's landscape, aware of oneself in relation to that landscape, with a purity and intensity that makes time stop still.

Each of the stories we have gathered here, in this book, had for us, in the moment of telling them, writing them and listening to them, that time-stopping quality. It was a breath-stopping, heart-stopping quality that made us weep for the feeling of trueness, of *being there*. It is not an accident that collective biography works best with early stories, since this was when we had the clearest access to being present in the moment. Because the memory-work is collective activity rather than the lonely activity that poetry, fiction writing or painting can be, the particular quality of listening with mindful and bodily attention to the other, from a position of mindful and bodily presence, is vital to its success.

It is not desirable to lay down rules of practice for collective biography such that ethics committees might seize upon them and impose them. The ethics of collective biography must emerge from an ethic of listening and of presence that cannot be mandated or imposed. Ethical reflexivity is always active rather than passive and must be developed moment by moment within the group's practices. It may nevertheless be helpful for me to spell out some of my own guidelines for successful practice that I have developed over many workshops, and that go on developing in the workshops in which I am currently participating. I offer the following list of practical tips in the spirit of ongoing development of collective biography as emergent practice:

- Participation must always be voluntary. Collective biography is not for everyone. I have had students who have successfully completed outstanding theses who preferred other modes of interaction and support. I have colleagues who love what we come up with but who would not be bothered to do such personally and collectively demanding work.
- The topics must always be negotiated among the members of any particular workshop. The participants can only immerse themselves in the process if the question is of interest to them and seems worth the hard work of delving into it.
- It is important for the leader to veto topics that may lead to emotions that the group is unable to deal with. I learned this to my considerable chagrin when a group I was working with insisted on examining the topic of fear. This is not to say that fear could not be dealt with through collective biography, but that that particular group did not know each other well enough and had not developed sufficient trust and care to manage the fallout that occurred.
- This previous point brings me to the importance of the group's dynamics. The practice of living together and working together helped create the knowledge of and care for each other that sustained us each through moments of anxiety and grief when they did arise. We did not all live in though, as such proximity did not suit everyone. Nevertheless the comfortable atmosphere and the demands of shared cooking and eating supported the ethic of mutual care. At one workshop, Helen's partner also lived in and supported the group through doing

the shopping as well as contributing to cooking and washing up, and we all thought this a marvellous innovation.

- The time and place of the workshop are integral to its functioning. Now that I have left the far north of Australia, for example, and am living in a busy city, the practices must shift to suit this new context. I find participants want the workshops shortened to two or three days – which can only work if they already know and trust each other and are familiar with the theoretical challenges of post-structuralist theory. In the papers collected here the authors came together from diverse locations in Australia and Europe, so the extended time together and group living facilitated the work of creating and sustaining a workable collective.

- I always carefully timetable the days of the workshop so that other needs, of families or for exercise or rest, can be accommodated. During our Island workshops, I believed, for example, that a swim in the middle of the day and a walk on the beach in the evening was something I could not do without. Not everyone shared this idea of exercise as necessity and some spent their breaks quite differently. This freedom of the body to do what it needs in the spaces between the hard and focused work, seems to me very important. The emotions of the memories and the task of listening requires time off to let the new images and ideas settle. The intensive group work makes for some an urgent necessity to be alone, while others settle comfortably into talk and the layering of more knowledge of each other's lives in the spaces in between.

- As leader I also believed it was important for the group to have time when I was not there. As became evident in Chapter 6, participants had anxieties about me that they needed to discuss with other members of the group. I was both an equal participant in the memory-work and the leader, and this often required a delicate stepping back as well as a decisive movement forward. Knowing when to be silent and absent was as important as the particular quality of being there.

- The responsibility of the leader for leadership is important. Taking major responsibility for planning, for working out the memory questions to be asked, for organizing the accommodation, for making the timetable, for keeping everyone to the timetable, for giving complete attention to the memories and to the forms of writing that enable each memory to unfold, and for making sure food arrangements have been taken care of and that everyone understands their own responsibilities to the others, and for making sure the process of collaborative writing goes through to the completion of a paper that goes to the heart of the matter we were working on . . . all of this and more falls to the leader. Having said that, it is crucial for the success of the group that each member contributes actively to the success of the workshop. To this end, the leader must above all listen and be responsive to each of the others, while still accepting the responsibility to ensure that the work is being accomplished.

Returning, then, to the concept of ethical reflexivity, one of the main contributions of collective biography has been to investigate the ways in which subjects are locked into normative patterns and to explore how the work we do might decompose some aspects of that normative power. Bodily and mental habits serve to lock subjects into familiar patterns of behaviour and thought. These habituated practices may be within the realm of conscious awareness or they may be unreflected on. The modes of thought, or rationalities, through which those habits and habitual ways of being are understood are frequently tied to ideas of 'real' or essential selves, and are perceived as unchangeable. In the social domain such practices are monitored and managed through forms of government, including self-government, that reward and punish particular ways of being. These forms of government and the behaviours that they perpetuate and police are historically (and culturally) specific, but are generally experienced as the only way things could be within one's own culture. Collective biography develops the practice of viewing language as a complex practice through which reality is discursively constituted and understood. The collective work of talking, writing, reading and questioning makes visible the patterns and habitual ways of thinking and speaking our selves into the world that we are immersed in, including those to which we might be passionately attached. Through this collective work we begin to see the extent to which these practices and ways of thinking and being are both habituated and discursively constituted. In this process they are dislodged from the natural (and inevitable) world and opened up for critical scrutiny and revision. That kind of reflexive work can be difficult and uncomfortable; but as the prized possession of one's essential self slips out of one's (tenuous) grasp, another power emerges. Whereas poststructuralism has been perceived as antithetical to the possibility of radical social action, through our collective biographies we have experienced a freedom from the weighty sense of inevitability and with it a strong sense of agency, though one that is always 'radically conditioned' (Butler, 1997a: 15).

As a framework for interrogating everyday lived experience, collective biography dislodges the familiar, making bodily and mental habits visible *as habits*, reflexively opening them up to scrutiny. It affords a mode of thought that shows those bodily and mental habits to be historically specific and discursively constituted. The gaze is turned on particular forms of discourse through which such ways of thinking and being could have come to be seen by subjects as normal and desirable. In this dual movement, of letting go of the accomplishment of the unified essential self, and the making visible of the ways discourses work on us and shape us up as appropriate(d) subjects, we understand more acutely our vulnerability to normative discourses, and our vulnerability to each other. In this dual movement we can, as well, begin to recognize the 'enigmatic traces of others' (Butler, 2004: 46) in ourselves, and in doing so accept our partial foreignness to ourselves. Having done so, we can greet each other with recognition of our common location in discourse – of our shared, enigmatic traces – and our mutual vulnerability to the need for recognition. We can also shrug off, now and then, the sense of inevitability of the way things are and move towards the kind of democratic engagement that welcomes multiplicity and difference, and remains open to that which is yet to unfold.

Present social and moral orders are not inevitable. They do not grant viable lives to everyone. So-called democratic countries are currently caught in their own fundamentalism, their own rhetoric of inevitability, their own inability to see otherwise. The practices of collective biography enable us to examine the ways we become caught in those apparent inevitabilities and they enable us to carry forward the project of imagining alternatives. They do so through a set of practices in which we afford each other a profound recognition in the shared moments of being that are encapsulated in our stories, through a practice of making visible the common threads of being that come from the power of normative discourses to shape the way things are, and through a shared commitment to the belief that the world can be otherwise.

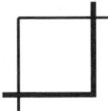

Notes

1 Written by Bronwyn Davies and Susanne Gannon.
2 Written by Bronwyn Davies and Susanne Gannon.
3 Published as: Davies, B., Dormer, S., Gannon, S., Laws, C., Lenz-Taguchi, H., McCann, H. and Rocco, S. (2001) Becoming schoolgirls: the ambivalent process of subjectification, *Gender and Education*, 13(2): 167–182.
4 Written by Bronwyn Davies, Susanne Gannon, Helen McCann, Phoenix de Carteret, Danielle Stewart and Barb Watson.
5 The value of sisterly love for brothers is repeated elsewhere in this novel, in particular in the moral lecture given to Meg by Mr Gillett immediately prior to Judy's death (Turner, [1894] 1983: 171–176).
6 We were, as children, divided over the transformation of these girls. Some of us refused to read the sequels where they had become boring women and wives. Others of us devoured the sequels, not having found the transformation problematic.
7 This imagined child is very similar to the ideal subject of neo-liberalism. That subject, as Rose points out, is capable of 'bearing the serious burdens of liberty', 'however apparently external and implacable may be the constraints, obstacles and limitations that are encountered, each individual must render his or her life meaningful, as if it were the outcome of individual choices made in the furtherance of a biographical project of self-realization' (Rose, 1991: 12).
8 In contrast, there are two men who teach her older sister Meg to be more loving and forgiving.
9 Published as: Davies, B., Browne, J., Gannon, S., Honan, E. and Somerville, M. (2005) Embodied women at work in neoliberal times and places, *Gender, Work and Organization*, 12(4), 343–362.
10 New managerialism, which is also referred to as neo-liberalism in the United Kingdom and Total Quality Management in the United States, is a system of government of individuals invented during the Thatcher and Reagan years. It is analysed in detail by Dean (1999) and Rose (1999).
11 Written by Bronwyn Davies, Jenny Browne, Susanne Gannon, Eileen Honan and Margaret Somerville.
12 Published as: Davies, B., Browne, J., Gannon, S., Honan, E., Laws, C.,

Müller-Rockstroh, B. and Petersen, E.B. (2004). The ambivalent practices of reflexivity, *Qualitative Inquiry*, 10(3), 360–389.

13 Written by Bronwyn Davies and Susanne Gannon in consultation with the collective.

14 An earlier version of this chapter was published as: Davies, B., Flemmen A., Gannon, S., Laws, C. and Watson, B. (2002) Working on the ground. A collective biography of feminine subjectivities: mapping the traces of power and knowledge, *Social Semiotics*, 12(3): 291–313.

15 Published as: Davies, B., Browne, J., Gannon, S., Hopkins, L., McCann, H. and Wihlborg, M. (2006) Constituting the feminist subject in poststructuralist discourse, *Feminism and Psychology*, 16(1).

16 Written by Bronwyn Davies.

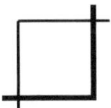

References

Barthes, R. (1975) *The Pleasure of the Text* (R. Miller, trans). New York: The Noonday Press.

Barthes, R. (1977a) *Image, Music, Text* (S. Heath, trans). London: Fontana.

Barthes, R. (1977b) *Roland Barthes by Roland Barthes* (R. Howard, trans). Berkeley, CA: University of California Press.

Barthes, R. (1977c) *A Lover's Discourse: Fragments* (R. Howard, trans). London: Penguin.

Barthes, R. (1985) *The Grain of the Voice: Interviews 1962–1980* (L. Coverdale, trans). Berkeley, CA: University of California Press.

Barthes, R. (1989) *The Rustle of Language* (R. Howard, trans). Berkeley, CA: University of California Press.

Bearne, E. and Watson, V. (eds) (2000) *Where Texts and Children Meet*. London: Routledge.

Behar, R. (1993) *Translated Woman: Crossing the Border with Esperanza's Story*. Boston, MA: Beacon Press.

Bell, S. (1994) *Reading, Writing and Rewriting the Prostitute Body*. Bloomington, IN: Indiana University Press.

Bennett, T. (1990) *Outside Literature*. London: Routledge.

Benstock, S. (1991) Authorizing autobiography, in R. Warhol and D. Price Herndl (eds), *Feminisms: An Anthology of Literary Theory and Criticism*. New Brunswick, NJ: Rutgers University Press, pp. 1040–1057.

Berger, P. and Luckmann, T. (1966) *The Social Construction of Reality*. Garden City, NY: Doubleday.

Bordo, S. (1997) The body and the reproduction of femininity, in K. Conboy, N. Median and S. Stanbury (eds), *Writing on the Body: Female Embodiment and Feminist Theory*. New York: Columbia University Press, pp. 90–110.

Browne, J. (2000) Bloody footprints: learning to be with women, unpublished MEd thesis, University of Canberra, Australia.

Brush, P. (1998) Metaphors of inscription: discipline, plasticity and the rhetoric of choice, *Feminist Review*, 58: 22–43.

Butler, J. (1990) *Gender Trouble: Feminism and the Subversion of Identity*. New York: Routledge.

Butler, J. (1992) Contingent foundations, in J. Butler and J.W. Scott (eds), *Feminists Theorize the Political*. New York: Routledge, pp. 3–21.

Butler, J. (1993) *Bodies that Matter: On the Discursive Limits of Sex*. New York: Routledge.

Butler, J. (1995a) Contingent foundations: feminism and the question of 'post-modernism', in S. Benhabib, J. Butler, D. Cornell and N. Fraser (eds), *Feminist Contentions: A Philosophical Exchange*. New York: Routledge, pp. 35–57.

Butler, J. (1995b) Conscience doth make subjects of us all, *Yale French Studies*, 88: 6–26.

Butler, J. (1995c) For a careful reading, in S. Benhabib, J. Butler, D. Cornell and N. Fraser (eds), *Feminist Contentions: A Philosophical Exchange*. New York: Routledge, pp. 127–143.

Butler, J. (1997a) *The Psychic Life of Power: Theories in Subjection*. Stanford, CA: Stanford University Press.

Butler, J. (1997b) Performative acts and gender constitution: an essay in phenomenology and feminist theory, in K. Conboy, N. Medina and S. Stanbury (eds), *Writing on the Body: Female Embodiment and Feminist Theory*. New York: Columbia University Press, pp. 401–417.

Butler, J. (2004) *Precarious Life: The Powers of Mourning and Violence*. London: Verso.

Byatt, A.S. and Sodré, I. (1995) *Imagining Characters: Six Conversations about Women Writers*. London: Vintage.

Carter, E. (1987) Translator's Foreword, in F. Haug et al. (eds), *Female Sexualization: A Collective Work of Memory*. London: Verso, pp. 11–20.

Chiapello, E. and Fairclough, N. (2002) Understanding the new management ideology: a transdisciplinary contribution from critical discourse analysis and new sociology of capitalism, *Discourse and Society*, 13(2): 185–208.

Cixous, H. (1990) Difficult joys, in H. Wilcox, K. McWatters, A. Thompson and L.R. Williams (eds), *The Body and the Text: Hélène Cixous Readings and Teaching*. Hemel Hempstead: Harvester Wheatsheaf, pp. 5–30.

Cixous, H. (1991) *'Coming to Writing' and Other Essays* (S. Cornell, D. Jenson, A. Liddle and S. Sellers, trans). Cambridge, MA: Harvard University Press.

Cixous, H. and Calle-Gruber, M. (1997) *Rootprints: Memory and Life Writing*. London and New York: Routledge.

Cixous, H. and Derrida, J. (2001) *Veils: Cultural Memory in the Present* (G. Bennington, trans). Stanford, CA: Stanford University Press.

Clough, P. (1994) *Feminist Thought: Desire, Power and Academic Discourse*. Cambridge, MA: Blackwell.

Colebrook, C. (2002) *Understanding Deleuze*. Sydney: Allen & Unwin.

Comte-Sponville, A. (2002) *A Short Treatise on the Great Virtues: The Uses of Philosophy in Everyday Life*. London: William Heinemann.

Crawford, J., Kippax, S., Onyx, J., Gault, U. and Benton, P. (1992) *Emotion and Gender: Constructing Meaning from Memory*. London: Sage.

Crozier, M., Huntington, S.P. and Watanuki, J. (1975) *The Crisis of Democracy: Report on the Governability of Democracies*. New York: New York University Press.

Daniels, J. (2000) 'Harming young minds': moral dilemmas and cultural concerns, in E. Bearne and V. Watson (eds), *Where Texts and Children Meet*. London: Routledge, pp. 161–171.

Davies, B. (1987) Marriage and the construction of reality revisited: an exercise in rewriting social theory to include women's experience, *Educational Philosophy and Theory*, 19(1): 20–28.

Davies, B. ([1989] 2003) *Frogs and Snails and Feminist Tales: Preschool Children and Gender*. Sydney: Allen & Unwin. (Second edition 2003, Cresskill, NJ: Hampton Press.)

Davies, B. ([1993] 2003) *Shards of Glass. Children Reading and Writing beyond Gendered Identity*. Sydney: Allen & Unwin. (Second edition 2003, Cresskill, NJ: Hampton Press.)

Davies, B. (1994) *Poststructuralist Theory and Classroom Practice*. Geelong, Victoria: Deakin University Press.

Davies, B. (1997) The subject of poststructuralism: a reply to Alison Jones, *Gender and Education*, 9(1): 271–283.

Davies, B. (1998) Psychology's subject: a commentary on the relativism/realism debate, in I. Parker (ed.), *Social Constructionism, Discourse and Realism*. London: Sage, pp. 133–145.

Davies, B. (2000a) *(In)scribing Body/Landscape Relations*. Walnut Creek, CA: Alta Mira Press.

Davies, B. (2000b) *A Body of Writing: 1990–1999*. Walnut Creek, CA: Alta Mira Press.

Davies, B. (2005) The fairy who wouldn't fly: a story of subjection and agency, *Journal of Early Childhood Literacy*, 5(2): 151–174.

Davies, B. and Bansel, P. (2005) The time of their lives? Academic workers in neoliberal time(s), *Health Sociology Review*, 14(1): 47–58.

Davies, B. and Davies, C. (forthcoming) Having or being had by experience, in M. MacLure (ed.), *The Educational Future and Innovative Qualitative Research: International Perspectives*.

Davies, B. and Gannon, S. (2005) Feminism/poststructuralism, in C. Lewin and B. Somekh (eds), *Research Methods in the Social Sciences*. London: Sage, pp. 318–325.

Davies, B. and Petersen, E. (2005a) Neoliberal discourse in the academy: the forestalling of collective resistance, *Learning and Teaching in the Social Sciences*, 2(2).

Davies, B. and Petersen, E. (2005b) Intellectual workers (un)doing neoliberal discourse, *International Journal of Critical Psychology*, 13: 32–54.

Davies, B., Browne, J., Gannon, S., Honan, E., Laws, C., Müller-Rockstroh, B. and Petersen, E.B. (2004) The ambivalent practices of reflexivity, *Qualitative Inquiry*, 10(3): 360–389.

Davies, B., Browne, J., Gannon, S., Honan, E. and Somerville, M. (2005) Embodied women at work in neoliberal times and places, *Gender, Work and Organization*, 12(4): 343–362.

Davies, B., Browne, J., Gannon, S., Hopkins, L., McCann, H. and Wihlborg, M. (2006) Constituting 'the subject' in poststructuralist discourse, *Feminism and Psychology*, 16(1).

Davies, B., Dormer, S., Gannon, S., Laws, C., Lenz-Taguchi, H., McCann, H. and Rocco, S. (2001) Becoming schoolgirls: the ambivalent project of subjectification, *Gender and Education*, 13(2): 167–182.

Davies, B., Flemmen, A., Gannon, S., Laws, C. and Watson, B. (2002) Working on the ground. A collective biography of feminine subjectivities: mapping the traces of power and knowledge, *Social Semiotics*, 12(3): 291–313.

Dean, M. (1999) *Governmentality: Power and Rule in Modern Society*. Sage: London.

Deleuze, G. (1988) *Foucault* (S. Hand, trans). London: Athlone Press.

Deleuze, G. (1992) What is a dispositif?, in T.J. Armstrong (ed.), *Michel Foucault Philosopher*. New York: Harvester Wheatsheaf, pp. 159–168.

Deleuze, G. (1995) *Negotiations 1972–1990* (M. Joughlin, trans). New York: Columbia University Press.

Deleuze, G. and Guattari, F. (1987) *A Thousand Plateaus. Capitalism and Schizophrenia*. London: Athlone Press.

Deleuze, G. and Guattari, F. (1995) Gilles Deleuze and Félix Guattari on *Anti-Oedipus*, in G. Deleuze, *Negotiations 1972–1990*. New York: Columbia University Press, pp. 13–24.

Denzin, N. (1997) *Interpretive Ethnography: Ethnographic Practices for the 21st Century*. Thousand Oaks, CA: Sage.

Denzin, N.K. (2003) *Performance Ethnography: Critical Pedagogy and the Politics of Culture*. Thousand Oaks, CA: Sage.

Denzin, N.K. and Lincoln, Y.S. (2000) *Handbook of Qualitative Research*, 2nd edn. Thousand Oaks, CA: Sage.

Derrida, J. (1976) *Of Grammatology* (G. Spivak, trans). Baltimore, MD: Johns Hopkins University Press.

Derrida, J. (1978) Structure, sign and play in the discourse of the human sciences, in *Writing and Difference* (A. Bass, trans). Chicago, IL: Chicago University Press, pp. 278–293.

Derrida, J. (1993) *Aporias*. Stanford, CA: Stanford University Press.

Ellis, C. (2004) *The Autoethnographic I: A Methodological Novel about Autoethnography*. Walnut Creek, CA: Alta Mira Press.

Ellwood, C. (2006) Coming out and coming undone: sexualities and reflexivities in language education research, *Journal of Language, Identity and Education*, 5(1), special issue.

Fairclough, N. (2000) Representations of change in neoliberal discourse (author's unpublished translation of) Represenciones del cambio en discurso neoliberal, *Cuadernos de Relaciones Laborales*, 16: 13–36.

Foucault, M. (1978) *The History of Sexuality. Volume 1: An Introduction* (R. Hurley, trans). London: Penguin.

Foucault, M. (1979) *Discipline and Punish: The Birth of the Prison* (A. Sheridan, trans). New York: Vintage.

Foucault, M. (1980a) Two lectures, in C. Gordon (ed.), *Power/Knowledge: Selected Interviews and Other Writings 1972–77 by Michel Foucault* (C. Gordon, L. Marshall, J. Mepham and K. Soper, trans). Brighton: Harvester Press, pp. 78–108.

Foucault, M. (1980b) Prison talk, in C. Gordon (ed.), *Power/Knowledge: Selected Interviews and Other Writings 1972–1977 by Michel Foucault* (C. Gordon, L. Marshall, J. Mepham and K. Soper, trans). Brighton: Harvester Press, pp. 37–54.

Foucault, M. (1980c) Truth and power, in C. Gordon (ed.), *Power/Knowledge: Selected Interviews and Other Writings 1972–77 by Michel Foucault* (C. Gordon, L. Marshall, J. Mepham and K. Soper, trans). Brighton: Harvester Press, pp. 109–133.

Foucault, M. (1980d) Body/power, in C. Gordon (ed.), *Power/Knowledge: Selected Interviews and Other Writings 1972–77 by Michel Foucault* (C. Gordon, L. Marshall, J. Mepham and K. Soper, trans). Brighton: Harvester Press, pp. 56–62.

Foucault, M. (1980e) Power and strategies, in C. Gordon (ed.), *Power/Knowledge: Selected Interviews and Other Writings 1972–77 by Michel Foucault* (C. Gordon, L. Marshall, J. Mepham and K. Soper, trans). Brighton: Harvester Press, pp. 134–145.

Foucault, M. (1981) *Omnes et singulatim*: towards a criticism of 'political reason', in S.M. McMurrin (ed.), *The Tanner Lectures on Human Values 11*. Cambridge: Cambridge University Press, pp. 223–254.

Foucault, M. (1982) The subject and power, in H.L. Dreyfus and P. Rabinow (eds), *Michel Foucault: Beyond Structuralism and Hermeneutics*. Brighton: Harvester Press, pp. 208–226.

Foucault, M. (1985) *The History of Sexuality. Volume 2: The Use of Pleasure* (R. Hurley, trans). London: Penguin.

Foucault, M. (1986) *The History of Sexuality. Volume 3: The Care of the Self* (R. Hurley, trans). London: Penguin.

Foucault, M. (1988) Technologies of the self, in L. Martin, H. Gutman and P. Hutton (eds), *Technologies of the Self: A Seminar with Michel Foucault*. London: Tavistock Publications, pp. 16–49.

Foucault, M. (1997a) Technologies of the self, in P. Rabinow (ed.), *Michel Foucault: Ethics, Subjectivity and Truth. Essential Works of Foucault 1954–1984. Vol 1* (R. Hurley, trans). New York: New Press, pp. 223–252.

Foucault, M. (1997b) On the genealogy of ethics: an overview of work in progress, in P. Rabinow (ed.), *Michel Foucault: Ethics, Subjectivity and Truth. Essential Works of Foucault 1954–1984. Vol 1*. London: Penguin, pp. 253–280.

Foucault, M. (1997c) What is enlightenment?, in P. Rabinow (ed.), *Michel Foucault: Ethics, Subjectivity and Truth. Essential Works of Foucault 1954–1984. Vol 1* (C. Porter, trans). New York: New Press, pp. 303–319.

Foucault, M. (1997d) The ethics of the concern for self as a practice of freedom, in P. Rabinow (ed.), *Michel Foucault: Ethics, Subjectivity and Truth. Essential Works of Foucault 1954–1984. Vol 1* (P. Aranov and D. McGrawth, trans). New York: New Press, pp. 281–301.

Foucault, M. (1998a) Nietzsche, genealogy, history, in P. Rabinow (ed.), *Michel Foucault: Aesthetics. Essential Works of Foucault 1954–1984. Vol 2* (D. Brouchard and S. Simon, trans). London: Penguin, pp. 369–391.

Foucault, M. (1998b) The order of things, in J.D Faubion (ed.), *Michel Foucault: Aesthetics. Essential Works of Foucault 1954–1984. Vol 2* (J. Johnston, trans). New York: New Press, pp. 261–267.

Foucault, M. (2000a) So is it important to think?, in J.D. Faubion (ed.), *Michel Foucault: Power. Essential Works of Foucault 1954–1984. Vol 3*. New York: New Press, pp. 454–458.

Foucault, M. (2000b) The subject and power, in Faubion, J.D. (ed.), *Michel Foucault: Power. Essential Works of Foucault 1954–1984. Vol 3*. New York: New Press, pp. 326–348.

Gannon, S. (2001) (Re)presenting the collective girl, *Qualitative Inquiry*, 7(6): 787–800.

Gannon, S. (2003) Flesh and the text: poststructuralist theory and writing research, unpublished PhD thesis, James Cook University, Australia.

Gannon, S. (2004) Crossing 'boundaries' with the collective girl: a poetic intervention into sex education, *Sex Education*, 4(1): 81–99.

Gannon, S. (2006) The (im)possibilities of writing the self writing: French post-structural theory and autoethnography, *Cultural studies ↔ Critical methodologies*, 5(2)

Gannon, S. and Davies, B. (forthcoming) Postmodern, poststructural and critical perspectives, in S.N. Hesse-Biber (ed.), *Handbook of Feminist Research: Theory and Praxis*. Thousand Oaks, CA: Sage.

Gargett, A. (2002) Eternal feminine: Natacha Merritt 'digital diaries'; postfeminist Deleuzian figurations, *Parallax*, 8(4): 32–45.

Gatens, M. (1996) *Imaginary Bodies: Ethics, Power and Corporeality*. London: Routledge.

Gordon, C. (2000) Introduction, in J.D. Faubion (ed.), *Michel Foucault: Power. Essential Works of Foucault 1954–1984. Vol 3*. New York: New Press, pp. xi–xli.

Grosz, E. (1994) *Volatile Bodies: Toward a Corporeal Feminism*. Sydney: Allen & Unwin.

Grosz, E. (1995) *Space, Time and Perversion*. New York: Routledge.

Guertin, C. (1999) Gesturing toward the visual virtual reality, hypertext and embodied feminist criticism, *Surfaces*, 8: 2–18.

Hammersley, M. (2001) Some questions about evidence-based practice in education, paper presented to the Annual Conference of the British Educational Research Association, Leeds, 13–15 September.

Harré, R. and Secord, P. (1972) *The Explanation of Social Behaviour*. Oxford: Blackwell.

Hartsock, N. (1987) Rethinking modernism: minority versus majority theories, *Cultural Critique*, 7: 187–206.

Haug, F., Andersen, S., Bünz-Elfferding, A., Hauser, K., Lang, U., Laudan, M., Lüdemann, M., Meir, U., Nemitz, B., Niehoff, E., Prinz, R., Rathzel, N., Scheu, M. and Thomas, C. (eds) (1987) *Female Sexualization: A Collective Work of Memory* (E. Carter, trans). London: Verso Press.

Henriques, J., Hollway, W., Urwin, C., Venn, C. and Walkerdine, V. ([1984] 1998) *Changing the Subject: Psychology, Social Regulation and Subjectivity*. London: Methuen.

Honan, E. (2001) (Im)plausibilities: a rhizo-textual analysis of the Queensland English syllabus, unpublished PhD thesis, James Cook University, Australia.

Hunt, P. (2001) *Children's Literature*. Oxford: Blackwell.

Irigaray, L. (1985) *This Sex Which Is Not One*. Ithaca, NY: Cornell University Press.

Jefferies, J. (1999) *The Scentual Way to Success: An Aromatherapy Experience for Business and Life*. Townsville, Queensland: Living Energy Natural Therapies.

Jones, A. (1997) Teaching poststructuralist feminist theory in education: student resistances, *Gender and Education*, 9(1): 262–269.

Kant, I. (1964) *Groundwork of the Metaphysics of Morals* (H. Patton, trans). New York: Harper Torchbooks/Academy Library.

Kearney, R. (1994) Jacques Derrida, in R. Kearney (ed.), *Dialogues with Contemporary Continental Philosophers: The Phenomenological Heritage*. Manchester: Manchester University Press.

Keith, L. (2001) *Take Up Thy Bed and Walk: Death, Disability and Cure in Classic Fiction for Girls*. London: The Women's Press.

Kristeva, J. (1981) Women's time (A. Jardine, trans), *Signs*, 7(1): 13–35.

Lather, P. (1993) Fertile obsession: validity after poststructuralism, *The Sociological Quarterly*, 34(4): 673–693.

Lather, P. (2000) Against empathy, voice and authenticity, *Kvinder, Køn and Forskning*, 9(4): 16–25.

Lather, P. (2004) This *is* your father's paradigm: government intrusion and the case of qualitative research in education, *Qualitative Inquiry*, 10(1): 15–34.

Laws, C. and Davies, B. (2000) Poststructuralist theory in practice: working with 'behaviourally disturbed' children, *International Journal of Qualitative Studies in Education*, 13(3): 205–221.

Lewin, C. and Somekh, B. (eds) (2005) *Research Methods in the Social Sciences*. London: Sage.

Marcus, G.E. (1994) What comes (just) after 'post'? The case of ethnography, in N.K. Denzin and Y.S. Lincoln (eds), *The Handbook of Qualitative Research*. Thousand Oaks, CA: Sage, pp. 563–574.

Martin, E. (1997) Designing flexibility: science and work in an age of flexible accumulation, *Science and Culture*, 6(28): 327–362.

Martin, R. (1988) Truth, power, self: an interview with Michel Foucault, in L.H Martin, H. Gutman and P.H. Hutton (eds), *Technologies of the Self: A Seminar with Michel Foucault*. Amherst, MA: University of Massachusetts Press, pp. 9–15.

McWilliam, E. (1996) Admitting impediments: or things to do with bodies in the classroom, *Cambridge Journal of Education*, 26(3): 367–378.

McWilliam, E. (1999) *Pedagogical Pleasures*. New York: Peter Lang.

McWilliam, E. (2000) Laughing within reason: on pleasure, women and academic performance, in E. St Pierre and W. Pillow (eds), *Working the Ruins: Feminist Poststructural Theory and Methods in Education*. New York: Routledge, pp. 164–178.

Meadmore, D., Hatcher, C. and McWilliam, E. (2000) Getting tense about genealogy, *International Journal of Qualitative Studies in Education*, 13(5): 463–476.

Mills, C.W. (1959) *The Sociological Imagination*. New York: Oxford University Press.

Montgomery, L.M. ([1925] 1994) *Anne of Green Gables*. London: Puffin Books.

Muecke, S. (2002) The fall: ficticritical writing, *Parallax*, 25(4): 108–112.

Novick, P. (1988) *That Noble Dream: The Objectivity Question and the American Historical Profession*. Cambridge: Cambridge University Press

Onyx, J. and Small, J. (2001) Memory-work: the method, *Qualitative Inquiry*, 7(6): 773–786.

Parker, I. (ed.) (1998) *Social Constructionism, Discourse and Realism*. London: Sage.

Pillow, W. (2003) Confession, catharsis or cure? Rethinking the uses of reflexivity as methodological power in qualitative research, *International Journal of Qualitative Studies in Education*, 16(2): 175–196.

Pinch, T. and Pinch, T. (1988) Reservations about reflexivity and new literary forms or Why let the devil have all the good tunes?, in S. Woolgar (ed.), *Knowledge and Reflexivity: New Frontiers in the Sociology of Knowledge*, London: Sage, pp. 178–198.

Porter, E.H. ([1913] 1994) *Pollyanna*. London: Puffin Classics.

Probyn, E. (2000) *Carnal Appetites: FoodSexIdentities*. London: Routledge.

Rabinow, P. (1997) Introduction, in P. Rabinow (ed.), *Michel Foucault: Ethics, Subjectivity and Truth. Essential Works of Foucault 1954–1984. Vol 1*. London: Penguin, pp. x–xlv.

Richardson, L. (1997) *Fields of Play*. New Brunswick, NJ: Rutgers University Press.

Richer, P. (1992) An introduction to deconstructionist psychology, in S. Kvale (ed.), *Psychology and postmodernism*. London: Sage, pp. 110–118.

Rose, N. (1991) *Governing the Soul: The Shaping of the Private Self*. London: Routledge.

Rose, N. (1999) *Powers of Freedom*. Cambridge: Cambridge University Press.

Rushdie, S. (1991) *Haroun and the Sea of Stories*. London: Penguin.

Sartre, J.P. (1963) *The Problem of Method*. London: Methuen.

Saul, J.R. (2005) *The Collapse of Globalism and the Reinvention of the World*. London: Viking.

Scheurich, J.J. (1997) *Research Method in the Postmodern*. London: Falmer Press.

Schmelzer, M. (1993) Panopticism and postmodern pedagogy, in J. Caputo and M. Yount (eds), *Foucault and the Critique of Institutions*. University Park, PA: Pennsylvania State University Press, pp. 126–136.

Schratz, M., Walker, R. and Schratz-Hadwich, B. (1995) Collective memory-work: the self as a re/source for re/search, in M. Schratz and R. Walker (eds), *Research as Social Change: New Opportunities for Qualitative Research*. London: Routledge, pp. 39–64.

Scott, J. (1992) Experience, in J. Butler and J. Scott (eds), *Feminists Theorize the Political*. New York: Routledge, pp. 22–40.

Sklar, H. (1980) Overview, in H. Sklar (ed.), *Trilateralism: The Trilateral Commission and Elite Planning for World Management*. Montreal: Black Rose Books, pp. 1–58.

Somerville, M. (2005) Postmodern emergent methodologies, paper presented to the First International Congress of Qualitative Inquiry, Urbana-Champaign, 5–7 May.

Somerville, M. and Bernoth, M. (2001) Safe bodies: solving a workplace learning dilemma, in F. Beven, C. Kanes and D. Roebuck (eds), *Knowledge Demands for the New Economy, Refereed Conference Publication, 9th Post-Compulsory Education and Training Conference*, Griffith University, Queensland: Griffith University Press.

Spivak, G. (1991) Theory in the margin: Coetzee's Foe reading Defoe's Crusoe/Roxana, in J. Arac and B. Johnson (eds), *Consequences of Theory*. Baltimore, MD: Johns Hopkins University Press, pp. 154–180.

St Pierre, E. (1997) Circling the text: nomadic writing practices, *Qualitative Inquiry*, 3(4): 403–417.

St Pierre, E. (2000) Poststructuralist feminism in education, *International Journal of Qualitative Studies in Education*, 13(5): 477–515.

Stanley, L. and Wise, S. (1983) *Breaking Out: Feminist Consciousness and Feminist Research*. London: Routledge & Kegan Paul.

Stephens, J. (1992) *Language and Ideology in Children's Fiction*. New York: Longman.

Stronach, I. and MacLure, M. (1997) *Educational Research Undone: The Postmodern Embrace*. Buckingham: Open University Press.

Trinh, M. (1989) *Woman, Native, Other*. Bloomington, IN: Indiana University Press.

Turner, E. ([1894] 1983) *Seven Little Australians*. Sydney: Lansdowne Press.

Venn, C. ([1984] 1998) The subject of psychology, in J. Henriques, W. Hollway, C. Urwin, C. Venn and V. Walkerdine (eds), *Changing the Subject: Psychology, Social Regulation and Subjectivity*. London: Methuen.

Visser, M. (2000) *The Geometry of Love*. London: Penguin.

Walkerdine, V. (1991) *Schoolgirl Fictions*. London: Verso.

Walkerdine, V. (1997) *Daddy's Girl. Young Girls and Popular Culture*. London: Macmillan Press.

Wallace, M. (1999) Women, work and training, unpublished PhD thesis, Deakin University, Australia.

Watson, V. (2000a) Introduction. Children's literature is dead: long live children's reading, in E. Bearne and V. Watson (eds), *Where Texts and Children Meet*. London: Routledge, pp. 1–7.

Watson, V. (2000b) By children, about children, for children, in E. Bearne and V. Watson (eds), *Where Texts and Children Meet*. London: Routledge, pp. 51–67.

Wax, R.H. (1971) *Doing Fieldwork: Warnings and Advice*. Chicago, IL: University of Chicago Press.

Weedon, C. ([1987] 1997) *Feminist Practice and Poststructuralist Theory*. Oxford, Blackwell.

Winefield, T., Gillespie, N., Stough, C., Dua, J. and Hapuararchchi, J. (2002) Occupational stress in Australian universities: a national survey: a report to the Vice Chancellors, National Tertiary Education Union, faculty and staff of Australian universities, and the Ministers for Education and Health. National Tertiary Education Union. www.unisa.edu.au/psychology/research/spirtfinal02.pdf (accessed 25 October 2005).

Wolkowitz, C. (2001) The working body as sign: historical snapshots, in K. Backett-Milburn and L. McKie (eds), *Constructing Gendered Bodies*. Basingstoke: Palgrave, pp. 85–103.

Ziarek, E.P. (2001) Rethinking dispossession: on being in one's skin, *Parallax*, 7(2): 3–19.

Zita, J. (1998) *Body Talk: Philosophical Reflections on Sex and Gender*. New York: Columbia University Press.

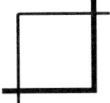

Index